Should we
Now Believe
THE
WARREN
REPORT?

Should We Now Believe THE WARREN REPORT?

by Stephen White

PREFACE BY WALTER CRONKITE

The Macmillan Company · New York
Collier-Macmillan Limited · London

FIRST PRINTING

The Macmillan Company, New York

Collier-Macmillan Canada Ltd., Toronto, Ontario

Printed in the United States of America

CONTENTS

PREFACE

by WALTER CRONKITE

The four one-hour television broadcasts which collectively became "A CBS News Inquiry: The Warren Report" were almost a year in preparation. Except for the four terrible days and nights following the assassination itself, American television had never mounted such a massive single effort. I believe that for every page of this book, there is a CBS News correspondent, producer, cameraman, writer, director, technician or executive who worked on "A CBS News Inquiry: The Warren Report." Almost any one of them could write a book about those broadcasts, and his personal involvement with them.

Most of those books would be passionate, perhaps anguished, for the assassination of John F. Kennedy is not a subject which our generation can, now or ever, approach in a spirit of ice-cold detachment. Most, though not all, of those books would agree as this one does with the central conclusions of the Warren Report and our own Inquiry: That beyond reasonable doubt, Lee Harvey Oswald did indeed kill the President, and that the overwhelming weight of evidence is that Oswald acted alone.

This is the book that did get written. Stephen White, who worked with us on the Inquiry from the beginning, has decided not simply to recount the astonishing year of work that went into it. That is another book, one I hope will still be written; it will be worth reading.

Instead, this reflective writer takes those four broadcasts as his starting point, and tries to assay what the assassination and its raucous, apparently endless aftermath can tell us about ourselves—as individuals, as Americans, and as the elements of mankind. To cut through the miasma of glandular thinking, and stimulate this kind of reasoned appraisal, was perhaps the central raison d'être of the entire CBS News Inquiry.

So that you can begin where Mr. White begins, the complete transcripts of those four broadcasts are bound into this volume; you might find it worthwhile, as I did, to leaf through them first, to bring the memories back into focus, before joining the author in his search for meaning. I have been fascinated, as I think you will be, by that search. For myself, I am willing to let those four broadcasts stand as the last, best reflection of what I, as a reporter, have been able to learn about the greatest, saddest newsstory of our lifetime . . . except for one final point:

All of us, in that legion who worked on the Inquiry are, in our broad outlook, at least, professional newsmen. For any one of us, it would have been the crowning moment of an entire career—of an entire lifetime—to discover that the Warren Report was wrong, to find that Oswald had *not* acted alone, to uncover a conspiracy that took the life of John F. Kennedy.

We could not.

ACKNOWLEDGMENT

This book is the result of a good deal of work and a good deal of thought, not all of it my own. Much of the information upon which it is based was gathered by a large staff who had no book at all in mind at the time but were occupied with the preparation of the four CBS News broadcasts upon which in some degree the book is based. Much of the thinking was equally collaborative, and took place during the course of intense discussions and—at times—furious arguments. From all of this I benefited directly, either by the sharpening that took place in my own thoughts as I defended them, or by the infusion of new notions from others. Clearly I owe a general acknowledgment to CBS News, and in particular to the Special Unit that prepared the Warren Report broadcasts.

More particularly, Mr. Richard Salant, President of CBS News, read the manuscript carefully and left a commentary of some sort on every page. Some of this commentary was approving, some highly critical, and some provocative. It is only fair to Mr. Salant to say that some of what he approved has vanished, much of what he criticized still remains, and I did not always pursue provocative lines he opened up. But there is no doubt that the book is much the better for his reading, and I am grateful for his assistance.

Miss Jane Bartels, of the Special Unit, read the book in its final form and tried to take care that all the facts were right. Any mistakes that remain have been added since she completed her task.

Finally, I owe an acknowledgment to Mr. Leslie Midgley that is most difficult to express. When the broadcasts were being prepared and when this book was first considered, Midgley was executive producer of the Special Unit (he has since become executive producer of the CBS Evening News). He and I began working together almost a quarter of a century ago, and although our paths diverged some years back we have persisted in the habit of calling upon one another when there has been a task to be done. The Warren Report broadcasts constituted the latest of these occasions, and I should be grieved if it turned out to be the last; I prefer to believe that somewhere, sometime, at some task Les and I will be at it again.

STEPHEN WHITE

February, 1968
La Jolla, California

THE PROBLEM OF DISSENT

This automatic reaction that there must be conspiracy somewhere, the prevalence of the devil theory of politics, this probably has increased among us. —Eric Sevareid

During the winter of 1966-67 and the spring of 1967, CBS News undertook an intensive investigation of the events surrounding the assassination of President John F. Kennedy. The evidence presented by the President's Commission on the Assassination of President Kennedy—the Warren Commission—was carefully restudied in the light of objections that had been raised against it. Men and women who might have had something significant to say about the assassination were sought out and interviewed. Experiments were conducted, some of them repetitions of those conducted earlier in behalf of the Commission, others entirely new and devised in behalf of CBS News.

The principal outcome of all this arduous effort was the preparation of four, hour-long television programs called "A CBS News Inquiry: The Warren Report," which were presented over the network on four successive evenings at 10 P.M., beginning June 25, 1967. The programs drew audiences that were large by any standards, and extraordinarily large by the standards of documentary programs: the Nielson ratings indicate that the first of the four programs was seen by 30,000,000 viewers and was among the top ten programs during that week; the others were not far behind. As television, as journalism, and as that complex hybrid television-journalism, the programs were resounding successes.

This book is another, and quite different, outcome. It rests just as firmly as the programs themselves upon the long months of study and investigation and rumination, it draws upon the same materials, and at times, as in its reports of experiments, tells in the medium of print much the story that was told earlier in the medium of television. For the most part its conclusions concerning all those matters with which the programs dealt extensively agree with conclusions drawn in the programs. Yet the purpose, and hence the style, of this book are quite distinct from the purpose and the style of the programs, despite the common origin.

The programs were intended to report, and they were constructed in terms of that intention. Facts were laboriously gathered and examined for relevancy; they were carefully ordered into a coherent whole, so that they might convey the maximum of information with the minimum of confusion; conclusions that appeared to be inescapably entailed by those facts were carefully set forth. This process—and it is an extremely intricate process when the medium is television—occupied much of the time of preparation, and its product filled all the first three programs and much of the fourth. So far as journalism is concerned, it is what television does best.

The fundamental question asked by the programs was: "Should the Report of the Warren Commission be accepted as a generally accurate account of the assassination of the President?" The answer that CBS News gave that questions was "Yes," with a few minor qualifications and no major qualifications.

But while those who were personally engaged in the preparation of the programs dealt with that question and the formulation of its answer, we found ourselves concerned with quite another problem, although one that was closely related to our principal task. Speaking now for myself alone (although I was by no means alone in finding myself caught up in these considerations) I became progressively more interested in the character of the widespread dissent against the Warren Report than in the specifics of that dissent, although it was the specifics of the dissent that entered most directly into the preparation of the programs. To put it somewhat more concretely, one of the specific areas of dissent, which is constantly cited, concerns the question of shots alleged to have been fired from what has come to be known as "the grassy knoll," which was in front of the President's car and to his right as the motorcade made its way down the slope of Elm

Street in Dallas. Looking into the question of the grassy knoll objectively, entirely in terms of the evidence, I found that it could not survive ten minutes of sober scrutiny, for on the one hand is the mountain of hard evidence that no shots came from that area, and on the other hand a few scraps of inferences that might with great ingenuity be tortured into an appearance of evidence that shots might have come from that area. And so in my mind the question of the grassy knoll gave way to what appeared to me to be a far larger question: Why does the legend survive? Why, in fact, does it appear to gain in strength with the passage of time?

The programs did not entirely ignore such questions. CBS News sought out a historian and a sociologist to comment upon just that kind of question, and for CBS News itself both Eric Sevareid and Walter Cronkite offered some commentary relevant to it. But it could not be deeply explored, in part because the programs were not so designed, and in part because such exploration is not in fact the kind of thing that television does best. The matter was touched upon, and little more. Yet it appeared to me that it was a question at least as significant, in its own way, as those the programs sought to answer.

That impression became more intense as the pattern of dissent clarified. Much of the dissent came from those who might charitably be called eccentrics, and less charitably lunatics. They were people, in some cases, who seemed to have wearied of flying saucers and were ready to turn to new diversions. Or they were those who manage, whatever the event, to see what others did not see, hear what others did not hear, and draw conclusions that normal people cannot possibly manage to draw. Or they were the paranoid, who see plots and conspiracies where the rest of us are likely to make out only the ordinary unexceptional course of events.

Another portion of the dissent came from those who might quite properly be suspected of direct self-interest. There was, and is, a market for dissent, and there is money or fame or position to be earned in that market. To those simple facts may be attributed at least a part of the attack upon the Warren Report.

But what was most surprising was the degree to which dissent existed among precisely those men and women from whom one would least have expected it. It is to be found widespread on

American campuses, for example, and among the professors as
well as the students. It is to be found in general among intellectuals, all of whom would maintain that a scrupulous attention to
the evidence lies at the heart of their customary attitudes. There
was an acute incongruity about all this, for it made bedfellows
out of the savant and the lunatic fringe: It was the lunatic fringe
that was assiduously uncovering the "evidence," and the student
and scholar who were uncritically accepting it.

It must be emphasized that from this last group dissent of this
particular kind is to be expected. And the presence of this group
within the pattern of dissent is the key. For now the dissent
against the Warren Report slips into place. The impression that
the dissent cannot rationally exist upon its own terms is justified,
for the dissent among this group does not in fact exist upon its
own terms: It exists by contagion. Dissent against the Warren
Report is merely one aspect of a far more general dissent. That
dissent is directed against the government itself, and in particular
toward the executive branch of the government.

There is among the young and among a large part of the intellectual leadership a growing belief that its government is engaged
in weaving webs of deception. The intensity with which that
belief is held can be attributed directly to the war in Vietnam.
It is, among those groups, a most unpopular war. The impropriety
of the war, its immorality, and its futility appear to them to be
manifest. Yet it is a war that, to these groups, the government
appears intent upon waging, against the best interests of the
United States.

It is a clear lesson of history that to wage any war, the forces
of propaganda must be called into play, and that propaganda
becomes all important within a democratic society if the war is
such that the mass of the people, adequately informed, would be
likely to rebel against it. Thus those who are deeply convinced of
the impropriety of the war in Vietnam are bound by the impera-
tives of their own position to believe that the government is
patiently and steadily lying to the people about the causes, the
course, and the impact of the war. It is an assertion that the
government is engaged in a plot directed against its own citizens,
and as the depth of the commitment against the war becomes
more profound, and more bound up with emotion, the assertion

of just that kind of plot becomes more unrestrained and more divorced from rational assessment.

It is not my intention in this book to deal in any way with the war in Vietnam, or with the variety of attitudes that are held concerning that war. That the war has created a division among the American people, and that a symptom of that division is the growing disenchantment among some Americans with their government, are not matters of opinion or of attitude. They are observable facts. As facts, they are intimately related to the dissent about the Warren Report.

Among those same groups that are profoundly opposed to the war in Vietnam, there is the further incitement of the personal style of President Johnson. He is, in the first place, not the kind of President to which they are accustomed, or would like to be accustomed. Those who found themselves attracted by the wit, the thoughtfulness, and the urbanity of Adlai Stevenson, or by the intellectual sharpness and the youthful drive of Kennedy, are not likely to feel any kinship to the Texas Populist with his air of empty rhetoric and his false *bonhomie*, and his preference for working deviously and behind the scenes. (I do not offer any of these three assessments as equitable: they are the impressions that the men convey rather than any claim to estimate the realities behind those impressions.)

To put it as bluntly as it can be put, there exists then, among a large body of men and women, the belief—indeed, the dogma—that the government has much to lie about, and that its President is one who would not hesitate to countenance those lies. So far as the Warren Report is concerned, there is also a murky underground stream, not necessarily consciously recognized, that associates the death of Kennedy with the elevation of Johnson and that flows in and around the notion that this, too, fits into a pattern of deceit and conspiracy.

Given the postulates with which they work, these men and women are obliged to suspect the Warren Report. If it is the act of a dishonest government, than the Report, too, must be dishonest. And having once adopted such a working principle, one is a good deal less likely to question seriously the nature of the specific objections to the Warren Report, since the Report has already been defined as false; one is a great deal less finicky about bedfellows, for all are staunch enemies of the powers that be.

There arises, then, a kind of reciprocity between the lunatic fringe and the categorical dissenter. The lunatic fringe provides the "evidence." The intellectual, the liberal, because that evidence is to its liking, accepts it uncritically, and in doing so lends a kind of respectability to the lunatic fringe, which it could never hope to gain by its own efforts.

In between lies the great mass of the American people. On the whole they are inclined to accept the good faith of their government with regard to the war in Vietnam, although the war itself is not necessarily to their liking. They feel no sharp alienation from the personal style of President Johnson, and would be resistant to a direct attack upon him.

They have neither the time nor the patience to read the Warren Report, and they will certainly not set out to read the twenty-six volumes that cover the hearings and the documents. But they do respond to controversy, and the dissent against the Warren Report is eminently something to talk about, something to read about when it is presented in the racy fashion of the dissenter and the critic; it has much of the attraction of the detective novel. Dissent, moreover, is respectable, for serious, sober men of science and scholarship share it.

Through the Warren Report, accordingly, a spirit of general distrust toward the government and its executive branch is being fostered among a far wider public than would engage in such distrust as a consequence of the Vietnam war or any other government action. It is a mirror image of the intellectual's own process of thought. "A government that lies so blatantly, so unconscionably, about the Vietnam war," says the intellectual, "can not possibly have told the truth about the assassination." And there is the real current danger that the general public will dutifully respond, "A government that lied about the assassination can not possibly be telling the truth about the Vietnam war—or for that matter about anything else." In the world of logic the two statements, taken together, cancel each other out and come to exactly nothing. In the real world of emotion and half-thoughts, they reinforce each other, gaining each moment in energy as they resonate back and forth.

It was to just this phenomenon that Seymour Lipset, professor of sociology at Harvard, alluded in a discussion that took place as he was being interviewed for the fourth of the programs.

I think [the assassination and its aftermath] will leave a certain proportion of people who, for the rest of their lives, will disbelieve what the set of the political and social establishment says.

To understand this problem, I think one has to use the notion some sociologists have advanced, the notion of the generation. The idea of the generation is that people of a certain age group tend to get many of the experiences that form their attitudes for the rest of their lives at a fairly early age—a point at which they come to political maturity, around twenty-one, going up some years or down some years, depending on who the individuals are.

Today, for example, we can locate the depression generation—people for whom the depression was a key formative experience. No matter what has happened since, the fact that we have had twenty or thirty years of prosperity doesn't eliminate that phenomenon—people who were one of ten or twenty million unemployed and are still reacting to it.

One might suggest that for a lot of young people today, those people involved in anti-war movements, a cynicism has developed about American institutions through this combination of their attitude toward the war and the Kennedy assassination. They will develop a cynicism about American institutions that will stay with them for the rest of their lives, even though the issues may disappear. So that for a given generation we will have a group that will be receptive to belief in negative things about the system—belief in clots within the system.

Some have suggested, for example, in relation to the depression, that an experience similar to the Kennedy one was the Sacco-Vanzetti trial that went on in Massachusetts for most of the 'twenties. A lot of students were involved in this then. And many young people came to believe that the state of Massachusetts, helped by the Supreme Court and various other high agencies, had deliberately framed two innocent Italian workers and sent them to their death for murder. The feelings about the Sacco-Vanzetti case were very bitter, very intense. Well, the people who came to believe that the American judicial system was one that could frame people were seemingly receptive to believing other negative things about the society. It's been argued that the very strong support some Leftist movements got, once the depression broke out, among a lot of intellectuals and young people, occurred in part because the Sacco-Vanzetti case had already broken many of them from their belief in the system.

Oné might argue that if we were to go into another depression, we'd have a receptive generation to add to their cynicism. I think that is one of the potential long-term consequences of this kind of division. I think that if the war continues, to some extent the question of what the potential is relates to how long the war goes on. The longer the war goes on, the more possibility there is for producing a very bitter, fairly large group, who would then remain a potential source of support for radical extremism for much of their lives.

In his summation at the close of the broadcasts, Walter Cronkite spoke to much the same point:

√   We have found . . . that there has been a loss of morale, a loss of confidence among the American people toward their own government and the men who serve it. And that is perhaps more wounding than the assassination itself.

As Mr. Cronkite implies, the larger question of the nature of the dissent against the Warren Report transcends the questions of the specifics of that dissent. It is with that larger question, upon which the broadcasts merely touched, that this book is intended to deal.

In a sense, the book begins where the broadcasts left off. The broadcasts examined the specifics of dissent, and came to the general conclusion that they were irrational. The full text of the four broadcasts is included in this book, and the manner in which that general conclusion was reached is set forth in that text, just as it was presented over the network.

The broadcasts were intended to account and to narrate. The book, encompassing the material in the broadcasts, is frankly intended to persuade. I have tried to look more deeply into the reasons for the concentration of dissent upon certain points within the account given by the Warren Commission. I have tried to state how people are led, or misled, to give to certain aspects of the dissent a totally unwarranted credulity, and correspondingly how they are led, or misled, to overlook or to discount the mountain of evidence the Warren Commission accumulated.

I hope to be able to persuade those of the dissenters whose minds remain open, or who had open minds to begin with, that they must apply those minds fairly and honestly to an assessment of the facts, and equally important, to an assessment of their own emotional or instinctive responses to the facts. In order to do this, I have ranged fairly widely. I have repeated some of the material that went into the broadcasts, with more attention to detail than the time allotted for the broadcasts permitted. But I have engaged also in general discussions of such matters as conspiracy, and probability, and the characteristics of eyewitness testimony.

I ask of the reader only thoughtfulness. If, after thoughtful appraisal of what appeared in the broadcasts and what is written here, he chooses still to dissent, he is well within his rights. I will then believe he is grievously mistaken, but he in turn will believe I am grievously mistaken (and publicly so!) and that is surely no worse than a stand-off for him. And we will certainly agree that, wherever we take our stand, it is no trivial matter.

THE SELECTION OF A COMMISSION

When the President selected the Commissioners, he chose men of unblemished reputation and very high standing [who] would have no reason whatsoever to be expedient or to search for political truths.

—Arlen Specter
Staff lawyer, Warren Commission

The events, as the Warren Report tells the story, took place as follows.

On November 22, 1963, President John F. Kennedy was driven through downtown Dallas in an open limousine. By 12:30 P.M. his motorcade was passing through Dealey Plaza, just outside the main business section, en route to the Trade Mart, where the President was to make a speech. At the President's left in the back seat of the limousine was his wife; in front of him on a jump seat was John H. Connally, Governor of Texas, and next to the Governor, Mrs. Connally. From a sixth-floor window Lee Harvey Oswald looked down on Dealey Plaza and the approaching motorcade. Oswald, once a Marine, later a defector to Russia, was now an employee of the school book warehouse in which he stood. In his hands was a cheap Mannlicher-Carcano rifle, bought a few months before from a mail-order house in Chicago. Oswald had made a special trip the previous evening to the house where his wife was living with friends, and where some of his personal effects were stored; he had brought the rifle to work with him that morning. As the President's car turned the corner six stories below, Oswald fired three shots in rapid sequence. One shot struck the President, passed through his neck without doing serious damage, then penetrated Governor Connally's chest and wrist before coming to rest in the Governor's thigh. Another shot went wild. A third shot struck the President in the back of his head, inflicting a fatal wound. The car raced to Parkland Hospital, four miles away, where a half an hour later the President was declared dead. Meanwhile Oswald hid his rifle among the cartons in the warehouse, walked hastily down the stairs, and made his way by foot, bus, and taxi to his home some three miles away. There he picked up a pistol and set out again on foot. A few blocks away he was hailed by Officer J. D. Tippit; when the officer left his police car Oswald shot and killed him. Continuing on foot he came at last to a motion picture theater, which he entered to escape the pursuit that was already in progress; a telephone call by the ticket-seller brought the police. After a brief struggle Oswald was subdued and arrested. That was Friday. On Sunday morning he was being transferred from the police station to the county jail when Jack Ruby slipped unnoticed into the basement of the station, just as Oswald was being led to a waiting car. Ruby, acting in a kind of frenzy compounded of hatred for the President's killer and pity for the President's widow, shot and killed Oswald.

It is with all these events, and others that preceded and followed the crime, and with the official report issued by the President's Commission on the Assassination of President Kennedy that this book will deal. The account contained in the paragraph above is the account given by that Commission—the Warren Commission—in twenty-seven fat blue volumes. As the Commission tells it, it is incredibly detailed. It is worthy of note that there are people who believe almost none of it. If that statement rings of exaggeration, we can quote Mark Lane, lawyer and self-appointed counsel to Lee Harvey Oswald; this is what he told CBS News:

> There is one conclusion, one basic conclusion that the Commission reached, I think, which can be supported by the facts, and that was the Commission's conclusion that Ruby killed Oswald. But, of course, that took place on television. It would have been difficult to deny that. But outside of that, there's not an important conclusion which can be supported by the facts, and this is the problem.

It is worth a moment to consider the significance of Mr. Lane's remarks, for he is saying a good deal more than simply that the Warren Commission was mistaken. Any commission can make a mistake. A bad commission can be expected to make many mistakes. But to make *only* mistakes (except in that single instance where a mistake was totally impossible) is not the sort of result that a commission can stumble into. No commission, however inept, could err as consistently as that. Total error can only be deliberate error; what Mark Lane is charging is that the Warren Commission deliberately withheld the truth. His statement is an accusation of conspiracy, entered into by seven distinguished men for purposes which must also be enfolded within the conspiracy, for Mr. Lane at no point attempts to make them clear.

Mr. Lane is by no means the only critic.

There is Richard Popkin, who writes that there were not one but two Oswalds.

Harold Weisberg believes in at least two assassins, and in FBI and CIA complicity.

Joachim Joesten believes that the murder (with which Oswald had nothing to do) was committed by a conspiracy of oil magnates.

Leo Sauvage writes that Oswald was framed, and that a right-wing conspiracy explains the assassination.

William Turner, ex-FBI agent, writes that a paramilitary operation, with riflemen firing from at least three angles, murdered the President.

Barbara Garson, in *MacBird*, at least hints that President Johnson was the dark figure behind the conspiracy.

And the list continues. I have heard one man seriously maintain that Governor Connally shot the President, and at least one other insists the President was not shot at all.

Then come the scattergun critics, who do not appear to believe much of anything except that, if the Warren Report asserts something, it must be wrong. Some, like Sylvia Meagher, have given over the major part of their time and effort (since the assassination) to the simple task of refuting anything and everything the Warren Commission maintains. They have set up a kind of loose association, a network which circulates information among its members and is dedicated, apparently, to the utter confusion of any official statement concerning the death of President Kennedy.

Anything that can be disputed is disputed. Consider the bare account given in the opening paragraph of this chapter. By one critic or another it is maintained that Oswald was not on the sixth floor of the Texas School Book Depository, that he did not have a rifle, that the rifle found in the building was a Mauser and not a Mannlicher-Carcano, that Oswald fired no shots, that no shots came from the depository, that two shots, four shots, six shots, up to twenty-two shots, were fired, that Oswald left the building before the assassination, that Oswald did not shoot Officer Tippit, that Officer Tippit was part of the conspiracy, that Ruby was part of the conspiracy. And this is only the beginning: the bare criticisms of the bare account. The Commission's twenty-seven volumes are impressive, but the literature of dissent is more copious by far.

The target of all this literature is the American public, and on that public it has had its effect. The critics with full-fledged theories of their own are numbered in the dozens, the scattergun critics in perhaps the thousands. But those who are simply dubious or skeptical, and those who have come to the conclusion that information of substance is being deliberately withheld from them by the government, number in the tens of millions.

So far as the great majority of the doubters are concerned, it is to neither the Warren Report nor the literature of dissent that they are responding. Mark Lane has had a bestseller in *Rush to Judgment*, but perhaps only a handful of people have read all the volumes issued by the Warren Commission—2,136 copies have been sold—and the other books have had only modest sales. But the literature of dissent—sensational, raucous, violent in tone and in implication—has had its effect in a more indirect fashion. It has created an atmosphere of deep distrust to which almost every sector of American opinion seems to be in some degree vulnerable. Most of those who doubt, even though they doubt strongly, cannot verbalize their dissent. They seem to say merely that they do not believe the Warren Report, and stumble if they are asked to go on from there.

It is fundamentally with this situation, rather than with the assassination itself, that this book will deal. It is not intended in any formal fashion to be a counterrebuttal to the critics—that is to say, there will be no attempt to seize upon the criticisms, one by one, and establish in some fashion or another the degree of their validity. Such a task would be unbearably tedious in the performance, and equally tedious in the reading. What is more, it would be utterly fruitless.

The purpose of the book is not to convince critics that their dissent is groundless, although it will turn out that most of it is exactly that. Rather, I will attempt here to dispel some of the fog that has been generated by the irresponsible, in the hope that once that fog has been dispelled the American people will once more be able to look rationally at the facts. Not all the fog will be dispelled, because some fog must always remain—that is always the case where human beings and human events are concerned. Where there is legitimate reason for doubt, I will try to say so candidly.

In the end, one may be certain that skeptics will remain, even concerning matters where this book will maintain that no skepticism is justified. That is all right too. But perhaps this book will help them know a little better just what it is they are being skeptical about.

Lyndon B. Johnson had been President of the United States for exactly one week when he announced the appointment of a commission, under the leadership of Chief Justice Earl Warren, to "ascertain, evaluate and report on" the facts that concerned the assassination of his predecessor. That action was forced upon him, if only because, in the absence of a Presidential Commission, there might well be several such investigations, conducted by the state of Texas, by the House and Senate, acting either jointly or separately, and by some such branch of the Executive as the Federal Bureau of Investigation. No one familiar with history, even if his familiarity was limited to the assassination of President Lincoln, could hope that this more recent tragedy would ever be fully explained, or explained at all to the satisfaction of every analyst. It was necessary that there be an official account, and highly advisable that there be only one.

Superficially, and in the charge that the President laid upon it, the Warren Commission was established to act as a fact-finding body. Its purposes, however, were far more profound. Representative government of the sort embodied in the United States Constitution is a kind of compact between citizens and those who act in their name. Powers are delegated with the implicit understanding that they will be exercised to the fullest extent possible in an open and a straightforward manner. Political and legal institutions are organized in a fashion that will assure openness, and the press is assured special treatment upon the principle that it will help maintain a constant pressure against those who may wish, whatever their purpose, to close the government or any portion of the society it serves.

For the most part the system works, if not perfectly at least to the satisfaction of most of those who are engaged. There is the general assumption that we all know most of what is going on, and that we would be able to find out most of the rest. A good deal of residual skepticism abides, to be sure, but even that skepticism assumes the normal workings of the system: "They are trying to hide something from us, but they won't get away with it." The statement itself is intended to point out that "they" are indeed not getting away with it.

The equilibrium of the relationship between representatives and represented begins to totter, however, whenever there is a sharp discontinuity in political events. As citizens observing the political process, we may be emotionally distressed by events, but as long as they take place in what appears to be a reasonable order, we feel we comprehend them; so long as B follows in some orderly manner from A, and C from B, we can understand the process and fit it into our fundamental understanding of our political system. To do so it is not even necessary to like A, or B, or C. But when B turns out to be the destruction of the major portion of our Pacific fleet in a predawn attack upon Pearl Harbor, and when we are not provided with any suitable antecedent A, we have a political crisis that is different in nature and may be far greater in significance than any military crisis arising out of the loss of capital ships.

There are those, of course, who do not feel the need for logical antecedents. Most of us do, however, and for many the first instinct is to set forth the simplest and (if the party in power is not to their liking) the most satisfying explanation: There *were* antecedents, but they have been kept secret from us. In this case, the argument goes, the compact between government and governed has been broken, and we are an Open Society no more. If enough people feel so, the government in power will fall at the next election; if they feel it deeply, more than the government will go—institutions that were once believed to be the very bulwarks of the governmental process itself may be torn down.

It is a remarkable aspect of human nature that the first thought, and often the only thought, is likely to be of governmental secrecy or of conspiracy, of which secrecy is the central element. It is true, of course, that the need for a logical explanation is immediately and fully met by postulating conspiracy. It is met equally well by postulating incompetence among the governors, but this is usually the last recourse of the questioners, although one would think that ordinary experience would make it the first. Another complete explanation is provided by religion: The event was the work of the hand of God. That was once the most popular of all explanations; it has fallen out of favor. It has been replaced in some quarters, however, by a comparable explanation, which attributes all events to the remorseless and unchangeable flow of history—a kind of fatalism with a gloss of scientism, which is generally known as Marxism.

Those are the kinds of explanation that rush in to fill the vacuum that is generated in the absence of real knowledge. Because most of them are threats to the stability of the society in which has taken place the event that calls for an explanation, it is at once necessary that an attempt be made to provide acceptable versions of the event. For its own selfish purposes a government in power must make that attempt, but it is not entirely or even primarily a matter of political self-interest, for it is the system of government itself, as well as those who enjoy positions of power within that system, that are threatened.

Because of considerations such as these, it would be naive to look upon the Warren Commission as no more than a fact-finding body. To fulfill its real mission, it had to do far more than find the facts: It had to convince the people of the United States that those facts constituted an acceptable explanation for the event with which the facts dealt, and that accordingly there was no further need to seek for antecedents to the event—the antecedents had been found, laid upon the table, and were fully available for further examination. In short, the Warren Commission was not only to write the book, it was to close the book, once and for all. That, at least, was the purpose that lay behind its creation.

In any absolute sense, neither one of the two halves of its tasks was truly within the power of the Commission to perform. Human events, even the simplest of them, are incredibly complex. Even for so simple an event as the exposure of these very words to any single reader, a whole inexplicable history forms the background. An account of the convergence of reader and printed page involves uncounted subsidiary events: What happened to you today that brings you precisely here at precisely this moment? What brings the book here? Why are you reading this book but not another? There is also the history of the book to account for. Each of those histories—and they are only two of the many that are involved—contains inconsistencies, contradictions, and above all a series of most incredible improbabilities. Yet this is the simplest of all events. There are few persons directly involved, there is the opportunity (if anybody should be foolish enough to wish to seize it) to study the event quietly and without distraction, there are no powerful forces involved to generate confusion, and perhaps most centrally there are no strong emotions involved. But consider instead a complex event—account for a marriage, if you will—and the absurdity of hoping for a categorical history becomes at once apparent. The best that can be looked for is a close approximation, and at times it will not indeed be very close.

Thus the Warren Commission began with an awareness that it would never provide a complete causal chain for the separate incidents that converged to result in the assassination of the President. There would in any case be gaps, inconsistencies, episodes that could be made plausible but never incontrovertible, and even events that appeared to be by no means plausible—which might, indeed, be very nearly unbelievable—but that represented nonetheless the closest thing to the truth that a scrupulously conducted investigation could provide.

Nor could the Commission, having done its best, hope for universal acceptance of its own version of the assassination. Most of us come to any event with a disposition for one explanation over any of the available alternatives. At the hour of the assassination, those who held deep antipathies for the radical right were immediately disposed to see a radical right plot at the heart of the murder; those whose antipathy was for the radical left looked for a leftist involvement. There are those who dislike Texas, and were prepared to accept an account of Texas hatreds and Texas gunplay. Russia was an immediately attractive suspect to some; Castro to others. Humans being what they are, it is probable that every sentient American, on first hearing the news, postulated an explanation that satisfied the body of his own biases, and would have experienced that incomparable "I told you so" feeling if his instincts had been borne out by the development of the news. The instincts, moreover, need not necessarily have been as tendentious as those that have so far been mentioned; the cool student of history might well have reacted to the first bulletins with the judgment that this assassination, like most Presidential assassinations and attempts at assassinations, was the work of some kind of lunatic. He, too, would then look in the news for those items that buttressed his initial conclusions.

For most of us, the facts as they became available would have forced us to withdraw, reluctantly or not, our original impressions. The weight of the evidence as it developed would militate immediately or bit by bit against maintaining the point of view that (in the bliss of ignorance) we were initially prepared to hold. But this outcome would depend only in part upon the weight of the evidence; there would also be the weight with which our own biases are maintained. The fervid Russia-hater would cling obstinately to his view—more accurately, his hope— that somehow and somewhere new evidence would be forthcoming that would reveal Russia, once and for all, to be the devil in the case.

At the extreme, of course, lies the paranoid. Since he sees all events in terms of his mania, he is not inclined to accept evidence that strikes at the mania itself. Whatever his initial version of an event, he is likely to cling to it, or if he alters it, to do so in a manner that constitutes merely a shift of ground, but not a shift of outlook. These are the irreducible dissenters, and little more need be said about them. The true problem is to recognize them when they appear.

For the Warren Commission these problems, even without considering the problems created by the true paranoic, were compounded by the nature of the evidence that unfolded in the first few days after the assassination. Anyone anxious to maintain the solution suggested by his own bias or his own emotions had at least a straw or two to cling to. Since the evidence was powerful that Oswald, somehow or another, was involved, there was at once a call for an explanation of Oswald himself, and Oswald had left behind him a path strewn with tidbits for the suspicious. There were Russian connections, anti-Russian connections, Castro connections, anti-Castro connections, FBI connections. He had written an angry letter to Governor Connally of Texas. He had—or had he?—tried to assassinate Major General Edwin Walker, one of the more voluble supporters of the radical right. There was even a record that at one time in his life he had been recommended for psychiatric care. Almost anyone who wished seriously to cling to his initial beliefs would be shaken from them only by some strong force; the Commission would have great need to persuade.

In all probability the Commission itself, reconnoitering warily the long road ahead of it, was aware of the ambushes it could expect to encounter. Perhaps still another may have occurred to the commissioners, since they are none of them naive men. In a world in which the media of communication offer huge rewards to those who feed them, there is money to be made by calculated dissent. So long as there are strong emotional urges to maintain a viewpoint, money in abundance will flow to those who are willing, by fair means or foul, to feed those emotions. To some, the assassination of the President might appear as merely one more opportunity to hustle a dollar, and an opportunity that promised, if it were well handled, to stretch out over the years.

At best, then, the Commission could expect trouble with a lunatic fringe, and perhaps with others who saw some pecuniary advantage in feeding the lunatic fringe and in extending it more deeply into the fabric. It could never, in any case, dispose of the lunatics; it could hope only to expose them as lunatics. And it is necessary to ask whether that hope was ever an entirely realistic one.

The question, in fact—and in its crude form it is a most difficult question—is whether we are not all more or less lunatic. We are members of a society that has been hammered for a generation with crisis and confrontation. There are powerful forces— Russia, more lately China—which glory in threats to bring us to ruin and which possess or threaten to possess means that make their threats something more than idle. Technology has created still other forces which appear to defy human direction, and which may destroy us simply by reason of our own inability to cope with them. Mass communications and the development of skills in manipulating the machinery of communications have given new powers to those who for one end or another—to sell political panaceas, to sell toothpaste—have a direct interest in unseating our reason. The rock of religion has, for many, crumbled under the impact of a science which can tell us how to do but not what to do, when to do, or whether to do. In many respects we appear to live in a world reason itself has made irrational.

Was there, in short, any audience with which the Commission could hope to engage in reasonable discussion? Or were its best efforts doomed to failure from the outset? This is certainly the most serious of all the questions that can be asked about the assassination of President Kennedy. We can survive the death of a great man—we must, after all, do exactly that, time after time, as each great man comes to the fullness of his powers, then declines and vanishes. But if lunacy has penetrated so deeply into our souls that we can no longer operate as reasonable men and women, there is certainly some question whether we can in the long run survive, and whether we should survive. The assassination poses just that question. It forces us to wonder how deeply sickness has struck into our souls.

To sum up, this inquiry into the work of the Warren Commission has three parts, to some extent quite independent of one another. First, does the account given in the Warren Report of the circumstances surrounding the assassination of President Kennedy come as close to being a true account as the Commission should have been able to come? Next, did the Commission, in determining what happened and in making the results of its determination known, perform in a manner that encouraged adherence to its conclusions? To put the same matter somewhat more obliquely, did the Commission exert itself sufficiently well and sufficiently wisely to draw the teeth of those who, it knew, would rise against its report? Finally, could the Commission at any time reasonably have hoped to convince the overwhelming majority of the American people that its account could be trusted —or even a respectable majority? The fact that these questions may be independent of each other is clear. One can conceive of the Commission emerging with an account mistaken in all significant respects, and yet gaining general acceptance. The world is full of myths, and universities are full of doctoral candidates seeking vainly—forever vainly—to dissipate them. (What is the "truth" about General Washington, or for all that about General Eisenhower?) To a large degree, these are three separate inquiries, united only in that they deal with much the same background of information.

This book relies heavily on two sources. One of them, as noted, is the investigation conducted in late 1966 and early 1967 by CBS News. The other is the publications of the Warren Commission itself. On the face of it this must appear surprising and perhaps illegitimate. It is possible and defensible only because the Commission itself took such great pains to make available a clear account of the evidence upon which it reached its conclusions. It has left that clear account even when the evidence appears at first reading or even at any reading to contradict the Commission's own conclusions. In relying upon the twenty-seven volumes of the Report, the hearings and the exhibits, we do no more than follow in the footsteps of those who are most critical of the Commission, for they too rely almost universally on evidence that the Commission has made available to them.

3 THE INVESTIGATION

I would say, after having prosecuted a great many cases, that seldom would you ever find a case which was as persuasive that Oswald was the assassin, and in fact the sole assassin, and we convict people in the criminal courts every day right here in City Hall, Philadelphia.

—Arlen Spector

Men are assassinated every day, and the police at once begin the routine business of finding out who did it and how. In most cases the facts are moderately easy to come by, although they may not always be available in a form sufficient to guarantee a conviction. In some cases the facts are hard to come by, and the police slowly diminish their efforts until they give the matter up as a bad job, for the police, after all, have only limited resources, and crime in general does not take a holiday while any one case is pursued.

When a President is assassinated, the conduct of the matter is somewhat different. The resources that are applied to ascertaining the facts are in effect the total resources of the society, and it is a good deal less likely that any available information will escape the searchers. This is double-edged, for it is equally unlikely that any available misinformation will escape them. The events linked to the assassination are no longer simple occurrences, but occurrences which are associated with intense feelings, with fears and hopes, perhaps with unshaped and unspoken intimations of personal guilt. Even the recollection of mundane pursuits, which were interrupted by the earliest news bulletin, takes on the flavor of the mystical and the unreal. Some of the ordinary hold on reality is shaken, and the dislocation extends to everything in the neighborhood.

Let me attempt, at the outset, to separate the assassination from the emotions it engendered. A man, riding in an automobile, is shot and killed. Most of the reports gathered at the vicinity of the crime, and those by far the most credible, indicate that the shots came from high in a building behind him; the building is searched and a rifle and three expended shells are found, the latter in a sniper's nest at an open sixth-floor window. The rifle's ownership is quickly traced; it is the possession of a man who worked in that building and had been seen on the sixth floor just before the assassination; he is no longer in the building slightly after the assassination.

Soon thereafter a policeman is shot near that man's home; the policeman's murderer is pursued quite closely to a motion picture theater where he is captured. In his possession is a handgun with bullets of the same manufacture as those that shot the policeman. Brought to a police station, he is identified as the same man who owned the rifle and worked in the building where the shots were fired.

In an ordinary murder, the heart of the matter would be established then and there. A certain amount of routine work would remain, for the courts are insistent upon form and procedure since their primary purpose is quite as much to protect the innocent as to punish the guilty. But to any reasonable man, unconstrained by legalistic rigors, there could be no reasonable doubt that the murderer had been found. Except for details, the case—more accurately, the two cases—would be closed.

In order to keep the case open, it becomes necessary at this early stage of the proceedings to introduce the notion of a conspiracy. The burden (in the real if not the legal sense) is now clearly upon those who wish, for whatever reasons they may have, to fly in the face of the obvious. The facts say clearly that the man now under arrest is the assassin. The facts are too plentiful and too diverse to have been rigged by a single individual; if they were rigged, they were rigged in concert.

This is, of course, a narrow view, and these remarks are limited to that narrow view: I am up to now asking only if the man in the window assassinated the man in the car. It is another question whether he did so as his own willful act, or with accomplices, or as part of a larger plot. The facts so far are consonant with any of these, and we must inquire further if we wish to know which is true, or most likely. But for the moment only the direct, immediate crime concerns us.

As long as I continue to deal with the man in the car and the man in the street, the notion of conspiracy to falsify the facts is too absurd to entertain. Rather, I would seek first to discover a motive for the murder, so that my sense of propriety would be satisfied. Propriety, after all, dictates that murders not be committed frivolously—there must be some reason. So I would search for the reason. If I found one, well and good. If I did not, I would put the murder down to sheer lunacy as we all did when a young man, not so very far from Dallas, fired shots at passers-by from the tower of a university building.

But let the man in the car be the President of the United States, and the suspicion of a conspiracy is not nearly so remote from common sense. There are powerful hatreds engendered in the neighborhood of a President. There are hundreds of millions of dollars to be gained or lost, depending—or more often merely believed to depend—upon the occupant of the Presidency. There are political causes, perhaps held to the point of fanaticism, which can be furthered or arrested in the White House. There is the simple matter of political partisanship, heightened in a few individuals to the point of insanity. (There was also, in this case, Dallas, where political partisanship in its most virulent form was endemic, and where not long before Texas matrons had spat upon Adlai Stevenson.)

The notion of a conspiracy could not be swept aside without further consideration. It is a measure of the importance of the Presidency that in the first few moments that followed the assassination, before even the simple facts I have so far stated were known, that notion was almost universally accepted, without thought and without wonder. I do not discount it out of hand now, or as I proceed.

It will be useful to consider, before proceeding further, the word *conspiracy* itself, and what it signifies and implies. The word itself, closely regarded, is easily recognized as a metaphor. It emphasizes one aspect in which a wide range of activities, in most respects quite distinct from one another, yet manage to resemble each other. The resemblance, of course, lies in the fact that, in each instance of a conspiracy, two or more persons are in concert to perform an act that is in some fashion conceived to be contrary to the general interest. But, except in a legalistic sense, that general resemblance may be far less significant than the particular differences.

Thus an individual who plans to rob a grocery store is merely planning to break the law; two individuals who plan to rob the same grocery store are conspiring. The substantive difference between the two cases is negligible. The effect upon society is equally negligible, since in some respects a conspiracy is more efficient than the act of a single person, and in other respects less efficient. In such circumstances, the notion of a conspiracy is little more than a legal device to assure that both participants, whatever the specific differences in the role they play in a given robbery, are subject to the same punishments.

The situation changes considerably if a group of men form an association with the general intent of performing robberies. Such a conspiracy—durable, purposeful, designed to foster a high degree of organization in the pursuit of criminal ends—is something quite different from the casual association of a pair of lawbreakers. A further step along the scale occurs when such a group engages in activities such as the recruitment into its ranks of officers of the law, or the use of returns from its activities to bribe police officers or judges, or to elect to office public representatives answerable to the group. The conspiracy takes on additional weight, for it is distorting social and political arrangements itself in the furtherance of its own ends. And still another step occurs when the criminal group assumes control over the society in which it finds itself, as the Mafia has done in Sicily from time to time, and perhaps in some American cities, or as (it may quite reasonably be argued) Hitler and his close associates managed when they assumed power in Germany.

In each case, the word *conspiracy* does admirably in making clear the similarities among all those groups. Yet those similarities are far less important than the differences they ignore. To use the one word to cover all of them, without further concern about each of the instances, is to engage in a great self-deception. Consequently, to say merely that an event is the result of a conspiracy is to say almost nothing at all, except that more than a single person was involved. To give any meaning to so general a charge, the nature of the conspiracy must be stated explicitly. It is not a small point. It may appear that a commentator calls upon *conspiracy* to account for a crime wave. Does he mean that most or all of the crimes are committed by criminals working in pairs? Or does he mean that a criminal group has taken possession of the city, its administration, its police, and its courts? Or is it something in between? Until he had made clear what he intends to signify, he has said nothing of any consequence.

There is a further remark to be made of the ordinary use of the word *conspiracy*. It implies the existence of individuals working not only in concert but secretly; they have banded *against* the rest of society, and must remain in some degree concealed from that society. Once it is premised that a conspiracy exists, it need only be permitted to increase in size and complexity to serve as a complete explanation for anything that ever has happened, is happening, or will happen. What is it that you most deeply and certainly know to be true? That the woman seated across the room from you is your wife? But no! She is a carefully constructed imitation of your wife, created by a plastic surgeon of unsurpassed skill. A thousand doctors, medical assistants, friends, neighbors, associates, police—all are in on the plot. But you talk to her, live with her—no one could possibly deceive you about your wife? My dear sir, you are in fact under the influence of a rare drug, which has been insinuated into you when you thought you were only taking aspirin. It affects your judgment. Actually, that woman is not even a reasonably fair imitation of your wife, but you no longer have the ability to discriminate. But why should anyone do this to you? I cannot tell you. It has to do with major political developments—which are, of course, being designed by members of the conspiracy.

Now all of this is in practice senseless, but it is logically quite sound. It is so sound, and this and other similar processes create such dilemmas for logicians, that they have been forced to provide rules against them. Generally speaking, the rule simply states that any process that can be used to prove *anything* cannot properly be used at all. If there is no conceivable logical way to falsify a proof, then it is not a proof. This may appear at first glance to be paradoxical, but it is nothing of the sort. It is quite reasonable. And in the case of conspiracy it is quite obvious,

once you begin to think about it, that it is true. You may end up
by involving everyone in the whole world, with the single exception of the victim, within the conspiracy, but there is nothing
logically wrong with that, except that it makes a strange kind of
conspiracy.

The word *conspiracy* has already occurred several times in
these pages, and it will often occur hereafter. I will try, however,
to stipulate in each case the kind of conspiracy that is under
consideration. And I will not accept as worthy of further consideration any of those theories in which the notion of conspiracy
runs wild; it is completely invalid to cope with awkward facts
merely by adding two or three thousand conspirators (·without
evidence, without even grounds for suspicion, but simply to make
a connected story) for there is literally no end to such a process.

But back to the assassination. The question at issue is the
identity of the assassin, and the question is not whether there
was a general conspiracy against the life of the President, but
whether as part of that conspiracy the identity of the assassin
was concealed, and an innocent man maneuvered into a posture
of deep-dyed guilt. I am not yet asking whether the President
was the victim of a plot. So far I ask only if Lee Harvey Oswald
was the victim of a plot. Can it, in other words, be reasonably
maintained that the mass of evidence converging upon the identification of Oswald as assassin was the creation of a conspiracy?

Consider only in part what such a conspiracy would have
entailed. As an example, take the identification of Oswald as
owner of a Mannlicher-Carcano rifle, serial number C2766. That
identification was made as follows.

When the rifle was found on the sixth floor, an investigation
revealed that Crescent Firearms in New York distributed Italian
military surplus and had in fact shipped a rifle with the serial
number in question to Klein's Sporting Goods in Chicago, which
then stepped forward to state that the rifle had been ordered by
mail reply to one of their advertisements. The order blank
directed that the rifle be sent to A. J. Hidell, at Post Office Box
2915 in Dallas, Texas. An accompanying money order was
signed A. J. Hidell. The United States Post Office in Dallas
identified the Post Office Box as having been issued, during the
time in question, to Lee H. Oswald. It had already been dis-

covered that in Oswald's possession, at the time of his arrest, was a forged Selective Service card bearing Oswald's picture but made out in the name of Hidell. Two handwriting experts later testified that the signatures on all those documents were written by the same man, and that the handwriting in all cases corresponded with the known handwriting of Lee Harvey Oswald.

Hypothesize, for the moment, that the rifle was in fact ordered by someone other than Lee Harvey Oswald, and see what such a hypothesis entails. At the outset it may seem forthright. But then the handwriting experts would have had to be in the general conspiracy, for they identified the handwriting to be Oswald's. One or more members of the staff of the Warren Commission must also be involved, for it was they who chose the handwriting expert, and obviously the choice of the wrong expert would have revealed the entire fraud. The Dallas police would have had to be deeply involved, for part of the identification rests on the discovery of the Hidell Selective Service card in Oswald's possession, and someone had to get to Oswald immediately after the capture to make certain it was planted there.

It must be recognized that the identification of the rifle is only one link in an almost endless chain of evidence. A conspiracy to plant the rifle could be but one of innumerable elements of a complete conspiracy. It would still be necessary, for example, to make sure that when the assassination was carried out Oswald was somewhere in the neighborhood and without a clear-cut alibi. Yet even that one single element—the conspiracy to attribute the rifle's ownership to Oswald—requires the collaboration of perhaps a half dozen men or more, scattered among the Warren Commission staff and the Dallas Police Department at the very least, and coordinating their activities. With hundreds or even thousands of such individual elements necessary to make up the total conspiracy, the number of people that would have had to be involved, and coordinated, begins to be staggering.

Now all of this is possible. Once one is permitted to roam at will in the green fields of conspiracy, everything is explicable. It is possible also that so widespread a conspiracy, with literally thousands of men involved, has remained tight-lipped and secure for all these years despite all the pressure and notoriety, all the occasions for second thoughts, all the temptations to indiscretion brought on by whisky, loving blonde companions, illness, or simple failure of memory. All this is quite possible.

And there are those who seriously maintain it. Jim Garrison, the District Attorney of New Orleans, who asserts stubbornly that the entire assassination is an open book to him and to his colleagues, has said that Oswald never fired that rifle; that he had nothing whatsoever to do with the assassination, and that he, Jim Garrison, will one day prove it. He has not yet done so, nor has he shown any signs of doing so.

Until he or someone else can provide facts as conclusive as those which arose in the hours that followed the assassination, the reasonable man must abide by the reasonable conclusion. What facts there are point to Oswald as the assassin.

It must be recognized that it is not a single fact that does so, but the convergence of a large body of facts. To dispute the conclusion in practice, it is not sufficient to cast doubt upon a single fact. It is necessary to destroy the conviction that arises when facts reinforce each other. It is the inner consistency of the account that makes it persuasive, and not the degree of certainty which applies to any single item.

Concerning the testimony on the point from which the rifle shots originated, many of those in Dealey Plaza, where the assassination took place, were uncertain; many believed the shots came from ahead of the car rather than behind it, many heard more shots than Oswald could possibly have fired. All that testimony must ultimately be accounted for, in part to satisfy our own instincts to seek the most complete possible account, and in part because the least possible vagueness must not be permitted to remain to beguile the irresponsible or tempt the unscrupulous. But regardless of the dissenting testimony, the persuasiveness of the account lies in the fact that eyewitnesses *did* place the point of origin high in the Texas Book Depository, and that their testimony converges with all the evidence of the rifle, of Oswald's movements, of the expended shells and every other fact in our possession. Nothing of any substance, except the all-explaining notion of a far-flung conspiracy, converges with the testimony of those who heard half a dozen shots from half a dozen points.

There remains some conflicting testimony that is extremely

difficult to reconcile with the facts, and perhaps can never be reconciled with the facts. For example, there is testimony concerning the package in which Oswald is alleged to have transported the rifle, which is often at odds with everything that can be ascertained. But the effect of such discrepancies, however disturbing they may be in relation to one fact or another, is almost imperceptible in relation to a whole body of facts which support each other at every point, and most of which are totally incontrovertible except by the inadmissible device of an open-ended conspiracy.

The case against Oswald was from the outset so compelling that it affected by force the manner in which the Warren Commission and its staff proceeded. Whatever may have been formally pretended, the staff could never have proceeded to an investigation intended to discover the assassin, for they knew the answer to that question from the outset. To have entered into a fantasy procedure, in which they imagined they had wiped from their minds all accumulated knowledge of the events associated with the assassination and were obliged to begin again from the beginning, would have been nothing more than a meaningless charade. The whole investigation was inevitably colored with the knowledge that the identity of the assassin was known. That knowledge, in fact, gave shape to the investigation.

But if that state of affairs appears at first blush to bring the objectivity of the investigation into question, consideration of the manner in which any investigation must be conducted will restore the equilibrium. It is tempting to consider an ideal investigation to be one in which a clutter of data, carefully collected and put in order, slowly begins to reveal conclusions which had previously gone unsuspected. But the mind of man works in quite another fashion. Whatever the matter under investigation, whether it is a heinous crime or the behavior of the nucleus of the atom, the investigator begins with a hypothesis and collects his data in terms of that hypothesis. So long as the data thus collected supports the hypothesis, the investigation proceeds smoothly. The moment data appear which contradict the hypothesis, that hypothesis is modified and a new one substituted. That is the normal procedure, and on the whole it is the only procedure that works.

If the identity of the assassin of the President had not been immediately known, the investigators would have had to hypothesize an assassin and proceed from there. They might well have decided, for example, that a member of a Dallas radical right movement was the most likely candidate, and embarked at once on the investigatory steps that such a hypothesis suggested. Whether we like it or not, some ordering principle is necessary if any investigation is to proceed, and if such a principle is not immediately evident, the investigator willy-nilly must invent one. What differentiated the Kennedy assassination was not that the investigation proceeded from an assumption as to the identity of the assassin, but that the assumption was far stronger than usual: It was a hypothesis teetering on the very edge of certainty.

That state of affairs might well lead to a completely perfunctory investigation. Had the assassination in Dealey Plaza been one in which an ordinary private citizen was struck down, one may be sure that the investigation would indeed have been perfunctory. The assassin being known, the prosecution would merely have accumulated what it needed to assure a conviction—tightened a few loose parts, met the formal requirements of the laws of evidence and the like. Those were obligations the Warren Commission did not face, for Oswald could not be tried. But the Commission had other and graver obligations, and its investigation—as its twenty-seven volumes testify—was anything but perfunctory. Whether it was expert as well as diligent is another question, with which the latter portion of this book deals.

Whatever the investigation, there are great virtues in possessing a strong hypothesis. It may at first appear paradoxical, but it is no less true that the mechanics of an earnest search for the truth work out to a ruthless attack upon the validity of the hypothesis which has generated the search. If you believe an associate to be honest and wish to make yourself sure of the fact, you do not seek out evidence of his honesty. What you look for is evidence of his dishonesty. You try your utmost to disprove your initial belief; if trying your utmost you fail to do so, then your belief in his honesty is established. There are no paradoxes to be found in such a procedure; on the contrary, there is no more efficient manner in which to proceed. It is the prime characteristic of an honest search for truth.

The trap lies in the phrase "try your utmost." If your belief in the honesty of your associate is strong enough, and above all if it has any kind of emotional overtones—if he is your favorite brother—you may not wish to try your utmost to disprove it, or you may not be able to try your utmost. You may find yourself overlooking evidences of dishonesty because you do not wish to see them, or rationalizing away evidences of dishonesty because you are not comfortable with them.

The Warren Commission was faced with that dilemma in its most troubling form. Since it was almost inconceivable that its hypothesis that Oswald was the assassin could be overturned, there was every temptation to brush aside brusquely anything that pointed in another direction. And since the hypothesis that Oswald was the assassin was politically a most favorable hypothesis, with the fewest undesirable connotations, there were emotional reasons that would reinforce the human tendency to see only that evidence that satisfied the hypothesis. No question of malice is implied—merely the question of human failings.

As this account proceeds to a detailed examination of the circumstances surrounding the assassination, I will show that the record of the Warren Commission—or more properly stated, the record of its staff—was a remarkably good one. There was a real attempt to develop all evidence that appeared to point *away* from Oswald. That evidence was accumulated, recorded, and published in its raw form; it constitutes ammunition for many of the attacks that are being made on the Commission. The record, however, was not entirely without flaw. There are occasions to be found when the Commission and its staff tried somewhat less than their utmost to gather unfavorable data.

At the very least, these occasions are blemishes. It remains to be determined whether they are any more than that. They cannot and do not affect the conclusion that Oswald assassinated the President, for something more than an occasional blemish is necessary to bring down the overwhelming case against Oswald. It may be, however, that in those blemishes lies in part the inability of the Warren Commission to persuade the American public.

Blemished or not, the investigation was carried out. Enormous efforts were undertaken to flesh out the bare bones of the basic account. What was required, at the outset, was further elucidation of the manner in which the President met his death. That Oswald shot the President was only the beginning: How often did he shoot? How often did he hit? Where did the bullets strike? Exactly how did the President die? And did this evidence, too, converge with the immediate evidence of the rifle, the circumstances, and the man?

Once more it should be repeated that there were two distinct purposes lying behind the search for further data. One was the pure obligation, answering as much to direct human needs as to any further end, to render the most complete possible account of a tragic event. The other was to withdraw from those who could be expected to question the report—to question *any* report—points of purchase from which to launch their inevitable attacks. The Commission had to find the truth and render it as close to unassailable as it possibly could.

And it should be kept in mind that those two purposes, although indeed distinct, were also inseparable. The most damaging outcome, for the Commission and for the ends it meant to serve, would have been the dissemination of falsehood. Any falsehood, even if it were trivial in itself, would lie in the path of society like a land mine, some day to detonate and bring down the whole Commission and all it stood for. The Commission had to be always aware that untruth would creep into its report, and it was something the Commission feared. For its own sake, if for no other, it could not knowingly include falsehoods. Devotion to the truth was a commitment that arose not necessarily from the inclinations of the individual Commissioners, but from the nature of the task. This much can be said as a matter of unalloyed common sense: The Commission, as a Commission, was honest. There is no small step away from that position. If it was not honest, it was a central part of a massive conspiracy.

THE CAMERA AND THE AUTOPSY

RATHER: *Is there any doubt that the wound at the back of the President's head was the entry wound?*

HUMES: *There is absolutely no doubt, sir.*

—Interview with Commander James J. Humes

Evidence, data, information about the assassination of President Kennedy are not difficult to come by. The assassination itself took place in the direct view of some hundreds of spectators who were scattered in and around Dealey Plaza to watch the Presidential motorcade. The Plaza itself, although the distortions inherent in photography and in television make it appear wide and roomy, is in fact quite compact. The artist's model, shown in the photograph section, gives the general dimensions and the salient features; it is drawn carefully to scale, and point-to-point measurements can readily be made with its help. No distances within the Plaza are really large, and no vantage point leaves a spectator much worse off than he would be in the cheaper seats of a good sized theater. So everyone who was present did indeed see and hear the assassination, and because the human recording apparatus is something less than perfect, the multiplicity of accounts means a multiplicity of conflicting stories.

Then too there is physical evidence of various kinds. There is a rifle and a handgun; cartridge cases, bullets, and bullet fragments. There are the documents which link the two firearms with Oswald, pictures of Oswald with the firearms. There are documents accumulated during the course of Oswald's life in the Marines and in Russia. There is the package in which Oswald is alleged to have carried the rifle to the School Book Depository.

34

There are palmprints. There are fibers from the blanket in which Oswald is alleged to have stored the rifle. Pictures and expert reports on all this physical evidence, and more, occupy page after page in the supplementary volumes of the Warren Report.

Of all this hard evidence, two constituent parts stand out in importance. One of these is a few inches of 8 millimeter color motion picture film, upon which an amateur cameraman named Abraham Zapruder was busily engaged in recording the Presidential motorcade when the tragedy unfolded. The other was the wounded body of the President himself, and the records of the autopsy performed on that body in Bethesda, Maryland. Both the Zapruder film and the autopsy are critical of the Warren Report, and of any discussion of the Warren Report. Neither the Zapruder film nor the records of the autopsy are freely available to the public or to those who are, for whatever reasons, students of the assassination.

The Zapruder film was bought from the amateur cameraman shortly after the assassination by Time, Inc., which paid for it a sum which has been estimated to be in excess of half a million dollars. Sums tend to grow when they are estimated rather than stated, and it may have been a great deal less—it could be a great deal less and still be substantial. Time, Inc., well within its legal rights, has refused permission to use the film in its original form, and has not been overly generous in permitting use of still pictures from the film. At the time of the four Warren Report broadcasts, CBS News, John A. Watters, general manager of *Life* magazine, wrote that in the view of Time, Inc., the film was an "invaluable corporate asset," and that rights to its use were not available "at any price." Consequently, prints made from the Zapruder film are not available for use in this book.

As a record of the event, the Zapruder film is superficially not very informative. Fate was kind to Mr. Zapruder in bringing him to the right place at the right time, and Mr. Zapruder, amateur or not, did a smooth and skillful job of tracking the President's car. But fate was also a bit malicious. During a critical part of the few seconds during which his film spun on its reels, the Presidential car passed behind a street sign, and cannot be seen. Focus is never sharp, and the picture must be puzzled out rather than viewed directly.

What it shows, upon immediate scrutiny, is the following: the Presidential car is seen turning the corner from Houston Street onto Elm Street, and beginning its descent toward the triple underpass. The President, his wife, Governor John Connally of Texas, and Mrs. Connally are seen responding to the crowds from the back of the car—the President and his wife from the back seats, the two Texans from the jump seats. The car then vanishes from view behind the street sign. When it emerges, the President is still erect but clutching his throat. The Governor appears to be turning toward the President. Then Governor Connally is seen to slump, and the President to sag. The car continues smoothly down the incline, until suddenly the President's skull explodes and fragments fly from it. The President's head moves backward a few inches, then he falls to his left and into the seat. By then the film has begun to run out, but it is no matter, for the car accelerated at once for the wild race to Parkland Hospital.

During that brief period of time the film had moved steadily through Mr. Zapruder's camera, one frame at a time, like a second hand marching around the rim of a pocket watch. And like such a second hand, it was a clock. Instead of counting seconds it counted frames, and one can say that two events were five frames apart on the Zapruder film just as one can say that they were so many seconds apart on the watch. The two statements are in all respects equivalent. It is not a metaphor to say that Mr. Zapruder's film is a clock of the assassination, for that is exactly what it is.

Because we are accustomed to measuring time in seconds rather than in frames, we would like to be able to convert Zapruder-time to something with which we are more familiar. In principle, the process is simplicity itself. We need only find the speed at which the film ran through the camera, and make a simple arithmetical computation. If the camera was running smoothly as it was designed to run, at 18.3 frames a second, then the interval between any two frames would be 1/18.3 second. All the other computations follow.

But what is simple in principle is not always simple in practice. As with any other clock, there are two questions to be resolved about the Zapruder clock. First, what is its relation to a standard clock? (The question of the nature of a standard clock need not be considered. It is the business of physicists and astronomers. There *are* standard clocks, which is really all that is necessary to know.) We ask that question about an ordinary pocket watch when we ask whether it is running fast or slow. The question is the same when the Zapruder clock is being considered: Was it running fast or slow? Second, whatever the speed of the clock, is it running smoothly at that speed? A clock may tick off minute after minute in exact conformity with a standard clock, and yet each second may differ from every other second. It may (many clocks do) run fast from 0 to 30 seconds, and then just slow enough from 30 to 60 seconds to balance. It is not easy to build a clock, even when you set out to do so. A camera, which is not designed primarily to serve as a clock, is immediately suspect when it is put to that use.

The questions are of great importance in relation to the Zapruder clock, because as far as the assassination is concerned it is the only clock we have. The film shows exactly the moment when the President was fatally wounded. Every other event shown in the film can be timed in reference to that known event by counting frames, so that we may say, for example, that Governor Connally sagged exactly fifty-five frames before the fatal shot. The Warren Commission did exactly that, counting the frames and giving each a number in serial order. The fatal shot occurred at frame 313; other events located on the film will be referred to by frame number throughout this book when the assassination is being considered. But other measurements of time, such as the measurement of the rate at which a rifle of a certain make can be accurately fired, have been made in seconds and not in frames, and to give those measurements significance we must be able to present Zapruder-time in seconds as well.

How good a clock was Zapruder's camera? The FBI undertook to find out at once, and reported that it had tested the camera and found it to be running at 18.3 frames a second, its rated speed. The camera then came into the possession of the Bell & Howell Company, its maker. When CBS News undertook the preparation of its programs, a natural skepticism led the staff to reopen the question. (The skepticism was natural simply because the camera is an inexpensive amateur model, and no such camera is dependable so far as speed is concerned; a variation of a frame or two a second makes no real difference in the quality of the picture.) Bell & Howell was unwilling to turn the camera over to CBS News for tests, but reported it had tested the camera once more, found it to be running at 18.3 frames a second, and turned it over to the National Archives, where it remains.

The CBS News producers assigned to the Warren project remained skeptical, and, because the camera was not available to them, fell back on the next best thing. In various camera shops nine Bell & Howell cameras were purchased at random, out of the same production lines as Zapruder's camera, and essentially identical to his. Those cameras were turned over to Charles Wycoff of Edgerton, Germeshausen and Greer in Cambridge, Massachusetts. Mr. Wycoff is an expert on cameras and films, and his company one of the country's outstanding research organizations in those and allied fields.

Using two independent methods, Mr. Wycoff checked the cameras. One of his methods was based on the simple principle of the stroboscope. A camera was wound, set running, and then viewed under the illumination of a bright flashing light. When the light flashes in exact synchronization with the passage of the frames of the film, each frame is illuminated when it is in precisely the same position as the frame that preceded it and the frame that is to succeed it. As a result, no motion is seen; an illusion is produced that the same frame is being seen over and over, standing stock still. The procedure, then, is to vary the rate of the flashes until the film stands still, and at that point the rate of the flashes is the rate at which the film is moving. Mr. Wycoff's device, called a Tachyscope, measures the rate of flashes with precision. It yields the speed of movement of the film to an accuracy of less than one hundredth of one percent.

The second method was one of direct measurement. A clock with a sweep hand capable of measuring time to one hundredth of a second was stationed in front of the camera to be tested. First the camera and then the clock was set running, and a motion picture of the clock taken. The film was developed, and upon it the first frame identified in which the clock could be seen to be running. Upon the remainder of the developed film it was only necessary to read the clock as it appeared on each frame to know the elapsed time. The method is less precise than the first, but yields nonetheless an accuracy of about 1 percent.

Mr. Wycoff reported that in general the cameras ran slow. Applying statistical methods to his results, he reported the speed of a Bell & Howell camera of that model might properly be estimated not at 18.3 frames a second, its rated speed, but more accurately at 17.0 frames a second, plus or minus two frames. It was his conviction that such a camera, selected at random, would run in general well below its rated speed, under optimum conditions. All this is interesting, and not without significance, but the fact remains that Mr. Wycoff did *not* test Zapruder's camera, and that for all he knows that might indeed be a camera that ran at 18.3 frames a second.

But Mr. Wycoff found something far more interesting. Whatever the speed of a camera, its optimum speed was likely to be greater than its speed under ordinary operating conditions. Wound to less than its full tension, permitted to accumulate dirt or scraps of film in its movement, the speed invariably fell, and in some cases fell sharply to twelve frames a second or less. In practice, as opposed to theory, camera speeds were consistently different from rated speeds or optimum speeds—and almost always on the low side, sometimes far down on the low side.

Mr. Wycoff concluded that failing the opportunity to test Zapruder's camera directly and under varying conditions—and it is exactly that which CBS News could not do, and which I do not know has ever been done—he concluded that the camera was in all likelihood running slower than its rated speed of 18.3 frames a second. This conclusion, which CBS News accepted, does not affect the utility of the Zapruder film as a clock. It does affect the conversion ratio for frames into seconds. It is the CBS News view that the film was probably passing through the camera at the rate of about 16.5 frames a second, and in using the Zapruder camera as a clock CBS News used that conversion factor. As we shall see, the matter is of some significance: It means that the events recorded on the Zapruder film may have taken a little longer to occur than the Warren Commission concluded, and in certain aspects that "little longer" becomes important.

I repeat that none of Mr. Wycoff's experiments are as decisive as tests on the Zapruder camera might have been. But since I cannot make such tests, I must fall back on what we have. I am in no way minimizing the significance of the Zapruder film, and I stress that it remains the sole clock that was running (so far as the record is concerned) while the assassination unfolded. And despite the comments, it remains a pretty satisfactory clock. I will make much use of it.

A few moments after he was fatally wounded, the President was rushed to Parkland Hospital, where a team of doctors, quite aware that they were engaged in a hopeless task, fought to keep him alive. But in all but the technical sense he was dead when he arrived, and in less than half an hour the doctors had no alternative but to acknowledge the fact. There followed an incredible episode in which the local coroner, who took the view that one murder was no different from another murder, attempted to prevent removal of the body. It was removed to a hearse, however, and transported to the airport, flown to Washington, and delivered to Bethesda Naval Hospital for autopsy.

It might have been far better, as far as history is concerned, if the autopsy had indeed been conducted at Parkland Hospital. Certainly some of the ambiguities that now surround the autopsy would have been avoided. It was not a matter that required the facilities or the expert attendants that could be found at Bethesda, for all the evidence appears to indicate that aside from the identity of the victim there was nothing out of the ordinary about the post-mortem examination. At Parkland the doctors who had treated the President would have been at hand, and a clear account of both the wounds and the treatment might have emerged. But all this is truly idle speculation. Those were moments of near-hysteria, when prudent people had to entertain the possibility that major actions against the American government might be under way; the staffs of both the late and the incumbent President were feverishly anxious to be back in Washington.

Bethesda had been selected by Jacqueline Kennedy, simply because her husband had been a naval man. At Bethesda, Commander James J. Humes, an experienced and respected pathologist, as senior pathologist and director of the laboratories, took charge of the autopsy. In view of the manner in which death occurred, he called in Lieutenant Colonel Pierre A. Finck, a forensic pathologist, to assist him. Forensic medicine deals with the legal aspects of medical matters, and in crimes of violence, where the matter may ultimately go to court, a forensic pathologist is presumed to know exactly what information will be of significance to the court. The third doctor at the autopsy was Commander J. Thornton Boswell, who was chief of pathology at Bethesda.

The record shows clearly that the autopsy was conducted in an efficient, orderly manner. The head wound was identified as the cause of death, and the examination showed beyond a shadow of a doubt that the bullet entered from the rear and exited from the front. These were matters that could be determined with complete precision by any doctor familiar with bullet wounds, and the record shows that there was never a scintilla of doubt.

The throat wounds, however, required puzzling out. Technically speaking, no gunshot wound at all was visible in the front of the neck; where such a wound might have been expected there was instead a passage cut through the throat into the windpipe. In back there was indeed a gunshot wound, but when an attempt was made to probe, no clear passage through the neck was found. But this initial confusion was more apparent than real, for it was no great matter for the doctors to establish what had happened. The wound in the back of the neck was clearly demonstrated to be an entry wound, for the bullet had carried with it shreds of cloth from the President's suit, and these were found embedded in the tissues. The lack of a clear passage was no mystery, for the bullet had passed through soft tissue and this necessarily closed back around the path. The passage cut into the throat in front was assumed to be a tracheotomy, performed in Parkland in an attempt to keep the President breathing; as a matter of common sense any surgical procedure is carried out through an existing wound, if there is one in an appropriate location, rather than wound the patient surgically at still another site. The doctors at Bethesda assumed that the Parkland doctors had done exactly that; Dr. Humes called Parkland the next morning to be quite sure, and was told that it was just as he had assumed. So far as the bullets were concerned, this completed the autopsy. Two wounds had been found, both entering the President's body from the rear and exiting from the front. Dr. Humes's notes were in order, and he was in a good position to prepare his report. For the record, he would also be able to consult color photographs and X-rays which were taken as the autopsy proceeded. Dr. Humes would have been quite justified in believing that the autopsy had been a job well done. No doubt he would have been incredulous if anyone had suggested how many storms were to break about his head.

The seed of the first storm had been sown, innocently enough, by Dr. Malcolm Perry, the senior attending physician at Parkland. Needless to say, the President had been accompanied to Dallas by the usual horde of newsmen. They had not come to cover an assassination, but when events produced an assassination they were instantly, overbearingly, uncontrollably ravenous for news. Almost without opposition from city officials, they turned Dallas into a madhouse. Their demands, undignified and unreasonable, resulted in the appearance before them of Dr. Perry, hustled to a press conference directly from the emergency room in which an hour earlier he had declared the President dead. Dr. Perry had conducted no examination of the President. He had tried to save his life, and had failed. He knew about the struggle to keep the President alive, but beyond that he had no information. Yet information was demanded of him.

This is his own account of his examination, as he told it in mid-1967 in an interview with Eddie Barker of KRLD, Dallas, for CBS News:

> **Dr. Perry:** I noted a wound when I came into the room, which was of the right posterior portion of the head. Of course, I did not examine it. Again, there was no time for cursory examination. If a patent airway cannot be secured, and the bleeding cannot be controlled—it really made little difference. Some things must take priority and precedence, and in this instance the airway and the bleeding must be controlled initially.
>
> **Barker:** What about the wound that you observed in the front of the President's neck? Would you tell me about that?
>
> **Perry:** Yes, of course. It was a very cursory examination. The emergency proceedings at hand necessitated immediate action. There was not time to do more than an extremely light examination.
>
> **Barker:** There's been a lot said and written about was this an exit wound or an entry wound? Would you discuss that with me?

Perry: Well, this is a difficult problem. The determination of entrance or exit frequently requires the ascertainment of trajectory. And of course, this I did not do. None of us did at the time. There was no time for such things.

The differentiation between an entrance and an exit wound is often made on a disparity in sizes, the exit wound being generally larger in the case of an expanding bullet. If, however, the bullet does not expand—if it is a full-jacketed bullet, for example, such as used commonly in the military—the caliber of the bullet on entrance and exit will frequently be the same. And without deformation of the bullet and without tumbling, the wounds would be very similar—and in many instances even a trained observer could not distinguish between the two.

Barker: Did it occur to you at the time, or did you think was this an entry wound or was this an exit wound?

Perry: Actually, I didn't really give it much thought. And I realize that perhaps it would have been better had I done so. But I actually applied my energies, and those of us there all did, to the problem at hand, and I didn't really concern myself too much with how it happened, or why. And for that reason, of course, I didn't think about cutting through the wound, which of course rendered it invalid as regards further examination and inspection. But it didn't even occur to me. I did what was expedient and what was necessary, and I didn't think much about it.

Barker: You did not turn the President over?

Perry: No, there was no reason to. There was not time with that problem, and there was really no reason to. It made very little difference to me, since my immediate concern was with an attempted resuscitation.

Dr. Perry's misfortune was that under the harassment of the press, less than an hour after the assassination, he said more than he knew. A transcript of the press conference was made at the time, and it shows that Dr. Perry, under urging, was a good deal more definite about the nature of the throat wound than his own account shows to have been warranted. At the conference he called it an entry wound, and pointed to the front of his throat in doing so. In a matter of minutes the story was on the wires and over the air. The reporters, relying upon what they had wrenched from Dr. Perry, stated flatly that the President had been shot in the front of his throat.

In the few seconds before Dr. Perry's scalpel cut into the wound, it had appeared to him to be similar to an entry wound. It *was* similiar to any entry wound. A bullet which passes only through soft tissue, striking nothing solid, emerging undeformed and still aligned in the direction of its trajectory, is quite likely to make an exit wound that looks like an entry wound. In cutting through the wound, Dr. Perry destroyed the local features at the site of the wound that would have revealed it, under scrutiny, to have been an exit wound. It made no real difference. Dr. Humes, in Bethesda, had found the entry wound, had noted the trajectory, had found no bullet in the neck, and thus had established beyond a doubt that the tracheotomy obscured what had originally been an exit wound. There was no doubt about it—or there would have been no doubt about it had not Dr. Perry, badgered into saying more than he knew, made his egregious error.

But Dr. Perry was not the only person to say more than he knew. As Dr. Humes and his assistants conducted the autopsy in Bethesda, the FBI and Secret Service were in attendance, sometimes in the room itself, more often in the corridor. There was, as we have indicated, a stage in the autopsy when the doctors were still in the process of determining the path of the bullet which struck the President's neck. The bullet hole at the back of the neck had been found and probed, but no passage through the neck could be found. The doctors themselves drew no conclusions from this—they merely went about their business. The FBI, not being medically trained, jumped directly to the conclusion that a bullet had entered the President's back and had somehow not passed through. The doctors had never suggested anything of the kind. They had said merely that no passage had been found. The FBI made its own unwarranted interpretation that no passage had taken place. Before Dr. Humes had issued his report, the FBI wrote one of its own. In it the FBI stated on no other basis than its own misunderstanding that a bullet had entered the President's back, penetrated a few inches, and then stopped.

This was what the FBI, in other moods, would call "an unevaluated report." An unevaluated report can be defined, somewhat maliciously, as a juicy morsel of gossip for which no evidence exists. FBI dockets are full to the brim with them, and the FBI is thoroughly casual about them. It was casual about this one. Within a week it knew the statement about the bullet was wrong, but when in January the FBI was asked to submit its own reports on the assassination for the files of the Warren Commission, it included material from this unevaluated report as simply and as ingenuously as it submitted a hundred others it had gathered during the few days that followed the assassination. (The volumes of testimony and documents are full of such reports, most of them clearly emanating from lunatics who plague the police after every serious crime.) As a consequence, the FBI managed to get into the record, as a formal FBI document, a statement that was of central significance to the account of the assassination, and that the FBI itself probably thought to be untrue.

That was by no means all the trouble that the wound in the back of the neck was to cause. The physicians, examining the wounds, carefully measured their locations and wrote the measurements down. Each measurement was made in terms of a specific anatomical structure: "So many centimeters below the lower mastoid process." They locate the wounds precisely. But as a matter of custom the location of the wounds is also marked, more or less approximately, on sheets of paper carrying standard stylized outlines of the human body. On one such outline Dr. Boswell marked the wound in the back of the neck. That marking is of no technical use, nor is it intended to be. Only the measurements have validity. The mark on the outline is meant merely as an aid to the memory when the report is finally prepared. And Dr. Boswell, taking no particular pains, made his mark not on the neck but some inches below it. That it was nothing more than a casual approximation is clearly indicated by the fact that the true measurements, which place the wound considerably higher, appear on the same sheet of paper. Dr. Humes, knowing that the mark carried no weight, was never consciously aware of the discrepancy, since he knew that anyone seeking to reconstruct the autopsy data from his notes would consider only the measurements and never the marks. But the mark is there, too low to represent an entrance wound that corresponded (given the known trajectory of the bullet) with the exit wound in front.

And finally, Dr. Humes was betrayed by the English language, as so many have been betrayed. The measurements are one thing, but in ordinary language the wound in back was low in the neck; the wound in front high in the neck. That is an accurate enough statement, as far as it goes. But to make it go all the way, place the index finger of one hand *low* on the back of your neck, and the index finger of the other hand *high* on the front of your neck, then look in a mirror. You are likely to be surprised to notice that your back finger is as high as or even higher than your front finger. The top of the neck, in fact, is some three or four inches higher in back than in front, depending upon what point to choose as the top of the neck. And since in practice all three words *neck, high,* and *low* are vague, there is no precision in any colloquial statement that uses them together. It is therefore not only possible but probable that a bullet traveling downward would enter the "neck" "low" in the back and exit "high" in the front.

I spoke earlier of how plausibility arises out of converging evidence. In these four instances, fate provided what appeared to be converging evidence. Dr. Perry stated the front wound was an entry wound. The FBI statement that the bullet entering the back of the neck did not pass through the neck implies that the front wound was inflicted from the front. Dr. Boswell's mark is not consonant with a bullet on a downward trajectory. The undeniable fact that the wound passed from low in the back of the neck to high in the front of the neck can be ignorantly taken to mean that the bullet was traveling upward. All this "evidence" converges to indicate that someone other than Oswald shot the President. None of it *is* evidence, for none of it squares with known facts. But if you do not know the facts, and particularly if these matters are presented in a manner that willfully conceals the facts, it all sounds very convincing.

Two further attacks are made on the credibility of the autopsy, one of them merely malicious, the second far more troubling. In preparing the autopsy, Dr. Humes proceeded as almost any normal person *would* proceed. Working from his notes, he wrote out a draft. Subsequently, working from that draft and his notes, he prepared a final version, in which the shortcomings, the mistakes, and the infelicities of the first draft were corrected. That draft having served its purpose, and not representing what he wished to appear as his final report, he quite naturally destroyed it. No possible criticism can be made of this procedure. No criticism has been made. Instead, it is repeatedly reported that Dr. Humes destroyed his notes. He did nothing of the sort. They are in the archives. To have destroyed them would have been irresponsible and would have subjected Dr. Humes to quite appropriate criticism, for the notes are the immediate record of the autopsy. The draft has no such status. It was merely a part of the process of preparing a report, and of no more significance than the typewriter or the pencil he used.

The matter of the color pictures and the X-rays is far more serious. After the autopsy they were turned over to the Kennedy family, who were quite understandably fearful that they would somehow appear in print, in all their horror and with all their power to revive dreadful memories. The Kennedys decided to withhold them from the public record. Recently they have been presented to the National Archives, but with the condition that they remain secret, except to authorized visitors, for five years. Thus they are not publicly available to confirm or deny the results of the autopsy. To those who wish to believe the worst, it all sounds suspicious. It becomes even more suspicious when it is realized that no member of the Warren Commission or its staff was permitted to see the color pictures or the X-rays, although some of the staff made every effort to do so. Only recently has it become known, by means of a comment made to CBS News by John J. McCloy, a member of the Commission, that not even Chief Justice Earl Warren saw the pictures and X-rays, although he permitted his Commission to gain the impression he had done so. To CBS News Mr. McCloy said:

> I think that if there's one thing that I would do over again, I would insist on those photographs and those X-rays having been produced before us. In the one respect, and only one respect there, I think we were perhaps oversensitive to what we understood was the sensitivities of the Kennedy family against the production of colored photographs of the body and so forth.

> But those exist. They're there. We had the best evidence in regard to that—the pathology in respect to the President's wounds. It was our own choice that we didn't subpoena these photographs, which were then in the hands of the Kennedy family. I say, I wish—I don't think we'd have subpoenaed them. We could have gotten—Mr. Justice Warren was talking to the Kennedy family about that at that time. I thought that he was really going to see them, but it turned out that he hadn't.

That evidence is not completely out of reach. As part of the investigation conducted by CBS News, permission was sought and granted for an interview with Commander Humes, now Captain Humes. He reported that he had reexamined the pictures and X-rays and saw nothing in them to lead him to change in any respect his original autopsy report. But Captain Humes is by no means a disinterested party. His report is not equivalent to that which might be given by someone unconnected with the Commission, and unassociated with the autopsy.

Certainly the feelings of the Kennedy family and the Kennedy children should be spared. But equally certainly, there should be means by which responsible persons might have access to the report, and the privilege to make public their conclusions.

The integrity of Captain Humes and the authenticity of his report are not at issue. The account I have given here should persuade any reader of both. The pictures and X-rays do, after all, exist, and while they do, it would be suicidal for anyone to lie about them. But I deal here, as I shall deal so often in this book, not with facts but with persuasiveness; with the need to draw the teeth of the malicious, the irresponsible, the lunatic. While important evidence is withheld, they will still be able to gnaw away at reality.

5 EYEWITNESSES

The Warren Commission had to choose between seriously conflicting accounts, and many of the critics think it chose badly.

—Dan Rather

A trained observer will ordinarily produce a moderately good record of an event to which he is paying attention. It is unlikely to be a perfect record. Two such observers, viewing the same event, will usually produce records that differ in their details, as anyone can verify who bothers to read both an Associated Press and a United Press-International account of even an uncomplicated happening. Not too unusually, the two accounts will differ in more than detail; there will be discrepancies of some substance that may ultimately prove quite difficult to resolve, and will survive to produce a conundrum for historians (after having been memorialized by *The New Yorker* in its "Which Paper Do You Read" department).

Even to produce this moderately good record, certain conditions must be met. First, the observer must be able to anticipate with some confidence most of what it is he is going to see. An event which follows a rigid pattern over most of its course, such as a sporting event, provides optimum conditions for the observer. Second, he must be paying attention—if possible, consciously restricting his attention to the portions of the event he can anticipate. Next, he must be as much as possible emotionally remote from the event, for there is wishful seeing and hearing just as truly as there is wishful thinking. Finally, he should make notes contemporaneous with the event, and flesh out those notes into a coherent account, recorded durably in one way or another, while they are still fresh in his mind. The quality of any account, like the quality of an egg, diminishes rapidly with time.

If all those conditions are met, the trained observer is quite likely—although by no means certain—to produce a moderately good record. If any of them is not met, the result may very well be a complete hash. Thus it is a matter of common experience that even at so rigidly patterned an occasion as a baseball game, an untoward incident is likely to produce nearly as many versions as there are observers. Let two ballplayers collide in pursuing a fly ball, for example, and the press box will debate until the end of the game the manner in which the collision took place and the consequences of the collision to the two men concerned and to the game. "We are checking with the dugout," the television announcer will say, "to find out what happened." Every journalist who has considered the matter is aware that his account relates what he *thought* he saw and heard; that if he is a responsible journalist it is his first duty to determine how nearly accurate his own impressions really were; and that in the end he will have only a reasonably good approximation to the truth.

There are further snares, even for the wary. As an observer repeats—in print or in the spoken word—his account of the event he witnessed, it both changes and hardens. The hardening process is simple; merely by repeating the account he persuades himself of the veracity of each item within it. Thus he may write initially that an event took place "at about 12:20," with the mental reservation that it might have been 12:10 and might also have been 12:30. But after a few repetitions it becomes "at 12:20," and after a few more "at exactly 12:20." All of us being no more than mortal men, this will happen in almost every case; it will happen all the more quickly and decisively if the exact time of the event is a matter of consequence.

The manner in which an account changes is far more subtle. In general, our own best friend is the editor who always stands by to improve the general tone of memory. Retold often enough, a story will change imperceptibly in a manner which exalts our own personal role. If upon some occasion I have played the fool and another man the hero, it is almost certain that any anecdote I create from the incident will ultimately take a form that reverses the roles. Any person who keeps a journal over any long period of time is shocked when he dares compare his current memory of an occurrence with the record he made at the time: shocked, dismayed, and embarrassed. Time, he will discover, has not softened the details of the occurrence, as one might expect, but has sharpened them, and in every case sharpened them in his own favor. We lie to no one as consistently and as successfully as we lie to ourselves, and we are helpless to prevent it.

In Dealey Plaza, when the Presidential motorcade moved through, there were several scores of men and women—perhaps two or three hundred in all—who had gathered to see the President pass. A few of them were trained observers: journalists, police officers, secret service men. Most of them were ordinary citizens, whose expertise, whatever it might have been, lay in quite other directions.

Trained or not, they all had a reasonably good notion of what to expect. The motorcade would pass; the President and his wife would smile and wave from the back seat; the Governor and his wife, from the jump seats. The onlookers planned to watch the President and Jackie, in affection or in hostility; they were anxious for some more intimate acquaintance with the object of their emotions, even though it would be limited to a passing glance at fifty or sixty feet. They expected to hear from the motorcade the roar of motorcycle engines and perhaps an occasional siren; from the crowd around them a patter of applause, and a babble of banal phrases. While they waited, their eyes swept the neighborhood passively, looking for nothing at all, intent upon nothing but the sounds that indicate the motorcade's approach.

Suddenly the pattern broke; the President was shot and fatally wounded. *The critical events took place in just about the time it takes a deliberate reader, not hurrying, to recite this sentence aloud.* For most observers, much or all that time had passed before they even began to realize something out of the ordinary had happened; some did not know, even when the Presidential car had accelerated out of the Plaza, that a murder had taken place. No one made any notes, but no matter; there had not been time to make notes. Anyone who reached for a pencil at the sound of the first shot might still be groping for it when the last shot rang through the air. And even in the moments that followed the assassination, there was no immediate means of gaining any kind of orientation, and of imposing some kind of pattern upon events; instead there was disorder, incipient hysteria, a general feeling that normal procedures had abruptly been wrenched awry. James Altgens, a professional photographer employed by the Associated Press, was so aghast he neglected to snap the shutter of his camera. Professional news photographers having trained themselves as they do, no greater dislocation of the psyche can be imagined.

A few minutes, a few hours, a few days, even a few months after the event, the men and women in the Plaza began telling what they had seen and heard: telling each other, telling the police, telling the press, ultimately, some of them, telling the Warren Commission. Their stories were wildly inconsistent. They had heard no shots, one shot, two, three, four, five, six. The shots had come from above, from the level, from the front, the side, the rear. The President had been struck once, twice, repeatedly. The shots had been fast, slow, equally spaced, erratic, in bursts. The President had fallen forward, lurched back, sagged to the side.

Some told their stories immediately and spontaneously. Others withheld them until they had gained knowledge of evidence that later developed and of differences in the interpretation of that evidence, unaware how deeply that further information might affect their own memories. Some found themselves suddenly important because their own recollections squared so admirably with official views that gradually took shape. Others found themselves courted because *their* recollections squared with widely proclaimed dissents to the official view. On every recollection, time worked its magic. Dim suspicions became sharply limned certainties. The shape made out vaguely in the corner of the eye became more distinct; with time it became recognizable as a man, his hair of such and such a color, wearing a shirt in such and such a way, performing such and such an act.

It is not necessary to suggest that anyone lied. Each person, it may be assumed without making any difference at all in the outcome, said exactly what he or she believed to be true. Nonetheless, most of the accounts were false in their important details. Any account that was accepted as the truth implied with utter finality the falsity of a host of others. There is nothing in the least invidious about this. It was the way it was; the way it always is.

Each eyewitness account was necessarily suspect. Yet each of them, and all of them taken together, were of great utility to the investigators, first the police and later the staff of the Warren Commission. No prudent man would conclude that they proved much of anything, but they might well lead the way to proof.

To begin with there was something that could be learned from all the eyewitness accounts that was not present in any single account. There might be details that recurred with a frequency that could not be immediately attributed to chance. If the preponderance of the observers heard exactly three shots, one might reasonably conclude that this was not a purely random effect, and that there was at least some reason to believe that three shots had been fired or that some real occurrence had taken place that would lead a skilled observer to hear three shots. (Two shots and an echo that could be clearly demonstrated, for example.) If, moreover, among the majority that heard three shots were most or all of the trained observers, the hypothesis would thereby be strengthened. If, finally, upon direct examination the observers who reported three shots transmitted by one means or another to the examiner a sense of sobriety, of responsibility, of veracity, or prudence, there would be that much more reason to give weight to their testimony; if those who heard four shots, or two shots, somehow left the examiner uneasy, unconvinced, experiencing perhaps an undefinable malaise, *their* testimony might be laid aside. Juries behave in exactly that way; it is what juries are for. All eyewitness testimony is suspect; a jury of ordinary men is trusted to determine which is more suspect than others. On the whole, it works fairly well.

It does not always show up well in the record. For the ordinary man, the ability to distinguish veracity from simulation, sincerity from self-aggrandizement, certainty from a false show of assurance, is accumulated by his own diversity of experience over the years. Far below the level of consciousness, he learns to look for and to recognize telltale indications, even though all the resources of the psyche of the person who confronts him are devoted to concealing just those indications. In cold print he has no such opportunity. Mannerisms, intonations, infinitesimal hesitations are lost, until one man's testimony is much like any other man's. There is the illusion that one witness is quite as worthy of credence as another, and at times a disposition to accept as gospel a gaudy tale which in face-to-face confrontation would not survive the first few words. The doctrine that there should be opportunity to confront witnesses is more than a mere formalism.

But eyewitness accounts, suspect or not, have still another value. To the diligent investigator they provide essential leads. They guide him in his search for evidence which is in some degree separable from the vagaries of human wills and human memories: substantial evidence, which can be held aloft and brandished. Told that three shots were fired, he knows to look for physical evidence of three shots. He may find it or not, but at the worst he is assisted by the self-evident heuristic principle that in conducting a search it is useful to be looking for something.

Thus, repeated testimony that shots came from what now is known as "the grassy knoll"—a slope overlooking Elm Street about one fourth the way around the compass from the Book Depository—led to an exhaustive search for physical evidence of those shots. That no physical evidence was found does not reduce the value of that search. The failure to find physical evidence is substantive in itself, for it adds to the conclusiveness of the physical evidence that was found. The twenty-six supplementary volumes of the Warren Report are concerned for the most part with the laborious account of all the false leads, all the plausible tales that turned out to be devoid of substance.

Yet there might easily have been fifty-six such volumes instead of twenty-six. The investigators, like any such investigators, were obliged sooner or later to call a halt to their search. As a matter of cold fact, to conduct any investigation, even the simplest, to its absolute conclusion would require infinite time, for the world of phenomena is infinitely rich and the recollections of the human mind infinitely diverse.

As an investigation proceeds, and as physical evidence accumulates, eyewitness testimony inevitably begins to sort itself out into "good" and "bad." "Good" testimony is testimony that fits into the pattern that is emerging. "Bad" testimony is testimony that disrupts that pattern. Here, above all, the physical evidence is paramount. If one witness maintains a passerby, now forever lost in the crowd, was tall, and another maintains he was short, there is little to choose between them. But if one maintains a murder was committed by gunshot, and the other reports a knifing, the presence of a bullet wound in the victim is determinative (except in the more *outré* murder mysteries).

Since an investigation is necessarily limited in time, and since the ideal product is a report which recounts in detail exactly what is presumed to have happened, a stage arrives in which the investigator will almost arbitrarily assign certain testimony to the category of "bad" from the moment that it comes to his attention. To take the extreme case, there was a report, probably in jest, that President John F. Kennedy was seen, early in 1967, at a party given in New York by Truman Capote. However circumstantial that eyewitness account, and however convinced the man who delivered it, there was little likelihood that it would be taken seriously, or pursued further. With infinite time and resources, such reports might be followed to their ultimate invalidation. With limited time and much to do, an investigator would be enormously frivolous to waste his efforts on any such endeavor.

Much of the criticism of the Warren Commission concerns itself with the failure of the Commission to hear the testimony of Mrs. Carolyn Walther. This is what she told CBS News:

Mrs. Walther: It was right there at our lunch hour, so we felt like we, you know, had plenty of time to see it and we rushed with our lunch. I think I got out on the street about 12:15 or 12:20—something along there.

And we were looking around, back and forth. People were talking and laughing, and in a very good mood. And I looked at this building and saw a man with a gun, and there was another man standing to his right. I could not see all of this man, and I couldn't see his face.

The other man was holding a short gun. It wasn't as long as a rifle. He was holding it pointed down, and he was kneeling in the window, or sitting. His arms were on the window. He was holding the gun in a downward position, and he was looking downward. ...

Just as I was looking at this man the people started shouting "Here he comes, here he comes." So I looked the other way and forgot about the man.

The President passed us, and he was smiling, and everybody was waving. Then the last of the cars went by, and I heard the shot. I thought it was a firecracker. Then I started back to work, and it was along the curb, and then two shots right together, and then another one. I'm sure there were four shots.

And then I said "It's gunshots." And people started screaming. . . .

I told them that I saw the man had light hair, or brown, and was wearing a white shirt. I explained to the FBI agents that I wasn't sure about that. That was my impression on thinking about it later. That I thought that was the way the man was dressed. This other man was wearing a brown suit. That was all I could see, half of this man's body from his shoulders to his hips. He was facing the window. Evidently he was looking out. But his face was in the upper part, where the glass was dirty, and I couldn't see his face. . . .

The first statement that I made, I said the man was on the fourth or fifth floor, and I still feel the same way.

Barker: When did you first talk to an officer about this?

Mrs. Walther: It was several days later. I don't remember just what day. I called them on the phone, and I talked to them one night. And they came to my place of employment the next day and talked to me. And they came again the next day and talked.

Mrs. Walther gave her account to FBI and police investigators before the Warren Commission began to meet. The staff of the Commission was aware of her testimony, but no member of either the Commission or its staff ever came in direct touch with her. Her testimony, in other words, was arbitrarily considered to be "bad," and was accordingly recorded but otherwise ignored.

There were internal problems with Mrs. Walther's account, in that she was accompanied to Dealey Plaza by a friend to whom she made no mention of the two men in the window, either when she first believed she saw them or in the moments that followed the assassination. This is somewhat unnatural, to say the least. Those who believe they have unique information usually rush to divulge it. Still, people do unnatural things—their foibles are not sufficient to rule them out as witnesses. The real problem with Mrs. Walther's statement is that it took the investigation nowhere at all, and that if it was accepted it made nonsense of a great deal of hard evidence. There were no physical signs, anywhere in the Book Depository, of two men and a rifle in the window she identified. There was no physical evidence of any action from that window: no shots that found a target, no unexpended shells. No one else saw anyone in that window; no one who worked in the Depository could account for two men in that window. In brief, Mrs. Walther was not heard because her testimony made no sense.

None of this is any reflection on Mrs. Walther. Undoubtedly she believes exactly what she says, and in a certain sense of the words she did indeed see two men at that window. All that can be said with assurance of Mrs. Walther is that it is most reasonable to assume that she was not a very good observer—like the rest of us.

In hindsight, it is tempting to assert that the Warren Commission should have paid more attention to Mrs. Walther, whether or not it considered her testimony to be useless. In doing so, they would have deprived those who assail the Report of the opportunity to use Mrs. Walther as a stick with which to beat the Commission. But that is indeed hindsight. The records reveal a dozen witnesses, all as sure of themselves and as destructive to the account given by the Commission as Mrs. Walther was. Critics have seized upon Mrs. Walther because in a sense she is the best of the counterwitnesses: She is a pleasant lady, she was standing in a favorable position when the motorcade passed, and she is subjectively quite certain of what she saw. But if Mrs. Walther had been denied them, by reason of careful and solicitous hearing from the staff of the Commission or the Commission itself, another would have been found to provide some flat contradiction of the Report. It would have been nothing more than a question of making a selection from those who were left, for there simply had to be witnesses with whom the Commission and its staff made no direct contact, and any one of them would have done almost as well as Mrs. Walther. It was a dilemma for the Commission from which there was never any escape.

It is only misleading to argue that the Commission accepted as gospel, evidence from eyewitnesses who were apparently at least as suspect as Mrs. Walther. The argument itself is sound enough. Any student of the Report, for example, must become uneasy at the testimony of the three men who stationed themselves at a fifth floor window in the Depository to watch the motorcade go by. Their stories dovetail admirably: They each heard three shots; they believed they were fired above them; one of them heard three shells hit the floor above them. It may well be so, but the uneasiness is engendered when one learns that the Warren Commission stimulated their memories by a reenactment that duplicated in detail the account to which the investigators themselves were by then committed, and in so doing may well have made concrete a recollection that had earlier been vague and indistinct. Here again, no reflection is intended upon Jarman, Norman, and Williams, who are saying nothing but what they believe. Yet essentially they are as suspect as witnesses as Mrs. Walther. The difference between the two cases is that the story told by the three workmen is powerfully corroborated by indisputable evidence, and Mrs. Walther's story is not—is, on the contrary, destroyed by indisputable evidence.

The point of the matter is that the Warren Report does not rely for the validity of its conclusions upon the recollections of inadvertent bystanders. These are called in, from time to time, to give "artistic verisimilitude to an otherwise bald and unconvincing narrative," although in fact they accomplish no such thing for the Commission any more than they did for Pooh-Bah. The accounts of bystanders in and around Dealey Plaza are little more than grillwork on a massive structure. The real question at issue is whether the structure itself is sound.

6 THE DIRECTION OF THE SHOTS

All of the shots came from the same place, from back over my right shoulder. They weren't in front of us, or they weren't at the side of us. There were no sounds like that emanating from those directions.

—Governor John Connally

An extraordinary amount of knowledge was accumulated within a few hours of the assassination. Yet in all, only the bare bones of the assassination were visible. Those bare bones appeared to be all that was required for a completely adequate reconstruction, but both prudence and natural curiosity demanded that the details be filled in. Particularly during those early hours it was easy to doubt that the story so far accumulated represented the whole story, and there was no foreknowledge of what might be revealed during the pursuit of further information.

The first need was to reconstruct the assassination in all its elements. The critical matters involved the direction from which the shots were fired (for although it was as certain as anything could be that *some* shots were fired from the Depository, it was by no means certain that they all came from there); the number of shots that were fired; and the time span of the assassination. These three elements in the reconstruction, listed serially here, are of course intimately connected. Strictly speaking, no one of the three can be considered in isolation from the other two, for considerations of time enter into a determination of number and direction, and considerations of number into a determination of direction and time. I will do my best to disentangle them, beginning with the question of the direction of the shots, and proceeding to deal with number and time in succeeding chapters.

So far as observers in Dealey Plaza are concerned, behavior, as distinct from the recollection of behavior, tells a fairly clear story. The Plaza itself was abounding in persons who were participants in the events, rather than mere bystanders: the Secret Service agents and the police in the Presidential cars and other cars, the Dallas police, and reporters either in the parade or at the side.

In the motorcade itself, the behavior was unambiguous; the driver in the President's car set out at once for Parkland Hospital, and the other cars followed. Among the police, the actions were somewhat more distraught. The most accurate statement might be that police rushed in all directions. Three of these appeared to be preferred directions; the railroad overpass, toward which the motorcade was proceeding when the shots were fired, the grassy knoll alongside the parade route, and the School Book Depository. Yet within a matter of minutes the first two of these were abandoned, and the School Book Depository was sealed off approximately twenty minutes after the assassination. Thereafter, detailed search took place primarily in and around the School Book Depository.

We are judging now from behavior, and not from the recollection of behavior. The behavior indicates clearly that in those first few minutes, the immediate indications led to the building and to the building alone. Officers searching the grassy knoll and the overpass simply exhausted the value of their activities in a moment or two; there was nothing further to do because there was nothing there. They were led, almost without conscious thought, to the building, because every item of information they gathered, whether from witnesses or participants, and the behavior of their fellows, led them to the building. Roy Truly, in charge of the building, was interviewed, and a check on occupants of the building began. About forty minutes after the assassination, on the cluttered sixth floor, the empty shell cases were found, and a few minutes later the rifle itself, carefully hidden.

The penetration of the building was so fast that Truly and an officer apparently met Oswald on his way down from the sixth floor. He was not arrested simply because Truly was able to identify him, and the officer, rattled by events, took an identification to signify innocence.

In short, the sum of several dozen individual decisions (during the few minutes that followed the shooting) was that the shots came from the building. Among those who had immediate responsibilities, there seemed to be little or no variation. Whatever the belief with which they began, they appeared almost unanimously to converge upon the building.

And simply because they behaved naturally, they sowed doubt among observers. The officer who, for one reason or another, believed that a shot or shots had come from the grassy knoll, had done the obvious thing: raced to the grassy knoll with his gun drawn, satisfied himself that his initial belief was probably mistaken, and made his way directly or indirectly to the School Book Depository, where the action was. Observers saw only that officers with their guns drawn had raced up the grassy knoll. They were not in the officers' skins, and did not feel the forces that then led the officers away from the grassy knoll. Instead they accepted a simple syllogism: Officers race up the grassy knoll, therefore the officers must have heard shots from the grassy knoll, therefore there must have *been* shots from the grassy knoll. From there the syllogism is taken over by human failings, and the observers decided they, too, had heard shots from the grassy knoll.

The fact is that it is never simple to tell where shots have come from. A person directly in line with a shot, or very nearly in line, will usually have a reasonably good notion; a person off to either side will be forced to guess, and only a trained observer is likely to guess accurately. Echoes and reverberations make it especially difficult, and Dealey Plaza, a small bowl surrounded by buildings and by concrete structures, might have been designed to create echoes and reverberations.

It is a further fact that no one in Dealey Plaza was ever able to report what he had heard, at least in a certain sense of the word, but was forced instead to fall back upon what he thought he heard. To some extent, one hears what one wishes to hear, as anyone knows who commonly conducts conversations in crowded rooms. The unexpected noise takes some time to make a conscious impression, particularly upon those whose attention is fixed elsewhere. It is probable that most of those in the Plaza were never conscious of gunshots while the gunshots themselves were reverberating; that only after the gunshots faded away was there any general realization that gunshots had been heard. Recollection, even after a few seconds, is subject to gross error, for it is almost always affected by the whole environment. Those who, upon their realization that they heard gunshots, saw officers rushing up the grassy knoll, would instinctively couple the two events. Completely outside any conscious interference—indeed, beyond the possibility of conscious interference—recollection would do the rest by merging the two perceptions: They would honestly and sincerely recall that they had "heard" gunshots from the grassy knoll. It is remarkable how many witnesses who report hearing shots from that direction couple their account with the memory of policemen rushing in that direction. They believe that in that manner they reinforce the validity of their recollection; in point of fact, they cast grave doubt upon it.

Among those in the best position to know—the occupants of the Presidential car, at whom the shots were directed and who were therefore directly in the trajectory—the recollection is unambiguous. The Governor, his wife, the driver, and the accompanying Secret Service man recollect clearly that the shots came from the direction of the Texas School Book Depository. So do the occupants of the following car.

The autopsy provided unambiguous evidence that the shots that struck home came from above and behind; that if there were shots from other directions, they missed their targets. The autopsy and the disputes that surround it have been considered earlier. It was the CBS News conclusion that there is no reasonable alternative beyond accepting the autopsy report or indulging in a belief in a conspiracy of enormous magnitude, shared by thousands of the country's most respected men and women. The techniques of determining entry and exit wounds are too well established, and the intensity of the autopsy was too great to permit the belief that careless errors were made. In particular, the skull wound and the Governor's wounds simply would not permit any explanation other than a shot from the rear and above, in each case.

Yet there is a single item of further evidence that troubles even the least skeptical critic. The Zapruder film appears to show fairly clearly that upon impact the President's head moved backward, *toward* the direction in which all other evidence asserts the bullet struck him. It is a universal experience that an object struck by a moving body moves itself in the direction of the projectile's motion, and not in opposition to that projectile. District Attorney Jim Garrison, earthy as always, put it to CBS News forcefully: "When I hit a golf ball with a driver," he said, "it doesn't move backwards."

The matter, of course, is far more complex than that. The golf ball does indeed move forward. But if Mr. Garrison should strike a block of gelatin with the sharp blade of a knife moving at high speed, he might find that the gelatin does not perceptibly move at all, although the knife passes through it; under other conditions he might find that the gelatin moves first forward and back, or even first backwards and then forward. The only natural law involved is the law of conservation of momentum, which establishes the relationship between velocities (and velocity involves both speed *and* direction) and masses before and after collision. The relationship is a simple one: The sums must be the same before and after.

The velocities and masses can be measured quite simply when the collision takes place between a golf ball and a golf club. With a skull and a bullet, the relationship is not so simple. The skull is a bony structure within which there are liquids and solids under restraint. A bullet entering the skull sets up all kinds of forces and counterforces. If they are such as to drive forward, at high velocity, a part of the skull, it may well be that the rest of the skull will move backward. To bear this out, a photograph was taken at one millionth of a second showing a bullet passing through an electric light bulb: an explosion occurred on the side of the bulb away from the point of entry of the bullet. That explosion, if the bulb were not restrained, might have driven the bulb slightly back. None of this is at all mysterious; it is ordinary high-school physics.

Thus most physicists will agree that considering only the interaction of a bullet and a human skull, there is a possibility, although only a slight possibility, that the skull will move backwards after the impact. But the matter goes further than that. The interaction that took place was between a human being and a bullet, and superficial physics will not do to explain it.

Consider once again Mr. Garrison's golf ball. Set a golf

ball on a tee and hit it forcefully with a club, and nothing out of the ordinary will happen. Set on the tee a plastic golf ball, and again nothing extraordinary will happen. But take a plastic ball, design it carefully to look like a real ball, and conceal the information from the man with the club. He, too, will hit it forcefully—and will quite probably tear a muscle or strain his wrist.

For in hitting a golf ball, or anything else, the whole body comes into play. At the moment of impact, the muscles brace powerfully to take up the shock. And if, for some reason, the shock does not take place—if the body has all the impressions of impact except the force of the impact itself—those braced muscles will drive the structure in the direction from which the blow was expected, and something will give. It is different in scale, although not in type, from the disastrous effect of stepping on a stair that is not there.

A somewhat analogous effect can be seen on a baseball field, when a batter is struck by a pitched ball in some relatively invulnerable spot: the forearm, perhaps. Often the impact knocks him off his feet and stretches him out in the batter's box. No physical analysis of impact on forearm would suggest that the consequence would be a prone batsman; he is on the ground because in the fraction of a second his whole neuromuscular system braced for the blow. It was internal energy, and not the energy of the batted ball, that sent him sprawling.

In short, the motion of a head struck by a bullet will depend in large part on the neuromuscular state of the man who is struck. What is present is no longer a simple collision, but a complicated nexus of forces and counterforces. In the President, it must have been complicated indeed. He had been struck, only a moment or two before, by an earlier bullet; his body was only then beginning to respond to that earlier impact. A bewildering series of messages was in transit from his brain to his nervous system and his muscular system, telling them perhaps to brace for the next blow, or to begin moving out of the line of fire. The muscles of his shoulders, his back and his neck were involved. A physicist and a physiologist, working together, might, if they knew all those messages and their consequences, work out in detail the effect on the motion of the President's head. But that knowledge is simply not available, in practice or even in principle.

There is indeed a mystery in the motion of the President's head after impact, but it is the ordinary kind of mystery that proceeds from inadequate knowledge. There is nothing in that motion that would lead a physiologist to deduce from it the direction of the bullet. *Given the fact that the bullet together with fragments of skull carried away most of the momentum along the direction of motion,* the skull itself might have moved in any direction at all.

In passing, it might be mentioned that related considerations rule out the earlier misunderstanding, indulged in by the FBI, that a bullet had penetrated a few inches into the President's back and had then stopped. Assuming that the entering bullet was traveling at full muzzle velocity, or very nearly, one would have to account for all its lost momentum. That momentum would have passed directly into the body of the President, almost in its totality, when the President was totally unprepared to receive it, and would inevitably have smashed him forward into the jump seats. The Zapruder film shows no such effect; it can be surely deduced from that alone that no such event took place.

The urge to demonstrate that shots came from a direction, or directions, other than the School Book Depository is, of course, merely one aspect of the more general urge to provide evidence for a conspiracy. The discovery that there were such shots would not in itself demonstrate a conspiracy—it is conceivable, although hardly likely, that two would-be assassins simply chanced to fix upon the same time and the same general location for an attempt on the President's life. It would constitute a powerful indication, however, that Oswald was not acting alone. It is important to any conspiracy theory in a somewhat more indirect fashion as well, for there is something indescribably sloppy about any conspiracy that depends upon a single rifleman, and not a particularly good one, operating with an ancient rifle. There is the feeling that anyone who planned at all would in all likelihood plan better than that.

In any case the search for a second assassin has proved to be unending. A favorite tool is the analysis of pictures taken, during the moments of the assassination, by the host of amateur and professional photographers clustered at the scene. Since all the cameras were focused upon the President, anything else is likely to be far out of focus. This is of great advantage to the searcher, for a sufficiently soft photograph can be considered full of un-revealed surprises.

The technique usually has been to scrutinize such a picture carefully until one is able to recognize, lurking behind fences, on fire escapes or in shadows a figure of a mysterious stranger, or better still, of several. An enormous enlargement is then made of the photograph, in an effort to make out more clearly the linea-ments of the suspect. The pattern in the enlargement is then utilized to drive the point home.

The procedure is futile enough to be almost tragic. The eye searching for patterns in a soft picture will find them, for the eye notoriously makes patterns out of what is presented to it, and the absence of detail in a picture enhances the process. Enlarge-ment, beyond a certain point, is completely without significance, particularly when the enlargement is made from a newspaper print of the photograph, as for some reason it customarily is. The dots of ink that go to make up the detail of a half-tone, un-noticeable when the picture is reproduced in normal size, swell up gigantically under enlargement until all sense of the picture itself is lost, and all that remains is an enigmatic pattern of black circles. Out of that enigmatic pattern, the imaginative eye can make anything at all that it pleases, for on that scale one picture looks like any other. Even when a negative is enlarged—and a negative of high quality—it remains true that information not on the negative is not to be found in the enlargement; a murky suggestion of a pattern obscured by shadow and structure remains exactly that and nothing more.

Other sophisticated processes can be used to detect motion between successive frames of motion picture film which would otherwise be obscured by the irregular movement of the camera mechanism, or a motion picture projector. One such film, the possession of United Press International, was carefully studied for UPI by Itek Corporation in Lexington, Massachusetts, which is customarily deeply engaged in creating optical devices for the United States defense forces and is therefore extremely knowl-edgeable about intelligence procedures as they are connected with photography. Itek studied, with all the sophistication at its command, film which was alleged to show a man with a rifle in the neighborhood of the grassy knoll. The deplorable facts are that nothing much would have been proved if such movement had been found where suspicious souls believed it to have occurred, and that in any case no such movement was found. Thus one set of pictures was cleanly disposed of; how many that leaves is almost anyone's guess. (A similar segment of motion picture film, alleged to show Oswald in motion at the sixth floor window, was analyzed in the same fashion by CBS News, and it, too, showed nothing at all.)

Presumably if such attempts should ever be crowned with success, those who stimulate them will assert they have demonstrated that shots were fired from a direction other than that which is generally accepted. Somewhere there seems to be an assumption that a person who appears obscured by shadow in a photograph is thereby manifested to be a shady character, capable of assassination; if he were a respectable person he would presumably have shown up more clearly in a photograph.

Of all the eyewitnesses, one in particular encourages those who stubbornly seek to have their faith rewarded on the grassy knoll. Mr. S. M. Holland, working on the railroad overpass at the time of the assassination, tells of seeing a puff of smoke, which he attributes to rifle or pistol fire, in the general direction of the grassy knoll; it hovered a few feet in the air before dispersing. Making his way to the picket fence at the rear of the knoll, he reports finding behind it a multitude of footsteps in the mud, and muddy footprints on the bumpers of two cars. Putting two and two together Mr. Holland deduces that a rifleman marched back and forth in the mud while he awaited the President, then bestrode the bumper and fired. Again, it should be presumed that in telling his story, Mr. Holland is saying nothing but what he believes is to be absolutely true. The credibility of his report, however, is low. No modern firearm produces puffs of smoke that hover in the air—the best one can expect is a very light, very fugitive puff which appears only directly at the muzzle of the gun and vanishes almost the moment it is seen. The scene of Mr. Holland's footprints had already been visited by police by the time he reached it. They saw nothing worth remarking, and the footprints in all likelihood were their own.

What can be said with all assurance is that no real evidence exists for gunshots other than those that came from the School Book Depository. The hard-bitten proponents of a conspiracy theory cannot do well without such gunshots, and they have searched desperately for evidence. They have produced none at all, aside from vague general statements from bystanders and the somewhat less vague, but still unsupported and generally unconvincing statement from Mr. Holland.

Some critics, usually those with military or police experience, take an even simpler line of approach. Out of their accumulated experience, they describe first how truly proficient assassins would plan an assassination: They would post riflemen in strategic locations, arrange for a triangulated field of fire, and bring the President under remorseless and inescapable attack. This being the prescribed manner in which to proceed, they conclude, it may be assumed that the conspirators proceeded precisely in that fashion. Thus William Turner, former FBI man and now a warm supporter of Jim Garrison, said:

> **Turner:** Now what happened there was that the Kennedy motorcade coming down there—the Kennedy limousine—there were shots from the rear, from either the Dallas School Book Depository or the Del-Mar, or the courthouse; and there were shots from the grassy knoll. This is triangulation. There is no escape from it, if it's properly executed.
>
> I think that the massive head wound, where the President's head was literally blown apart, came from a quartering angle on the grassy knoll. The bullet was a low-velocity dum-dum mercury fulminate hollow-nose, which were outlawed by the Hague Convention but which are used by paramilitary groups. And that the whole reaction is very consistent to this kind of weapon. That he was struck and his head doesn't go directly back but it goes back and over, which would be consistent with the shot from that direction and Newton's Laws of Motion.
>
> Now, I feel also that the escape was very simple. Number one, using a revolver or a pistol, the shells do not eject, they don't even have to bother to pick up their discharged shells. Number two, they can slip the gun under their coat and when everyone comes surging up they can just say, "He went that-a-way." Very simple. In fact, it's so simple it probably happened that way.

It can be very convincing if you desperately want to be convinced. If you pay attention, however, you find that Mr.

Turner is merely assuming everything he pretends to prove, and ignoring any evidence that does not fit his thesis.

In the end I can perhaps best sum up by asserting that of all the evidence mustered by the Warren Commission and its staff, that evidence that fixes the direction of the shots is least subject to real criticism. They all came from the sixth floor of the Texas School Book Depository Building.

THE NUMBER OF SHOTS

There were indeed three shots fired, as the Commission said . . . the one that apparently didn't hit anyone in the car was fired before the ones that hit the President. —Professor Luis Alvarez

Investigating the number of shots that were fired at the Presidential motorcade, two immediate clues constitute the starting point. One of these is the frequency with which bystanders specified three shots. Unanimity, to be sure, did not exist, but the preponderance of the bystanders who report three shots, and of those whose evidence seemed most believable—the trained observers, and those who were directly in the line of fire—there was something very close to unanimity. Of the latter group, Governor Connally, knowledgeable about firearms and unquestionably in the best position to know what was going on, *heard* only two shots but concedes he probably did not hear the shot that struck him.

The second clue was constituted by the three expended cartridges found in the sniper's nest on the sixth floor of the Book Depository building. Three expended cartridges is certainly strong evidence for three shots.

Yet neither clue, nor indeed the two clues taken together, was entirely conclusive. I have reiterated the skepticism with which any eyewitness account should be received, and it applies quite as well in this instance as in any other. Not only was Dealey Plaza a kind of echo chamber, but even under the best of conditions the number of shots fired from a rifle is by no means easy to determine by persons who are not paying close attention. There is a sharp report when the sound of the firing reaches the ear; there may be still another report when the bullet passes close by, and still a third when it strikes. Under the best of circumstances, it takes at least some care to distinguish all of these, and circumstances in Dealey Plaza were not the best. As for the three expended shells, although they indicated clearly that three shots had been fired, they did not necessarily prove that all three had been fired at the point where the shells were found. If Oswald had carried his rifle to the sixth floor with an expended cartridge casing in the firing chamber, his first act would have been to operate the bolt and eject it. The sequence bolt-fire-bolt-fire-bolt would have thus produced three casings but only two shots. Another possible sequence, beginning with a live shell in the chamber, would run fire-bolt-fire-bolt-fire-bolt-fire: This would produce four shots and three casings, leaving an expended casing in the chamber. It appears to be ruled out, however, by the fact that Oswald's rifle, when it was found hidden on the sixth floor, had a live shell in the firing chamber; the sequence at the window therefore had to end with the manipulation of the bolt. Altogether, the presence of three shells, taken at face value, does not uniquely specify three shots, but suggests three shots, and under the circumstances, certainly limits the choice to either two shots or three.

The evidence from the wounds is of course ambiguous, since the wound can tell only how many shots struck home, and not how many were fired. Even with that restriction, however, there can initially be no clear conclusion. The President was clearly shot twice, once in the head and once in the neck. Governor Connally had several wounds, which at first impression might be attributed to several bullets, but which could also have been caused by a single bullet, providing his body was in a quite specific position when the bullet struck. The position required is a natural position, and consonant with everything that appears in the Zapruder film. There is further evidence in that, while the Governor's chest wound was clearly caused by a bullet traveling at high velocity, the thigh and wrist wounds were not; the wrist wound, in fact, was almost certainly caused by a bullet which had lost most of its momentum, for a high-velocity bullet traveling at anything near muzzle velocity would have shattered the wrist, and the actual wound was trivial.

But although those facts, so recounted, suggest that three

bullets struck home—two upon the President, one upon the Governor—the conclusion is by no means necessary. The Warren Commission in fact decided that the wounds inflicted upon both men were the consequence of two rather than three bullets. That has come to be known as "the single-bullet theory." It is important in the Warren Commission's account of the assassination, and as much as any other single aspect of the Warren Report the prime target of critical dissent. I shall leave it for a chapter of its own, pausing here only to remark that the wounds themselves appear initially to be consistent with either two or three hits.

Finally, there is the evidence of the bullets themselves. In the car there were found two bullet fragments, one of which weighed 44.6 grains and the other 21.0 grains. Smaller lead particles and some lead residue were found as well, adding little to the full recovered weight. Bullets of the type used in Oswald's rifle weigh 160–161 grains, and the two fragments thus weighed approximately two fifths of the whole bullet. Both fragments were traced unambiguously to Oswald's rifle.

The Commission assumed that the two fragments came from the same bullet. There are sophisticated tests, involving scrutiny of the fragments under neutron irradiation, which might have added to the Commission's knowledge. Those tests, although they could not be used to prove that the two fragments had once been part of the same bullet, might have proved that they were not. (The situation is analogous to establishing paternity by means of a blood test on the child: If the child's blood type is consistent with that of the alleged father, nothing has been proved except that the allegation might be true; if the two blood types are inconsistent, parenthood has been conclusively ruled out.) The Commission did not bother with those tests, although it bothered with a good deal that was less significant. Thereby it dismissed an opportunity to disprove its own theories, and in so doing was without a doubt remiss.

Another bullet was found, almost intact, at Parkland Hospital. This, too, was traced to Oswald's rifle. The circumstances under which it was found are of some importance in regard to the single bullet theory, and I will consider them at the appropriate place.

There was also testimony that something struck the street near the motorcade, and even a mark on the curb at Main Street which might have been caused by a bullet, and which under spectrographic examination yielded signs of lead and antimony. In the absence of copper, with which the bullets were jacketed, it is most probable that a fragment rather than a full bullet struck the curbing, if anything at all did that was associated with the assassination. The third bullet, if there was one, is missing. No unambiguous evidence for its existence has ever been found.

The Commission, having missed its opportunity to prove the existence of three bullets by appropriate tests on the fragments, had to make up its mind on the basis of conflicting and inconclusive evidence. On the side of three bullets it had eyewitnesses, in some of whom it was reasonable to impose a good deal of trust; it had also the three cartridge casings. On the side of two bullets it had its own conclusions that only two shots struck home, and its own inability to find any convincing trace of a third bullet. The Commission chose to believe that three shots had been fired. The best that can be said about that choice is that it is consistent with what evidence there was before the Commission; the choice of two shots would have been just about as consistent.

Here the matter stood until late in 1966, when Dr. Luis Alvarez, professor of physics at the University of California at Berkeley, found himself in repeated discussions with his graduate students concerning the Warren Report and became interested in the variety of problems they raised. It was at about that time that *Life* magazine published large numbers of still pictures taken from the Zapruder film. Professor Alvarez is a man with a restless and inquiring mind, which has won him a worldwide reputation in such diverse matters as air traffic safety and the nature of the nucleus of the atom. He began to ask himself whether there might be, in the Zapruder film itself, evidence as to the number of shots which would not appear upon a simple examination of the film, however careful that simple examination might be.

Any explosion is accompanied by a shock wave, which can carry considerable energy. Even a modest explosion will break windows in its vicinity, and the shock wave from a nuclear explosion will tumble buildings. The shock wave from the detonation of a rifle bullet is on a considerably smaller scale, but Professor Alvarez had a hunch that it would be at least enough to flutter the flags on the motorcade vehicles, and his first examination of the Zapruder stills inclined him to believe he had discerned such a flutter. On behalf of CBS News he traveled to Washington to examine the high-quality stills from the Zapruder film that are available in the National Archives. He intended to study the flags, and to establish whether he could detect a series of discrete shock waves, which could plausibly be attributed to rifle fire.

Not for the first time in his or in any other scientist's experience, his initial hunch was a blind alley. The flags fluttered, but which flutters were due to shock waves, which to reflections of shock waves, which to vagrant breezes, and which to the slightly uneven motion of the vehicles, he was unable to determine. In the language of his own science, any signals that might have been present were totally obscured by noise.

But in the process of examining the film, Professor Alvarez made an unanticipated find. In almost any field of vision there can be found highlights of one kind or another—points of metal from which light reflects, or perhaps images so small as to appear on the negative almost without dimension. Professor Alvarez noted that in the stills from the Zapruder film certain highlights and small images could be clearly seen, but that on occasion these highlights, on a single frame of film or a few successive frames, turned from points of light to smears of light. His interpretation was that the phenomenon, whenever it appeared, signified a very slight convulsive movement of the camera in Mr. Zapruder's hand —slight because the phenomenon itself was slight; convulsive because the movements did not follow the slower, steadier hand movements that are made by almost anyone straining to hold an object, which could also be detected on the Zapruder film.

What caught his attention further was his impression that one such convulsive movement occurred at frame 318 in the Zapruder film. The film clearly shows the fatal shot striking the President at frame 313, and the gap of five frames between frames 313 and 318 amounts to approximately one third of a second, or something very like a reaction time. Was it possible, Professor Alvarez asked himself, that the quaver in Zapruder's hand was a direct consequence of the rifle shot? Could it be that either the sound or the shock wave, reaching Mr. Zapruder at about frame 318, had caused his hand to start slightly?

Professor Alvarez continued to examine the film, and meanwhile suggested to CBS News that an expert on films and cameras, in whose possession would be found the appropriate equipment, be asked to examine the film independently and to report on the manner in which the highlights behaved. For that purpose, CBS News retained Mr. Charles Wycoff, who has already been mentioned.

While Mr. Wycoff set about his work, CBS News arranged its own test. A car was stationed in the sun. A group of amateur cameramen were set to work photographing the car through Bell & Howell motion picture cameras, identical to that used by Mr. Zapruder. They were told to film away as steadily as they knew how, whatever happened. Then behind them and from a tower a rifleman fired shots toward the car, in no particular time pattern.

In most of the frames of their pictures, the highlights can be clearly seen. But in every case a few frames after a shot was fired the highlights turned to crescents of light. Each amateur cameraman was startled, some more and some less, into a sharp, involuntary movement that jerked the camera very slightly and very convulsively. Granted, the test is not the best that might be imagined, but it was the best that could practically be made, and for what it was worth it bore out Professor Alvarez's hypothesis.

Mr. Wycoff, meanwhile, reported that he had found similar streaking at three points of the Zapruder film, and other streaking, far less marked and easily distinguishable from the principal streaking, in two other places on the film. The three principal occurrences can be seen in frames 190, 227 and 318 of the Zapruder film.

It happens that all of these are significant frames. Assuming a reaction time of four or five frames, 318 is immediately significant, for it appears to indicate that the event to which Mr. Zapruder reacted took place at about frame 313 or 314—and the event at frame 313 is the fatal shot. The streaking at frame 227 signals an event at frame 222 or 223, and this also has a significance, although a less precise one. The Zapruder film last shows the President unwounded at frame 205, after which a road sign blocks the President from Zapruder's field of vision. At frame 225 the President comes into view again; he is clutching his throat. Some-

where between frame 205 and 225 he was shot—frame 222 falls
within that interval.

All this Mr. Wycoff knew. But frame 185 or 186 counted back
four or five frames from the phenomenon he observed at frame
190—had no significance for Mr. Wycoff at all. So far as he was
concerned when he made his investigation, it was nothing more
or less than a point at which his evidence indicated something
had happened that startled Mr. Zapruder and affected his hold on
the camera a few frames later. But frame 186 does have a significance, even though Mr. Wycoff then had no inkling of it. Its
significance is expressed in the pages of the Warren Report, where
an account is given, after tests, of what Oswald would have seen
through the sights of his rifle as the Presidential motorcade passed
before and below him. Just as this book does, the Warren Report
uses Zapruder frame numbers to fix events. The paragraph reads:

> . . . the agents (conducting the tests) concluded that at frame 166 of
> the Zapruder film the President passed beneath the foliage of a large
> oak tree and the point of impact on the President's back disappeared
> from the gunman's view as seen through the telescopic lens. *For a
> fleeting instant, the President came back in view in the telescopic lens
> at frame 186 as he appeared in an opening among the leaves.*

Frame 186, in other words, was not simply just another frame, as
Mr. Wycoff might have suspected. It represented, instead, a point
at which a gunman might well have fired a shot.

The two minor disturbances also included one point of interest. They were represented on a chart drawn by Mr. Wycoff as
he proceeded with his tests. It may be seen that the disturbances
at two particular frames are significantly less noticeable, in terms
of the length and duration of the streaking. One frame provides
nothing further than its own mute evidence. But the other frame
shows a slight, almost imperceptible slowing down of the
President's car, followed almost immediately by resumption of
its normal parade speed. Professor Alvarez hypothesizes that both
the deceleration and the twitch of Mr. Zapruder's hand were
brought about by a siren, which caused the driver instinctively to
lift his foot from the accelerator—as we all do when we hear a
siren—and at the same time slightly startled Mr. Zapruder. A
tenuous hypothesis, to be sure, but not unreasonable. The earlier
slight disturbance in the first frame was in all possibility caused

by still another unexpected sound, which cannot be identified. In that fashion, all the evidence recorded on the Zapruder film is accountable.

How much to make of all this is a matter of taste and judgment. To call this investigation decisive would be to say a great deal more than the facts warrant. It is certainly suggestive, and certainly plausible. It is plausible enough for Professor Alvarez, who is a thoughtful man and whose record in framing hypotheses is good enough to have made him the youngest physicist ever made a member of the National Academy of Arts and Sciences. Professor Alvarez told CBS News:

> **Alvarez:** To me it means that there were indeed three shots fired, as the Commission said, and that the one that apparently didn't hit anyone in the car was fired before the one that hit the President, and not between the two shots that obviously hit the President.
>
> The Commission made no judgment, if I remember correctly, as to which of those two situations was the correct one. I think they favored the idea that the shot came between rather than ahead, but it seems to me quite clear from my own measurements that the shot that didn't hit anyone in the car and was never found, in fact, that this one came before the two that were observed to hit the President.

Mr. Wycoff, who made the detailed check upon Dr. Alvarez's hypothesis, concurs. He, too, believes that the evidence is persuasive, and that blurs on the Zapruder film constitute fair reason to believe that three shots were fired at about frames 186, 222, and 313 as fixed by the Zapruder film.

CBS News, too, concurred, believing that the examination of the Zapruder film, as suggested by Professor Alvarez and carried out by Mr. Wycoff, is enough to lead to a conclusion that three shots were fired at the Presidential limousine. These shots may have been as ineradicably marked in the Zapruder film as if he had caught the bullets in flight.

And I am not yet finished with the Alvarez-Wycoff analysis. I have fixed the direction and the number of the bullets; I have yet to fix the time that elapsed between the first and third shots. This is a matter of considerable moment, for it affects directly the physical likelihood that Oswald fired all three. I shall devote the next chapter to that point.

THE TIMING OF THE SHOTS

From our own tests we were convinced that a rifle like Oswald's could be fired in 5.6 seconds or less, and with reasonable accuracy, at a target moving much the same as the Presidential limousine.

—Walter Cronkite

The use of the Zapruder camera as a clock has already been considered. Employing it in that fashion, the conclusions we have already drawn from the Alvarez-Wycoff analysis of the film provides a means for establishing the exact timing of the shots, although the figures with which one emerges will depend upon the value that is assigned to the rate at which the camera can be presumed to have been running.

The computation is simple enough. If the first shot was fired at frame 186, there is a lapse of thirty-six frames until frame 222, when the second shot is assumed to have been fired; then another lapse of ninety-one frames until 313, when the last shot is *known* to have been fired. (About the last shot there is no ambiguity whatsoever.) The total elapsed time is to be measured by the passage of 127 frames, from 186 to 313.

At 18.3 frames a second, the speed at which both the FBI and Bell & Howell report the camera to run, these frame lapses indicate the passage of slightly less than two seconds between shots 1 and 2; and almost five seconds between 2 and 3; the total comes to approximately 6.9 seconds. At a rate of 16.5 frames a second, which CBS News believes to be somewhat closer to the true rate, the figures come to approximately 10 per cent more: 2.2 seconds between the first two shots; 5.5 seconds between the last two, and a total of about 7.6 seconds for the series. (Fractions of a second in the totals are lost in rounding off.) Any errors in these estimates are likely to be such as to add to the time available for the three shots, rather than reduce it.

These are not the figures at which the Warren Commission arrived. To understand the official account, we must take into consideration the very thin evidence upon which the Commission relied. There was, once more, the evidence of bystanders, as variegated here as in every other instance. All agreed the shots had come quickly. Some said they were evenly spaced, some that they were bunched in one way or another. So far as bunching was concerned, there was again difference of opinion. Some said the first two were closer together than the last two, some the opposite. (I ignore here those who heard more or less than three shots, since I have dealt with them earlier, and their evidence does not appear reliable.)

Clearly there was nothing here upon which to base any decision. The Commission was therefore forced to rely instead upon its own judgment in interpreting the tests made upon a moving car as seen through a telescopic sight from the sixth floor window of the School Book Depository building, together with the meager information that could be deduced from the Zapruder film. As we have already seen, at frame 166 of the Zapruder film the President, clearly unwounded, had proceeded to a point where a gunman in the sixth floor lost him to sight behind an oak tree. While the oak tree intervened, the gunman would have been able to discern the car, but not able to fix a target in his sights. At frame 186, a momentary opening in the trees revealed the President; the Commission judged that the moment passed too quickly to enable the gunman to get off a shot. At frame 205, the Zapruder film no longer shows the President, for a street sign intervenes. At frame 210, the President, still invisible in the Zapruder film, came once more into the gunman's view as the car passed from behind the tree. At frame 225 the President reappears in the Zapruder film. He is clearly wounded. At frame 313 the fatal shot is clearly seen.

The Commission concluded only that the first shot to hit was fired between frames 210 and 225, when the gunman could see the President but Zapruder could not. The Commission sets no time at all for the missing shot, but is inclined to believe that it occurred some time between frame 225 and frame 313.

To convert frame numbers to seconds, the Commission employs the rate of 18.3 frames a second, which gives it figures of 4.8 seconds in all if the first shot was fired at frame 225, and 5.6 seconds if it was fired at frame 210. These are in fact the conclusions of the Commission, in terms of its full account of the assassination, for although the Commission leaves open the possibility of a shot earlier than frame 210, it clearly does not think highly of it, and prefers to assume that the shots that struck the President were the first and last of three.

It is clear that once more I am anticipating the "single-bullet theory," for if one shot missed, a single bullet must then have inflicted two sets of wounds. Again I ask patience, for I shall come in time to the detail of the single-bullet theory. CBS News accepts it as valid, as did the Commission, and I shall be able to say exactly why. For the moment I ask that it be accepted here on faith, and utilize it in summing up the Commission and the CBS News reconstruction of the shooting.

The Commission believes that Oswald lurked in his sniper's nest as the President and the motorcade moved slowly along Houston Street toward him and directly in front of him. It is reasonable to assume that while all eyes were turned more or less in Oswald's direction, he was reluctant to expose himself. As the motorcade swung more than 90 degrees into Elm Street, the eyes swung away to follow it, but now, as Oswald brought his rifle into position, an oak tree obscured his view. The brief moment at frame 186 when the President was visible was not enough, and Oswald waited until at frame 210 he had a clear view of the President. He sighted, somewhere shortly after frame 210 he shot, at about frame 260 he shot again, at frame 313 he shot for the third and last time. His first shot struck the President in the back of the neck, passed through the neck and went on to strike Governor Connally. His second shot missed. His third shot killed the President.

The CBS News account follows the Commission account until the moment at frame 186 when the President appeared in the fleeting opening in the tree. Oswald had been tracking him approximately through the tree until that point. Now, nervous and trigger happy, he snapped off a shot, which understandably enough under the circumstances was wide of the mark. He was more patient the second time, and fired at frame 222, wounding the President and Governor Connally. But now, settled down to his business and aware that haste had prevented him from firing a truly lethal shot, he sighted carefully, and on his third shot at frame 313, brought off the assassination which had been his aim.

Ironically, the CBS News account, differing as it does from the Warren account, goes a good part of the way toward rescuing the Warren Commission from a dilemma of its own making, and subsequent experiments conducted by CBS News go some of the rest of the way. To comprehend the dilemma—and it is one of the major weaknesses of the Warren Report—we must consider both the Mannlicher-Carcano rifle with which the assassination was carried out, and something of the man who fired it.

The Warren Commission conducted a series of tests to ascertain the accuracy and the firing speed of the rifle used in the assassination. They were, by any account, an odd series. Oswald, according to the Commission's own account, had fired at a target below him, moving away from him at a known angle and at approximately a known speed, at a range that varied from approximately 60 to approximately 90 yards. The Commission never attempted to match those conditions. Instead, expert riflemen from the Infantry Weapons Evaluation Branch of the Ballistics Research Laboratory fired at fixed targets from an elevation lower than that of Oswald, and FBI experts fired first at fixed level targets at 15 yards and later at fixed targets at 100 yards.

Those tests showed, plainly enough, that the rifle, although far from an admirable weapon, was accurate enough for the task set it. But they showed also that few of the experts could bring off three shots in the 5.6 seconds that was the maximum allowed the assassin by the Commission if the second shot missed; that in fact it was a rare expert who could fire three shots in less than 6 seconds, and most of them took far longer, up to 8.25 seconds.

Oswald was in fact by no means an expert rifleman. He had attained the rank of sharpshooter in the Marines, which sounds far more impressive than it is, for that rank means little more than a familiarity with the rifle, and beyond that is the lowest rank a Marine can attain and still be trusted with a weapon. The Commission's own account required Oswald to outperform experts at their own trade.

Actually, the amount of adrenalin pumping thorugh Oswald's veins as he stood at his window must have been fantastic, and no tests can do justice to the performance a man might attain under such conditions. The Commission's story is not quite as unpersuasive as it sounds. Still, it is unpersuasive enough.

CBS News, too, conducted tests. In one sense they were gravely deficient; CBS News could not use the Mannlicher-Carcano rifle used by Oswald, but was forced instead to buy several Mannlicher-Carcano rifles, of exactly the same make and model, and in approximately the same physical condition. At the H. P. White Ballistic Laboratory, north of Bel Air, Maryland, a tower was constructed which provided the elevation of the sixth floor window over Elm Street; below it, at the proper angle and declination, a track along which ran targets at the speed of the President's car. To the best of its ability, CBS News duplicated the conditions that held at Dealey Plaza. Then a group of marksmen, some of them expert, some merely ordinarily proficient, were asked to fire three shots as quickly and as accurately as they were able.

The marksmen found the bolt on the rifle extremely difficult to manipulate—so difficult that of a series of thirty-seven attempts, there were seventeen cases where the rifleman was unable to get off three shots, or in some cases even two, before the target reached the end of its run. This was not disturbing. Oswald, too, *might* have been unable to get off three shots, but the cold fact is that he did; *his* rifle did not jam that afternoon.

But many of the riflemen were quite capable of firing three shots, as accurately as Oswald did or very nearly so, in times that were at or around five seconds. The average for all the completed series was 5.6 seconds, but included in that average was a technician who had one hit and two misses in 4.1 seconds, a state trooper who had two hits and one near miss in slightly under 5.0 seconds, and a technician who had three hits in 5.2 seconds. The series of three shots was rarely equally spaced, and a marksman often snapped off his second shot less than two seconds after his first, or his third shot less than two seconds after his second.

The results, in short, were simply not consistent with those reported by the Commission. CBS News cannot concede that 4.6 seconds is the minimum time required for a series of three shots, for we observed shorter intervals. CBS News cannot concede that 2.3 seconds is the minimum time for two shots, since time after time a sequence of two shots occurred in far less than that interval.

I cannot ascribe the difference in times to the differences in rifles. The Oswald rifle, handled, studied, and often assembled and disassembled before the tests, was, if anything, cleaner and in better working condition than the rifles CBS News used. It may be that the essential difference between the tests reported by the Commission and those conducted by CBS News was in the instructions given the marksmen, or the manner in which those instructions were followed. CBS News asked that the marksmen fire, as rapidly as they could consistent with accuracy, at a target that simulated in all respects that presented to Oswald. They were asked to do essentially what one would assume Oswald set out to do. The request may be fundamentally different from one which requires that the experimenter determine how quickly he can fire three shots, for now a part of the emphasis is upon completing the series, and the experimenter may devote a portion of his attention to assuring that the sequence will be completed. The CBS marksmen concentrated on working the bolt as *quickly* as they could, with the result that in some cases the test broke down entirely. The Commission reports may have been from marksmen who concentrated on working the bolt as *efficiently* as they could, which is not quite the same thing.

In any case, the reader can compare the manner in which the various series of tests was conducted, and come to his own conclusions. My own view is that the tests conducted by CBS News were better designed and better conducted, except in one very significant aspect. They did not have Oswald's rifle. That difference can not be minimized, but none the less I believe CBS News emerged with more dependable results.

In addition the CBS News account, setting the first shot as it does at frame 186, allows at least 6.9 seconds and possibly even more for the series of shots. What is hard to believe in the Commission account and after the Commission tests becomes credible in the CBS News account and after the CBS News tests. That Oswald, his blood racing, using a reasonably accurate weapon and given seven seconds or more in which to work, could have fired three shots of which one found its mark, one missed slightly, and one missed altogether, seems to me to be quite reasonable.

I am saying that Oswald, an admittedly mediocre marksman, outperformed upon this one occasion, experts against whom in competition he would not have had a ghost of a chance. The dissenters to the Warren Report have seized upon the high degree of improbability of this outcome. It was highly improbable—there can be no denying that fact. But it is entirely impermissible to infer that, merely because an event is improbable, it did not happen. There is no justification in logic or in everyday experience for any such inference, for the improbable happens all the time—there is, in fact, sound reason for stating that *only* the improbable happens.

The notion of probability is extremely complex. Even the mathematicians, whose business it is to deal with such matters, have never completely come to terms with it. In ordinary usage, there are frequently two fairly distinct concepts intermixed in the employment of the idea of probability, and one of them now and then gets in the way of the other.

Colloquially stated, a man who poses a probability is in most cases asserting the equivalent of a wager, real or theoretical. Even the meteorologist who intones "One chance in ten of rain today" can be taken to mean that on the basis of the current weather map and his own experience he would consider it to be a fair wager at odds of one to nine that rain will be forthcoming, and an equally fair wager at odds of nine to one that it will not be. This is all clear enough.

But the fact is that, once the day has passed, it has either rained, or it has not. The odds, whatever they may have been when the affair was one of prediction, are of no great significance when the occasion has passed into history. No matter how great the odds may have been against rain, once it has rained it has rained, and that is all there is to it. Odds estimate the future, but they do not govern the past.

In short, it is reasonable to say when one looks ahead that an event is improbable. Looking back on an event, it is equally reasonable to say that before it occurred it *was* improbable. But the event itself, as an occurrence, is a matter of record, and one cannot deny it happened by posing figures that show it should not have.

What is more, in the long view all events are highly improbable. Any state of the universe is a unique configuration of numberless atoms and electrons. The existence of one particular configuration, rather than any of the innumerable other possible configurations, is as unlikely an event as anything you might imagine. Yet the undeniable fact exists that one such state, however improbable it may be, exists at each moment of time, and is duly succeeded by another state.

Perhaps a simple example will make the point clear. At Aqueduct Race Track in New York, during the month just passed, some 250 horse races were run, and each of them was won by some horse or another; there were 250 winners. The chances of those 250 horses winning those 250 races are so small as to be almost beyond the imagination. A one dollar bet, parlayed on all 250 winners, would in theory come to a sum of money that exceeds, by the largest factor you could imagine, the total value of everything that exists on earth, with our investment in the moon and Mars included. Yet it happened. Not only did 250 horses win 250 races, but the matter is so commonplace that it may be difficult to see why so much point is being made of it here.

Anyone engaged in recording history, as distinct from someone engaged in predicting it, must be discreet in his use of probability considerations. His object, never quite attained, should be to eliminate them entirely, and to record, not what the odds tell him *should* have happened, but rather what *did* happen. Probability considerations serve to alert the historian, to the extent that an event which appears highly improbable should be scrutinized with extreme care. At times he will be forced to fall back entirely upon probability considerations, simply because important data are lacking. (Probability and ignorance are bedfellows, for once you *know* anything, the question of probability no longer arises.) But there is no justification for denying a hard fact simply because it could not have been predicted. It is a contingent universe, and we should all be aware of that.

The Warren Report, and this book, deal at every turn with events which are probabilities, because they deal at every turn with events which are not fully known. But it is essential to recognize, in the Warren Report and here, that the statement that an event was highly improbable is a comment upon the event, and not a claim or a pretense that it did not happen.

The account given here provides, almost as a by-product, an explanation for the one witness whose account is most troubling to the Commission. That witness, of course, is Governor Connally. His account is troubling not only for what it says but because it is Governor Connally who says it, for Governor Connally is a practiced hunter, familiar with rifles, and as one directly and painfully in the line of fire, he of all witnesses was in the best position to gain a clear impression of what was going on.

From the moment when he was first interviewed in the hospital, only two days after the assassination, Governor Connally has clung stubbornly to two statements. First, he has insisted that the shot that wounded him could not possibly have been the first shot, because he heard the first shot before he was wounded. Second, he heard only two shots.

His first assertion, which is the troubling assertion, is explained by the Commission as the result of a delayed reaction: Governor Connally, the Commission says, was wounded *before* he heard the first shot, but was unaware of the wound until *after* he heard it. The delayed reaction of itself is quite likely, but Governor Connally has insisted that in his case it was far too much of a good thing: He *heard* the shot, then had time to turn and try to look at the President before he himself was wounded. Nothing, says the Governor, will convince him otherwise.

The CBS reconstruction merely confirms the Governor's belief that the first shot missed. He did indeed hear the first shot and begin to turn; it was the second shot which struck him. He did not hear the second shot; his body was fully occupied reacting to the wound inflicted on it. By the time of the third shot, the sudden total disorder in his neurological functions had subsided, and his ear and brain recorded it. The Governor's recollections are quite justified: He heard and felt exactly what he says he did.

Thus the CBS News version of the assassination, based on evidence at least as good as any accumulated by the Commission, disposes of two major objections to the Warren Report as a whole. The time span is far more consistent with the capacity of the rifle, and the Governor's recollections are fully explained. Admittedly, one would prefer better evidence than is possessed by either the Commission or CBS News. But in the absence of such better evidence, the CBS version seems to be by far the preferable. I feel entirely justified in adopting it.

THE SINGLE-BULLET THEORY

Where did the bullet go? The probability is that it went into Governor Connally, because it struck nothing else in the car. That is the most compelling piece of evidence . . . because looking down the trajectory, as I did through Oswald's own rifle, the trajectory was such that it was almost certain that the bullet which came out of the President's neck with great velocity would have had to hit either the car or someone in the car.   —Arlen Specter
Staff lawyer, Warren Commission

I need no longer defer consideration of the single-bullet theory, troublesome, at first hearing thoroughly implausible, and yet an integral part of almost any reasoned analysis of the assassination.

The theory, simply stated, is that a single bullet fired from the Mannlicher-Carcano rifle passed first through the President's throat, then into the chest of Governor Connally, penetrating his chest from back to front, emerging to penetrate his wrist and finally to inflict a minor wound on his thigh.

The hypothesis of the single bullet was called into being in response to two real problems that faced the investigators. The first of these has to do specifically with the full account of the assassination adopted by the Warren Commission; the second is far more general, and would impose itself upon almost any rational account.

The Warren Commission decided, upon evidence which has already been presented here, that the assassin fired three bullets, the first of which occurred somewhere between frames 210 and 225 of the Zapruder film. The second bullet, the Commission was inclined to believe, was fired at some time during the interval.

The Zapruder film does not show the Governor between frames 207 and 222, while the field of vision from Zapruder's camera was blocked by a street sign. But that interval is less than one second, and the amount that a human body will ordinarily move in that time is quite limited. The Governor can be seen in frames directly preceding and directly succeeding the blocked frames, and the position of his body in the interval can be extrapolated with great confidence. The conclusion is that between frames 207 and 225 the Governor was in a position, physically, to have received the wounds he is known to have received. He continued in that position until frame 235, when he began to turn right; by frame 240 he was too far right to have received his injuries. Governor Connally himself believes he was hit between frames 232 and 234.

The dilemma begins to come clear. Putting the first shot to hit the President as far back as any evidence permits the Commission, at frame 210, and putting the shot that struck the Governor as far forward as possible, at frame 239, provides an interval of only twenty-nine frames between shots. At the camera speed adopted by the Commission, this comes to about 1.6 seconds. And to fire the Mannlicher-Carcano twice in a period of 1.6 seconds is more than any evidence will bear. There is the sheer physical necessity of finding time to work the bolt, to sight and to fire, and 1.6 seconds—which is the absolute maximum time the assassin would have had according to the Commission's own line of thought—is simply not to be credited. It will not help measurably to adopt the thesis, as we have already done, that the camera was running slowly, for an increment of 10 percent or so will not help the case sufficiently. Even further doubt, if that is necessary, is cast on the account by the Governor's testimony, for although it is reasonable that he should have placed the impact of the bullet somewhat later than the facts warrant simply because he may have felt a delayed reaction, he is unlikely to have placed it any earlier: If the Governor believes he felt the impact between frames 232 and 234, it is highly implausible that he was in fact shot later than that. This would lose a few more tenths of a second. The Commission simply could not adopt such a version of the Governor's wounds.

What we have considered so far is an intricate network of suppositions, in which one supposition can simply not find a place. But the second reason for hypothesizing a single-bullet theory is a good deal more compelling. The bullet that struck the President left the rifle at approximately 2,160 feet a second, and was traveling at 1,904 feet a second when it entered the President's neck. Here it encountered only soft tissue, and when it emerged most of its speed remained; tests conducted for the Commission indicate that speed to have been in the neighborhood of 1,775 feet a second. The trajectory of the bullet is known; the bullet passed through the President at an angle of approximately 18 degrees, as shown in the accompanying chart. It emerged, in short, as a high-speed missile, traveling a course that would take it into the middle of the car.

So far as Governor Connally was concerned, the situation was precisely that which would have obtained if a gunman, seated a few feet behind him, had fired a rifle directly into the Governor's back. One would not expect such a gunman to miss the Governor entirely. Still, he might do so. But what a miss it would have to be! For the bullet, fired from a few feet back, would have to miss, not only the Governor, but also the car in which he rode to meet the conditions that obtained in the actual case. For the hard fact is that no trace of that high velocity bullet is to be found in the car—a bullet certainly capable of wreaking major damage on anything it struck.

One could account for this only by postulating that the bullet, on leaving the President's neck, was deflected through an angle of some 30 or 40 degrees by something upon which it left no visible mark. But such an event would appear to be in violation of all the laws of physics applied to all the materials in the vicinity of the President and the Governor. It simply cannot be reasonably maintained. In the end the logical demands that led to postulating a single-bullet theory turn out to be in fact the most powerful evidence for that theory.

Other evidence, highly suggestive, is at hand. If the position of the President, the Governor, and the assassin are reconstructed, the trajectory of a high-speed bullet is reasonably such as to inflict all the recorded wounds, allowing merely for the expected minor deflections of the bullet as it passed through neck, chest, and wrist. It is more than merely consistent for such a bullet; the alternative would have to be that Oswald fired two successive bullets that followed almost precisely the same trajectory, despite the fact that car and occupants would have moved in the interval, or more absurd still (for it is this sort of thing that critics of the single-bullet theory maintain) that two separate riflemen, firing simultaneously, got off shots that followed almost precisely the same trajectory.

Governor Connally has been in the past the principal objector to the single-bullet theory among those who are disposed to accept as authentic the Warren Report. His objections, however, have been based principally upon the associated assertion that it was the first bullet fired that caused all the damage. As I have stated, Governor Connally maintains that he heard the first bullet and turned in response to it, and that therefore that bullet could not have struck him. That objection, at least in that specific form, is fully met by the CBS News version of the assassination, which makes the second bullet, rather than the first, the bullet that struck. But the Governor's objections remain in another form. He maintains that he was struck between frames 232 and 234, and not at frame 222 as this version asserts. To meet this further objection, one must postulate a delayed reaction of something more than nine but less than twelve frames, which means that the Governor had been wounded somewhere between one half and two thirds of a second before he became aware of it. There is nothing troubling about such a hypothesis; reaction times of that sort are too common to warrant comment. The Governor himself was in any case not reacting well, for although his wrist had been penetrated by a bullet, he himself was not aware of the wound until the following day, when he noticed the wrist in bandages. Two thirds of a second, after all, is not very much time—a good deal less time than it takes to begin drawing a breath.

The single-bullet theory has come under further attack for still another reason. At Parkland Hospital, under circumstances which the Report itself did little to make clear, a nearly intact bullet was found after the President and the Governor had been carried to emergency rooms. In the broadcasts the manner in which the bullet turned up is fully related. It is an interesting story, and one that does no credit to the Secret Service. I shall say here only that the bullet in question clearly came from the stretcher on which Governor Connally was carried to the emergency room, and can be reasonably assumed to be the bullet that wounded him. It may be seen from a close examination of it that the bullet itself is almost totally undeformed and intact, except for a few grains of lead, which are missing from the back.

The bullet was carefully examined by ballistics experts, and was unambiguously found to be a bullet fired from Oswald's rifle "to the exclusion of all others." To those untutored in ballistics, it is a troublesome exhibit, for it is superficially difficult to conceive of a bullet which passes through the neck of one man, the chest and wrist of another, penetrates the thigh and emerges from this long history as unmarked and as unaffected as this bullet appears to be.

Yet no ballistics expert is so troubled. A full-jacketed bullet, wholly sheathed in copper, which does not make direct impact with hard structure can go a long way and do a good deal of damage without itself showing much effect. It is one more case where an effect which appears surprising to the uninitiated is accepted as an ordinary matter of course among those whose experience is broad. What it amounts to is that the bullet, with its tough protective shield, was never subjected to an abrupt change of momentum: It slowed up a little in passing through the President's neck, slowed up gradually a good deal more as it passed successively through the Governor's chest and wrist, and finally struck the Governor's thigh almost spent. There were at no time forces exerted upon it sufficient to deform it to any great extent; merely continuous small forces which robbed it bit by bit of its energy.

CBS News went to some pains to recreate a part of the path taken by the bullet, using carefully measured blocks of gelatin to simulate the resistance offered by tissue, and other artifacts to represent clothing and bone structure. The tests were conducted by Dr. Alfred G. Olivier, chief of wound ballistics at Edgewood Arsenal. The object was to line up targets simulating the President's neck and the Governor's chest, wrist, and thigh. Dr. Olivier reported:

> **Olivier:** When the bullet struck the simulated neck, it was perfectly stable, passed through making a small track in the gelatin. . . . It was a small entrance and a small exit, as described in the autopsy report.
>
> After the bullet left this simulated neck and passed from this dense medium into air, which is less dense, then it had a chance to start to tip and by the time it struck [the next] block it was tipped. By the

time it had passed through . . . it had lost considerable velocity, and entered the simulated wrist. In some cases, it passed through the "wrist," in other cases it lodged in the "wrist." Behind the wrist we had another gelatin block, representing the Governor's thigh. In none of the cases did [a bullet] actually penetrate that, but it would have taken very little more velocity to have caused a similar wound.

I think that [these tests] very strongly show that one bullet could have caused all the wounds.

Dr. Olivier's conclusion at first glance appears to contradict his tests: Although none of his test bullets penetrated the gelatin block that simulated the Governor's thigh, he concludes nonetheless that the real bullet fired by Oswald could have done so. The inconsistency is not a real one. Dr. Olivier conducted tests in which the charge in the shell (modified to take account of the lessened distance from muzzle to target in the experiment), the density of the targets, and the spacing of the targets were all approximations. He could not, under those circumstances, expect precise results. What he got was an approximate answer, which was entirely consistent, within its margin of error, with the single-bullet theory. If in his tests the bullets had all stopped inside the "chest," then the behavior stipulated by the single-bullet theory would have lain outside his margin of error, and would have been inadmissible. The manner in which his tests were conducted, and the conclusions he drew from them, are totally straightforward. They are characteristic of all simulations, for it is impossible to get more accuracy out of the results than you can build into the simulation.

It should be added here (I will note later that it was not added in the account of these tests given over the air) that the bullets used in the simulation emerged from the tests undeformed, like the bullet that the Commission asserts passed through the President and the Governor. A picture of two test bullets appears in the photograph section.

The contending alternative to the single-bullet theory holds (in its most persuasive form) that three bullets were fired, of which the first struck the President, the second struck the Governor, and the third killed the President. Of all those who adhere to that alternative, Mrs. John Connally is indisputably the least readily dismissed, for no one was in any better position to observe the events than Mrs. Connally, directly in the line of fire. Mrs. Connally's recollection is clear and distinct:

> **Mrs. Connally:** The first sound, the first shot, I heard, and turned and looked right into the President's face.
>
> He was clutching his throat and just slumped down. He just had a—a look of nothingness on his face. He didn't say anything. But that was the first shot.
>
> The second shot, that hit John—well, of course I could see him covered with blood, and his reaction to the second shot. The third shot, even though I didn't see the President, I felt the matter all over me and I could see it all over the car.
>
> So I'll just have to say that I think there were three shots, and that I had a reaction to three shots. And that's just what I believe.

All that can be said is that her testimony must be evaluated. The events she describes took place in a few brief seconds, during which she was assailed by unexpected sounds and harrowing sights. Under such conditions, a perfect recollection would be surprising. That there should be some reversal of the order of events is almost to be predicted: Mrs. Connally heard unexpected sounds, saw two wounded men, and only afterward could hope to sort out what it was that happened.

It is not a question of "accepting" one person's testimony and "denying" another's—in this case Mrs. Connally's. Neither testimony is either accepted or denied; both are studied with respect to all the evidence. Mrs. Connally's eyewitness account can be easily comprehended in the light of what we all know of the way the human mind works; it can not be comprehended, taken at face value, in the light of all the other evidence.

And all that sustains the theory of three bullets and three hits is the testimony of Mrs. Connally and speculations in which any one of us can indulge. The arguments against three hits are powerful. To almost all at CBS News the single-bullet theory is thoroughly convincing. There is no evidence which stands as any real barrier to its adoption, and all the hard evidence is thoroughly consistent with it. The negative consideration—if the bullet that struck the President did *not* strike Governor Connally, what became of it?—is extremely compelling. Like so much in the Warren

Report—like so much in the account of any complex event—it can never be proved beyond the possibility of doubt that a single bullet struck both men. But by the evidence that exists, it is imposed upon us to believe that it did.

The Warren Commission was gravely troubled by the single-bullet theory, and it has been well established that the Commission wrangled long over the manner in which its statement of the theory would be phrased. The paragraph as it appears in the Report is worth quoting in full:

> Although it is not necessary to any essential findings of the Commission to determine just which shot hit Governor Connally, there is very persuasive evidence from the experts to indicate that the same bullet which pierced the President's throat also caused Governor Connally's wounds. However, Governor Connally's testimony and certain other factors have given rise to some difference of opinion as to this probability but there is no question in the mind of any member of the Commission that all the shots which caused the President's and Governor Connally's wounds were fired from the sixth floor window of the Texas School Book Depository.

Perhaps no official government document has included so remarkable a paragraph. If there were no other accounts to assert that the Commission had trouble reaching agreement on the substance of the single-bullet theory, a casual scrutiny of the paragraph would make it obvious. In the style of the modern literary critic, let us subject it to textual analysis.

The first sentence is carefully designed to give the impression that it says something it simply does not say, simply because there is in fact no substantive connection between the clause that begins with the word "*although*" and the rest of the sentence. The *although* clause deals with the question of which of the three shots struck the Governor—whether it was the first shot, the second shot, or the third shot. The latter half of the sentence deals with the question of whether a single shot—the first, the second, *or* the third—struck both men. These are two different matters entirely, and the sentence as a whole is equivalent to one that would read, "Although Lyndon B. Johnson was Vice President, the assassination took place on a Friday."

The second sentence leans over backward to qualify itself. It begins with *however* and later includes a *but*. It passed the

Commission, but it would never pass a respectable grammarian. The sentence refers also to mysterious "other factors" which are specified neither in the paragraph nor anywhere else in the Report.

Finally, the paragraph concludes with the statement that all the shots which inflicted wounds were fired from the sixth floor window of the Texas School Book Depository. In itself this is unexceptionable, but in context it is startling, since precisely the same statement was made only a few paragraphs before. In fact the section of the Report headed *Conclusions*, of which the paragraph now under examination is numbered 3, contains that statement in almost the same words as item number 1. Something impelled the Commission to repeat it almost compulsively, and that something is not hard to find.

The fact being concealed is that, whatever the *although* sentence struggles to imply to the contrary, the Commission clearly believed the single-bullet theory to be necessary to its essential findings. The Commission had mustered powerful evidence to show that the President was first shot between frames 210 and 225. (It is irrelevant in this connection that CBS News believes that significant portions of the evidence were not available to the Commission. The point here is that the Commission itself was convinced.) The Commission also had mustered powerful evidence that showed clearly the impossibility of attributing to Oswald a second shot in time to wound the Governor when it is clear he was wounded. It follows necessarily, then, that *if* two separate shots were fired and struck home upon the President and the Governor, one of those shots must have been fired by an assassin other than Oswald. In short, in the full fabric of the official account, destruction of the single-bullet theory seems to lead remorselessly to a second assassin.

That, of course, is precisely the reason why the critics of the Report have made so violent an attack on the single-bullet theory. In the view of these critics, to demolish the single-bullet theory is to open the floodgates; thereafter (still in *their* view) anything goes.

If the Commission had been less rattled at that particular juncture of its report-writing, it would have contented itself with the simple sentence: "There is very persuasive evidence from the experts to indicate that the same bullet which pierced the President's throat also caused Governor Connally's wounds." That is all that can be said about the single-bullet theory, and all that it is needful to say. Anything more is deceptive and misleading.

It is my view that the single-bullet theory is one moderately sized piece of an enormous jigsaw puzzle. It is a piece that seems to fit perfectly. It is possible that however perfectly it fits, it does not belong in the puzzle, and that there is another piece, not yet found and perhaps forever to be missing, which also fits and which really belongs. But in either case, the puzzle itself, considered as a whole, does not change. The missing piece, if there is one, cannot be sufficient to change "A Stag at Bay" to "The Taj Mahal by Moonlight."

Whatever may have been the "certain other factors" that troubled the Commission, the one they specify is accounted for in the version of the assassination provided and asserted by CBS News. The Governor's recollections no longer do violence to the single-bullet theory. And this, you will recall, is a by-product of that version; CBS News did not design it for any such purpose.

And to recur to the question of "necessary" and "not necessary," I am inclined to reiterate that those terms are not applicable within the account as a whole, or indeed within any account of any event, taken as a whole. What is significant is not any single item of the theory, but the general independence of those items and the fact they converge to create a single, coherent account. Command a thousand honorable brick-makers to make bricks, and a thousand honorable bricklayers to lay them, and the resulting structure, if it is large enough and coherent enough, will not fall because one or two or several bricks are faulty or badly laid. No one brick is "necessary" or "not necessary." Those who attempt to convey that impression are misleading, or worse.

With the single-bullet theory, in any case, the sheer mechanics of the assassination are complete. The "how," in its most direct sense, has been told. But the questions that remain are at least as significant as those that have been answered.

10 LEE HARVEY OSWALD

*The Warren Commission could not give Lee Harvey Oswald
his day in court and the protection of our laws. . . . We do
not have that reliance. We must depend upon our own judgments and look into our own consciences.*

—Walter Cronkite

Anyone who immerses himself in the details of the Kennedy
assassination, as so many members of the staff of CBS News im-
mersed themselves for so many months, turns away at last from
the details of ballistic tests, autopsy procedures, and eyewitness
accounts to fix his attention finally on Lee Harvey Oswald. In the
end, the most lasting image is that of a meager, pallid man, who
stands in the shadows of the warehouse corner, fingering his
twelve-dollar rifle and its seven-dollar telescopic sight, and waits
for the motorcade to swing slowly around the corner and present
to him a clean, unobserved shot at the back of the President's
head. It may be that this as much as anything else cries out for
explanation.

The Warren Commission went to extraordinary lengths to
recount, down to the last detail, the life and death of Lee Harvey
Oswald. It is there in the twenty-seven volumes, summarized at
the outset, narrated in detail by witnesses and documents. Those
who are obsessed with the notion of a grand conspiracy and read
it avidly, seeking out inconsistencies, (as if there were any life in
which inconsistencies were absent) or justifying by one item or
another their own interpretation of Oswald's defection to Russia,
or his trip to Mexico, or any other aspect of his errant life. But it
is not in the items that the interest lies, nor is it in the items that
insight into the assassination is to be found. One must look, to
the extent that one can do so, to the whole man.

There is the impression that Oswald had grasped, sometime early in his life, an enormous idea, and that idea in the end was his undoing. He had come to realize, heaven knows how, that man is capable of imposing changes in his environment merely by means of the operation of his own mind. It is a staggering notion. It is certainly a notion that most men never get. Above all, men who are forced to engage in a daily struggle for survival, as Oswald was engaged during the greatest part of his mature life, do not usually entertain such a notion. It is their hands and the sweat of their brows that work to change their own environments, and not the speculative activities of their minds. Yet the notion was born, somehow, in Oswald, and it took command of him.

He went on, of course, to the next step: He made the general notion a specific notion, and read it to signify that *his* mind, Oswald's mind, was capable of this miracle. It was natural that he feel so. Few men are innately modest, and Oswald did not come from a modest household. On the contrary, he was encouraged from infancy to be vain. But there is no evidence, in all the account of his life, that Oswald's mind was up to the ambitions he had for it. The brutal fact is that he seemed to have a quite ordinary mind. There is no record that he did anything well, mental or physical. By any but the lowest standards, he was a dismal incompetent. "He was a pretty good order-filler," his colleagues at the Book Depository were to say of him later, and this was the nearest thing to a tribute he ever earned.

Born into other circumstances, all of this might not have mattered so much. An upper-middle-class Oswald, or an Oswald born into a subculture that placed high value on intellectual achievement, would have progressed smoothly through high school, college and graduate school, and perhaps developed an interest in political science and devoted his life to it. Surrounded by men and women whose principal occupation was the exercise of mental powers, Oswald would have bent himself happily to the same pursuits, a respected and unexceptional man. He would have attended seminars, written learned papers, impressed youth with the breadth of his knowledge and wisdom, and in all carved himself a comfortable niche. Endowed as he was, nothing much would have come of it in the end, but no one would have noticed, and in any case few would have been in any position to be sure. The appearance of intellectual activity is socially quite as acceptable as intellectual activity itself, and often a good deal less abrasive. In his worst days, Oswald was not fundamentally a difficult man. On the whole he was rather anxious to please. Pursuing our fantasy to the end, we might predict he would have ended up president of the appropriate professional society, and have been quoted from time to time in national news magazines.

But that kind of opportunity never presented itself. Mrs. Oswald did not understand and could not help her son, nor could the companions he found in the shabby corners of whatever city chanced to be his home, nor the overburdened teachers in the neighborhood schools. (One might imagine that one good teacher might have made a difference, but it is probably not so—there was far too much working against Oswald.) In New York they were acute enough to notice something troubling about the boy, and recommended psychiatric care, but Mrs. Oswald knew better than that and the opportunity, for whatever it might have been worth, was lost.

He tried, but there was no one to provide him with the basic instruments that he needed. He read weighty books, and never quite understood what they were trying to say. He joined the Marines, more than likely in the desperate hope that among many men he would find a few who would listen and respond as he groped his way. He found no one who spoke the language he knew very well existed somewhere. He ran away to Russia, the country born of intellectual debate and nourished on polemics. Russia accepted him grudgingly as a worker, but showed no interest in what he sincerely believed to be deep thoughts. He married a Russian girl—was not every Russian born to intellectualism?—only to find she cared less about the intellect than his colleagues in the Marines. It was pretty clothes and refrigerators that really occupied her mind. He tried conversing with himself by keeping a journal, but it is witless and devoid of content.

Always looking for intellectual nourishment, he dabbled in political activities, but never could he shoulder his way among the elite. To the end he clung to his vision. Under arrest he was stubbornly legalistic, the lawyer of his choice was a well-known intellectual, he maintained an air of superiority toward his captors. Whatever else may have happened to Oswald, it is almost certain that he died still convinced he was the better man.

In the Warren Report, and thereafter in almost every account written of Oswald, he is characterized as a "loner." If this is intended as a description of his way of life, it is hardly arguable. Oswald could lay claim, at the time of the assassination, to no close friend, and not even to associates with whom he might simply and unaffectedly pass his time. His marriage was disintegrating, and had been for many months. He was clearly aware of the fact, and clearly making no headway in coping with it. His days were spent at a trivial job, where he found no one who could qualify as anything more than a forced acquaintance; his leisure in a small, mean furnished room, where he was not even on conversational terms with his landlady. It is difficult to conceive of more lonely a man.

But when one speaks of a "loner," one ordinarily understands it to signify a man who has chosen to go it alone, who has withdrawn from the society of his fellows and created for himself a life in which he alone plays any significant part. In those terms, it is as clear as anything in the Commission account of his life that Oswald was nothing of the sort. He possessed, on the contrary, an enormous urge to. be a part of his society. He had traveled to find a society that would accept him on his own terms. He had tried Russia, and they would not have him. In all probability he had made an earnest attempt to reach Cuba, and Cuba too was not interested. With the Paines, friends of his wife, he had sought out discussion societies, friendship societies—they would not have him and in the end the Paines would not have him either. He corresponded widely with people who appeared to him to be of importance, although none of the correspondence thrived. He was, as all who knew him testified, inclined to be disputatious—again not often the characteristic of the man who seeks to withdraw.

In short, in his brief life Oswald appeared to have discovered that the world was made up of those with whom he wished to associate and who shunned him, and those with whom he did not wish to associate, and whom he shunned in turn. To any human being such a state of affairs would be agonizing. To Oswald, certain that his capabilities were such as to make of him, given the opportunity, a man of real consequence, the fate to which he was condemned tore at his soul. The world was awry, and he had been born to set it right. Yet it was becoming obvious to him that he had not the smallest hope of doing so. He could not even hope to be the village Hampden of whom the poet wrote, for Oswald did not have so much as a village.

And so, he must have decided, if he could not affect the world in which he lived in the manner for which he was so eminently suited, he would find himself another way. It was a grim decision, but it had its own kind of lunatic logic: He was born to make a difference; it was fated he make a difference; he *would* make a difference. In March of 1963 he invested a few hard-earned dollars in a cheap rifle.

Oswald was no lover of guns, no outdoors man, no devotee of rifle ranges. There is no sign that he was paranoid, no record that he imagined plots against his life, or enemies in ambush around him. The rifle was purchased because Oswald intended to assassinate someone. One power that he knew he possessed being denied its exercise, he would purchase himself another power that could not so easily be thwarted.

It is difficult to believe that he had President Kennedy selected for a target. Oswald had no animus toward Kennedy—at any rate, no more animus than he held toward anyone else who was doing the things Oswald thought he himself was so well fitted to do. Of the Presidents who had served during Oswald's lifetime, Kennedy perhaps came closest to Oswald's own idea of what a man should be and how he should behave. In March, and indeed until late in November, Oswald had no reason to believe that the cast of the dice would ever bring him to a time and place a strategist might have designed for the assassination of the President. In all likelihood, Oswald had no target at all in mind when he mailed away the money order for his rifle.

His wife, Marina Oswald, told the Warren Commission that in Dallas, a little more than two weeks after Oswald bought the rifle, he used it in an attempt on the life of Major General Edwin A. Walker, a leader of the Texas radical right, and that two weeks later he told her he might make an attempt on the life of Richard M. Nixon. There was indeed a rifle shot fired at General Walker which missed its mark, and there is some circumstantial evidence that Oswald might have fired it. Mr. Nixon was not in or near Dallas during the period in question, but Lyndon B. Johnson was, and it is possible that Mrs. Oswald, in telling her story, confused the incumbent Vice President with the man he succeeded in that office.

On the one hand, it seems quite consistent with Oswald's own political views that he should choose as his victim Walker, Nixon, or Johnson. He could not have had much love for any one of the three. On the other hand, the story of the Walker attempt depends pretty much on the testimony of Marina Oswald, and the story that Oswald might have had designs on Nixon-Johnson rests entirely upon her testimony. Marina Oswald at her best was not the most convincing witness in the world, and over the long period of time during which she was in intermittent touch with the Warren Commission, she did not wear well. A judgment on the accuracy of her accounts may fairly be left to the taste of the adjudicator.

What appears convincing is that sometime early in 1963 Oswald had made up his mind to kill someone important, and that only chance brought the President into his gunsights. In the most fundamental way, the assassination was a highly personal act, performed to satisfy Oswald's own needs, and all the surrounding circumstances were purely incidental. It is probable that only on Thursday, the day before the assassination, did Oswald come to realize that the parade would pass directly by the School Book Depository building, and that at that instant the vague intent took on form and shape. For everything about the assassination seems unplanned. There was a quick, otherwise unaccountable trip to Irving to pick up the rifle; a clumsy explanation for the package he carried back to Dallas with him; no plan of any kind for making an escape. All bear the marks of improvisation. Having killed the President, Oswald hurried back to his room to pick up a revolver, and thereafter appeared to have nothing at all in view. In the end he hid in the darkness of an empty theater and awaited his capture.

It goes without saying that all this is highly speculative, and carries only the amount of weight that a reader will freely give it. Yet some kind of speculation about Oswald is as much a necessity as the determination of the number and the nature of the

President's wounds. If one is to account for the assassination, one is obliged to account for the assassin.

Merely to say that Oswald had lost his hold on sanity, and that the murder was the act of a lunatic, is not sufficient. We have said that to raise the general cry of conspiracy is impermissible, not because conspiracy can not explain events, but because it can be employed to explain too much. Exactly the same can be said about the general cry of insanity; it can be called upon to explain any and every human action. We are being careful here not to raise that general cry. It was madness, but there was method in it.

One of the tragedies that culminated in Dealey Plaza was the tragedy of Lee Harvey Oswald. In the eye of eternity, it may be that it was the greater tragedy of the two. Kennedy, a hero, died the death of a hero and is enshrined. Oswald was a human being gone to waste. Tragedy is where one sees it.

There is one further note which can be offered only as a personal note, for it is entirely a matter of the writer's own recollection. I recall no general outburst of animus directed toward Oswald in the two days that he lived after the crime. There was some, of course, and a man who held animus assassinated Oswald in turn. But there was no outpouring of wrath that I recall directed toward the man who had killed a national hero, no thirst for Oswald's blood, no hysteria seeking for a means of striking back at Oswald or at those whom one might associate with Oswald. The general attitude appeared to be, not one of wrath, but of compassion. At the time it struck me as remarkable; today I sense it to have been instinctively correct.

With all this, the immediate account of the assassination is closed. We have the means, the method, and the tortured motive. It is difficult to conceive that in any important respect the account is mistaken.

11 THE CRITICS

[Oswald] did not touch a gun on that day. He was a decoy at first, and then he was a patsy, and then he was a victim.
—Jim Garrison

Attention has so far been concentrated, for the most part, on those aspects of the Warren Report that have drawn most of the critical fire, or in which the Commission itself has been charged with dereliction. I have concerned myself with the basic facts of the assassination: the number, direction, and timing of the shots; the single-bullet theory, and the nature of the man who committed the crime. If this is measured against the breadth of the critical attack, it might at first appear that I have merely scratched the surface. For every element in the Warren account that I have scrutinized, there are dozens which have aroused the fury of one dissenter or another.

This feeling of incompleteness, however, is more illusory than real. One must consider, to begin with, the nature of the critical attacks. They fall into certain categories, in which both motivations and modes of operation differ. We have already written something of the motivation. We must think now of the modes of operation.

Let me distinguish first those critics who are merely suspicious, or who have some kind of scholarly interest in the workings of the Warren Commission. For the most part the account given so far in this book covers much of the substance with which they are concerned, and an earnest attempt will be made during the rest of the book to cover all the rest.

But there is another kind of critic, and these the most vocal and the best known, whose suspicions are in fact prior to the

Warren Commission or its report, or even the assassination itself. They are the people married to a conspiracy theory of history, or politically at odds with their government (or perhaps any government), or immediately skeptical of any official explanation of any event (some of them divide their time between the Warren Report and flying saucers), or who descry the possibility of financial gain in dissent. Their mode of operation is quite distinct. They do not evaluate information and on the basis of that evaluation become suspicious. Instead they set out suspicious, and search for information upon which their suspicions can somehow be made to depend.

These people have rummaged diligently through the Warren Report, seeking out any scrap upon which a case can be built. They are not necessarily scrupulous: A sentence taken out of context can be readily put to their use; an assertion which is elsewhere flatly disproved can be restated, its disproof ignored. Some of them invent facts, others rely upon the ambiguities of the ordinary language to imply facts that are not so. Many of them, it may be added, are deluding themselves at least as actively as they seek to delude others. This is truest of all of those who use "photographic evidence" or "scientific evidence" to buttress their beliefs or claims.

Perhaps Mark Lane constitutes a group all his own. Mr. Lane maintains that his actions are the legitimate actions of an attorney for the defense. The defense has no need to produce a coherent account of what happened. That is the task of the prosecution, upon whom rests the burden of proof. The attorney for the defense is obliged only to destroy the prosecution's account. He is under no obligation to replace it with any rational account of his own. Hence the classic defense of the man accused of borrowing an intact vase and returning it broken: The lawyer maintained that his client had never borrowed the vase, that it had been damaged when he got it, and that it was undamaged when he returned it. That is of course frivolous, but it embodies the principle.

Mr. Lane's position is somewhat weakened by the fact that he has no client, and that in any event there is no one on trial. Taken at its face value, however, that position may maintain

Mr. Lane's dignity, but it does not alter his procedures—it merely denominates them common legal practice and makes them somehow respectable. Like his fellow critics, Mr. Lane rummages and emerges with whatever his rummaging can produce, abetted by an active imagination and carefully controlled scruples about telling the whole truth. What applies to his fellows applies quite as well to Mr. Lane.

The rebuttals to all these claims are to be found in the Warren Report, together with any evidence that may exist for the claims themselves. To track them down, one by one, would be a tedious and unprofitable undertaking, simply because the process of establishing the claims is such that for every claim put to rest, two new ones will arise. So long as the suspicions are independent of the evidence, this is bound to be the case.

What can be safely stated is that, almost without exception, the charges against the Warren Report, in this category at least, where they are not completely unscrupulous, can be found to rest on one or more of three bases. First, they can arise from a decision to accept as veridical testimony of one or more eyewitnesses which contradicts the Commission account. Thus, there is a witness who maintains he saw Oswald on the first floor of the School Book Depository when the assassination was committed. To the critic seeking substance for his suspicions, no more is necessary. Second, they can be referred to the fancied "laws of probability." The assertion here is that since it is improbable that a man could cover the route Oswald covered in the time it took him to do so—and indeed under the circumstances that obtained immediately after the assassination it *was* improbable—one may safely conclude that he did not cover that route. Third, and most frequently, there can be detected anywhere and everywhere the appeal to an undefined and open-ended conspiracy. Since Officer Tippit was patrolling a beat not ordinarily his own when he was shot, he must have been part of a conspiracy to do something or other. (What that something or other might have been varies with different critics.)

I have already stated why most of these, even if they were not brought into final doubt by other indisputable evidence, are not valid objections to the report. Thus even in isolation they

are not worth serious consideration. But of course they do not
exist in isolation. There is ample evidence that Oswald was on
the sixth and not the first floor. Whatever the probability may
have been, Oswald *did* cover the route, and was seen along
almost every point of it. Tippit was sent to the beat he was
patrolling simply because the officers who normally patrolled
that beat had themselves been dispatched toward Dealey Plaza,
where their presence might have been needed. One could go on
indefinitely stating and rebutting. It is to be hoped that the
reasons for not doing so are by now abundantly clear.

In a sense I have divided the dissenters to the Warren Report into the respectable and the unrespectable. But in terms of
sheer number, most dissenters are really in neither class. Their
dissent comes from nothing more substantial than a vague feeling
of dissatisfaction, and takes on substance by reference to the old
saw: "Where there's smoke, there's fire." Like most old saws,
that one constitutes a good general rule, but it can be most misleading in any specific case. All that one is really entitled to say
with certainty is that where there is smoke, there is smoke. Or
one can also say, with considerable confidence, that where there
is smoke there may very well be someone who wishes to convince
you that there is fire. The view that the Warren Report is suspect simply because so many books have been written calling
the Report suspect is a lazy view, and not one that can be defended except on grounds of human weakness. At the very least
those who hold such a view should be required to read both the
Warren Report itself and the books and articles which attack it,
with the intention of making some honest attempt to distinguish
between smoke and smoke screen. On the whole they have not
done so and will not do so. This means, of course, that they are
not likely to read this book, either, which makes one wonder why
it has been written.

All this has been harsh, and quite intentionally so, toward the
vast majority of the dissenters who have imposed themselves on
the public attention. It would be unreasonable and unfair to let
that harshness convey the impression that there can be no
respectable dissent to the Warren Report. There is in this book
considerable dissent, and there will be more on later pages, but
I hope that this book is respectable.

I have been harsh toward those whose opinions were effectively formed and hardened even before the assassination itself took place, and toward those who have not honestly made the effort necessary to entitle them to an opinion. But there are those who have looked at the evidence with some attention, and who still maintain (most of them) that although the Warren Commission may have told the truth and nothing but the truth, to the fullest extent that it was possible, it has still not told the whole truth.

To a large extent, such a position can be interpreted to mean that impressions of the assassination hastily formed during the first few days that followed it have not been overcome by all the efforts of the Warren Commission. In a refined sense it is an attack not upon the integrity of the Warren Commission, nor even upon the basic capacity of the Warren Commission, but upon the ability of the Warren Commission to communicate in persuasive form what its integrity and its capacity had brought to light. (That, obviously, can not be the view that the respectable critics themselves take, but it can very well be the way that it all appears to a disinterested observer.)

It was quite natural that suspicions should have been aroused in the hours and days that followed the assassination. Only a highly disciplined man would have been able, as news from Dallas poured into his eyes and ears, to withhold any opinion, and to wait patiently and stubbornly until all the evidence was in before forming some tentative hypothesis of his own.

I have already referred to some of the elements that fostered suspicion. Oswald had a background that could easily be interpreted to signify close Communist connections. He had, for example, sought Russian citizenship and attempted to renounce his American citizenship. American communism is, to some degree, a conspiracy against the form of government almost all of us support, and it is at least conceivable that such a conspiracy decide upon a political assassination to further its own ends. It is even more conceivable that such an assassination could have been the work of some individual who was part of no conspiracy, but who merely believed that in doing as he did he would be furthering the cause of American communism. (Something very much like that did in fact lead to the assassination of William

McKinley.) These, and particularly the latter, are by no means unreasonable suspicions, given Oswald's own history.

Paradoxically enough, suspicions of which the origin was diametrically different from that mentioned above were also in their own way quite reasonable. That Texas, and Dallas in particular, teem with right-wing fanaticism can scarcely be denied. Looking at Oswald, now, not as a Leftist, but more generally as a radical, it was not totally beyond reason to suspect that perhaps he had been the tool of right-wing conspiracy, or the product of right-wing conspiracy. In the East that conclusion was, in fact, the conclusion instinctively and usually reluctantly drawn by many. For more than a few it was with distinct relief that they learned that Oswald, so far as anyone knew, had no right-wing connections.

Such suspicions, and others as well, were immediately and powerfully reinforced by the entry of Ruby upon the scene. It is simply not easy to conceive of the assassination of an important prisoner in the basement of a police station as the product of a chance individual act. Almost inescapably, the mind seeks out a more reasonable explanation, and if one is not forthcoming, prefers to believe that it is being withheld, rather than that it simply does not exist.

It was difficult also to believe that the incredible behavior of the Dallas police, during the forty-eight hours that followed the assassination, was merely a natural phenomenon. By Sunday morning they had issued so many statements and counterstatements that even the sharpest mind might have been befuddled. They had never so much as attempted to exert any control over the press, which, as it could be guaranteed to do under such conditions, ran wild, sending to the four corners of the world a budget of rumors and speculation passing as fact. The police interviewed Oswald and kept no record of the interview, shared their own preliminary speculations with anyone who would listen, drew judgments where no judgments were defensible, and had so prejudiced Oswald's chances for a fair trial that had he lived he almost surely could not have been convicted. Then, to climax it all, the Dallas police lost their prisoner. It seemed to many, at the time, that it was impossible to credit all this to sheer ineptitude. Some larger force must have been at work.

Inadvertently, Earl Warren himself made the largest single contribution to the general atmosphere of suspicion. There are things that will not be revealed in our lifetime, he told the press, and then prudently decided to say no more. Prudent or not, he left it to the individual to speculate on what those things might be. Given the right temper of mind, such speculations can be horrifying. And to those already suspicious, their worst fears were reinforced when the Report itself was constantly promised to the public and constantly delayed; when the date of issuance was announced and withdrawn. The whole management of the Report itself was not such as to engender confidence.

In short, there *were,* and are, reasonable grounds for suspicion. It is on the whole the contention of this book that most of those grounds for suspicion do not survive fair-minded examination, and that those few that do survive such examination are in fact suspicions concerning matters peripheral to the central issue. But since the suspicions are themselves rational, those who hold them are entitled to do so, and those whom a fair-minded examination does not persuade have every right in the world to remain suspicious.

There are also suspicions of another kind, represented best among the critics by Edward Jay Epstein. Mr. Epstein's suspicion is a fundamental one. It concerns the problem of a government engaged in an investigation which might threaten that government itself. How, in practice, is such an examination to be carried out? That is the question Mr. Epstein asked, first as a master's degree thesis and then in a book. Answers to such a question are well worth seeking, and whatever the opinion may be of the skill with which Mr. Epstein conducted his inquiry, there can be no doubt that the inquiry itself is a laudable activity. The philosophical question that occurs at the end of such an inquiry is a troubling one: Does a government have the right to withhold the truth, or to knowingly disseminate a lie, when the matter at stake is the nation's own faith in that government? The practical question is quite as troubling: Under such circumstances, is it all but a foregone conclusion that the government will indeed withhold the truth or disseminate a lie?

In posing just those questions, Mr. Epstein strips away any pretense that the Warren Commission was not a political commission, engaged in a political inquiry, or that the Warren Report is not a political document. It is absurd to weave pretenses that are intended to obscure those facts, and equally absurd to read any kind of menacing connotations in the word *political*. The death of a President is a political event, and an inquiry into the circumstances surrounding that death is a political inquiry. It serves no useful purpose to produce denials of the obvious. And Mr. Epstein's suspicions that political activity may not always be an entirely forthright activity are reasonable. Those suspicions, if they are to be resolved at all, can be resolved only by examination of the acts of the Commission and the conduct of its inquiry, and not by any statement that two and two in this case, and in this case only, do not make four.

President Johnson, in his choice of men to serve on the Warren Commission and most clearly in his choice of chairman, made every effort to preclude any accusation that the Commission had been partisan. It is not charged, by Mr. Epstein, or by anyone else, that party politics was involved in either the inquiry or the report. But the charge has been made that politics in its broader sense was indeed intimately involved, particularly as the investigation encroached upon the affairs of the Federal Bureau of Investigation and the Central Intelligence Agency. Except in their most extravagant forms, which need not detain us here, those charges do not bear upon the essentials of the assassination itself, and I must defer my own consideration of them until I am better able to place them in context.

Finally, one last wellspring of suspicion. Anyone's response to evidence is affected, more powerfully than he may suspect, by his own history and the history of his own subculture. In most of the world, experience both personal and collective indicates that the assassination of a ruler is more often than not a conspiratorial act and part of a grand design to overthrow a government by violence. It may be a central part of that design, as when the assassination is a vital element in a *coup d'état*, as it was for example when Diem was assassinated in South Vietnam. It may be intended to act at one or more removes, as when the assassination itself is one act of terror among many, the sum of which is to be a general breakdown in public faith in the government. Less frequently it may represent the belief that the removal of one man will of itself bring about far-reaching governmental changes, as was the belief when an attempt was made a few years back on the life of General de Gaulle.

It was therefore entirely natural that in most of the world, and even in the Latin and Slavic areas of our own Western European culture, the assumption was made that the assassination of President Kennedy fell into one or more of those patterns. Since in the outcome the assassination was not part of a *coup d'état* or a general atmosphere of terror, and since the consequences were a stress upon continuity in government rather than far-reaching change, it is concluded that the conspiracy failed and that the American Government, like any government under such conditions, is now anxiously striving to conceal the fact that a conspiracy had existed.

It is highly probable that only the passage of generations will erase those suspicions abroad, and that indeed they will never be erased. No matter how readily the case for a conspiracy can be refuted, it can arouse nothing but skepticism among those to whom the discussion itself appears superfluous, since to them an *a priori* case had been made. In this respect, foreign criticism falls in many cases into a category we have already discussed: The critics were prepared to be suspicious long before the event itself, and their suspicions are neither aroused nor allayed by the investigation or the Report, for they exist independent of the facts. Nothing very much can be done about it.

With this I leave consideration of what I have called the unrespectable suspicions, and I confine our attention to those we can reasonably consider respectable. There are enough of them to keep us busy.

12 CONSPIRACY

The Commission . . . left the door open on the question of conspiracy just a crack. The words do not preclude the possibility of conspiracy. They don't say that the Commission concluded there was no conspiracy, or that Oswald was the sole assassin. They only say that the Commission could find no evidence that others were involved. —Walter Cronkite

It is time now to pay closer heed to the theories of conspiracy that have been attached to the assassination of President Kennedy. I have written of the obligation of anyone who intends to give serious consideration to a conspiracy theory. He must specify what he means, and he must do so in a fashion that can honestly be seen to contain a line of thought. Above all he is precluded from buttressing his theory indefinitely by the mere accumulation of new conspirators, for the use of such a process, since by its very nature it will not serve to prove anything at all, in its essence proves nothing at all.

I must repeat, for the viewpoint may be obscured by the harshness with which these pages treat the open-ended conspiracy theory, that to suspect a conspiracy at work was not only reasonable but indeed almost inevitable during the hours that followed immediately upon the assassination. President Johnson himself, and the White House staff, acted in Dallas like men who feared a *coup d'état* was in the making. Even at this long lapse of time, it is a task well worth undertaking to scrutinize the evidence and to see what emerges, for the notion of certain kinds of conspiracy is by no means frivolous, and indeed it remains to this day quite possible that some kind of conspiracy will be uncovered. "*Some kind* of conspiracy," you will note, and it is to the recognition that conspiracies come in many forms and shapes that we must be careful to cling. Whatever may be true of roses, it is simply not the case that a conspiracy is a conspiracy is a conspiracy.

It was maintained in the last chapter that there is no tradition in the United States, or in the recent history of Anglo-Saxon and Scandinavian countries, for the transfer of political power by force or by conspiracy. Nonetheless, the idea of a full-fledged conspiracy, or of somewhat less categorical conspiratorial schemes, in close proximity to the center of power, is by no means far-fetched. Of such we do in fact have experience, although as in most such experience of conspiracy thwarted or held in check, the history is somewhat ambiguous and capable even after the passage of time of arousing emotions.

Explicitly, there was good reason to believe that during the years of the depression some kind of conspiratorial activity closely associated with communism went on in Washington, and that the conspirators themselves had to some extent penetrated the government and were engaged in activities that were at times illegal, and at other times plainly contrary to the public interest as it was generally conceived, and hence at the very least highly improper.

This is touchy ground. How near the seats of power that conspiracy really was, how much discipline existed within it, how profound and carefully conceived its plans, no one really quite knows. Most of the information that exists comes from those who maintain they were part of the conspiracy (that point will recur later) and for many reasons it is suspect. It is touchy above all because much that the conspirators wished to achieve would have attracted the support of a large portion of the American people (never large enough, however, to constitute even a strong minority) if it had not been sought by methods that were indeed conspiratorial and that were led (or conceived by the conspirators themselves to be led) in the interests of a foreign country. There was, and there still is, a disposition among many to hope deeply that the men and women involved were not in fact conspirators, but loyal American citizens. That hope can be quite quickly transformed into a belief.

Nevertheless, there is far too much evidence that a conspiracy of sorts did exist to enable the matter to be casually dismissed. What is perhaps of even more consequence is that there existed

then, and exists today, a widespread conviction among the
American people that such a conspiracy once commanded a certain amount of leverage in Washington and was working feverishly and effectively—if in the end unsucessfully—to assume
control of the American Government. Even the least panicky
observer must bear in mind that the possibility of another such
conspiracy is not to be disregarded, and that in certain circumstances it might well adopt the tactic of political assassination
or worse.

It is in this context that one might quite reasonably examine
the assassination of President Kennedy for evidence of conspiracy. One would then hypothesize a relatively small body of men,
close to or at the seats of power, with certain specific ends in
view, to whom it appeared that the assassination of President
Kennedy would serve those ends. Such a group might be, for
example, ultra-leftist or ultra-rightist; its members might be
agents of a foreign government which had some good reason to
wish President Kennedy replaced; they might be a coherent
group of some kind within the government, such as the Army,
the FBI, the CIA, which had over the passage of time generated
in the shadows of its own will and its own purposes and was now
determined to give them effect. None of these is impossible.
There are many governments in being today which trace their
origins to one or another such conspiracy. Our own government's
birth can be interpreted as the consequence of a left-wing conspiracy against King George III.

All this is quite conceivable, although perhaps only with
great reluctance, until the moment that one begins to fit the
assassination itself into it. Then any hypothesis of that sort begins
to crumble. No small group, however clever and however dedicated, could have hoped to bring off such an act as the assassination of a President and still remain an undetected, undisturbed
conspiracy. It could not have hoped to cover its traces without
broadening itself to the point of absurdity: without, in short,
becoming the kind of open-ended conspiracy of which I have
spoken, welcoming new members by the battalion as their services became needed. A conspiracy, when it moves to direct any
sensational activity, must succeed in its major aims or be exposed.
There are circumstances when exposure does not matter, as when

the matter is one of espionage by an enemy government. Exposure may be inconvenient but there is a fundamental indifference about it. But when the conspiracy exists to transfer power, any blatant overt act must eliminate much of the secrecy within which the conspirators obscured themselves. The conspiracy has been exposed. If its act has succeeded in effecting the transfer of power, exposure is no matter, for the conspirators now become patriots. If the act has failed, and power has not been transferred, the conspiracy is now in the open to be rooted out, or opposed, or tolerated as the possessors of power may determine. When German generals conspired in 1944 to eliminate Hitler, they did so knowing that whether they failed or succeeded, they could certainly not hope to retain secrecy; they did not have the option of trying and then falling back into further furtive conspiracy if Hitler survived.

One might stretch his imagination to conceive a group risking its own destruction by mounting a Presidential assassination, perhaps in the belief that if it were successfully brought off, events themselves would proceed in such a fashion that the ends of the conspiracy would be achieved and secrecy would be no longer necessary. Given this country and the outlook of its people, such a belief would be somewhat lunatic, but lunatic beliefs are not novel. But now Oswald will not fit the hypothesis. Lunatic or not, a conspiracy would scarcely risk its own being by entrusting its sole important single act to a chance passerby, exposed in an open window and equipped with an ancient rifle and defective sights. (As I have already said, it will not do to make Oswald an integral part of the conspiracy, for to explain Oswald would then require a conspiratorial group larger than all outdoors.) Evidence or no evidence, to believe in any of the conspiracies I am now considering, one must believe in an assassin other than Oswald, and I believe we simply cannot do anything of the sort.

The final possibility might be that the assassination was in fact a success; that power was effectively transferred; that the conspirators are now conspiring further to keep secret their initial conspiracy. In a sense, of course, power was transferred: from Kennedy to Johnson, from Massachusetts to Texas, from men and women with one personal style to men and women with another. Such transfers of power take place quite normally, in an orderly fashion, every four or eight years. It may be, too, that in recent months a certain amount of power has transferred from civilians to military, but it is clear that such transfers also take place from time to time, and there are outside events to explain much of that transfer. Certainly, there has been no sign of a radical transfer of power, such as a conspiracy might seek to effect.

It is repugnant even to examine this line of thought, for what it clearly says, of course, is that Johnson conspired to assassinate Kennedy. In the name of all that is holy to God and man, how is he supposed to have done it, and to have kept it secret? Are Congress, the entire administration (many of them still owing allegiance to Kennedy), the press, the colleges and universities, the Army, the Navy, the FBI, every local police force, even the Kennedy family—are they all part of the conspiracy? Did Johnson himself, living a public life from the days of his youth, begin to plan this conspiracy when he first ran for office in Texas? And are all these conspirators—not hundreds, not thousands, not even millions, but tens of millions, so dependable that not one of them produces the hard evidence that some of them must have, or provides a guide to those who wish to find such evidence? I wrote earlier of the communist conspiracy in the Thirties—almost every item of it has been revealed, directly or indirectly, by members of the conspiracy themselves. Is this *conspiracy* made up of millions of men and women with whom this deepest of secrets is forever safe?

We come this quickly to the utterly irrational. Whatever your best efforts, the hypothesis of a small conspiratorial group—indeed, of any definable conspiratorial group with definable conspiratorial aims—can not be maintained by sane men. It will simply not remain the hypothesis with which one began; it bursts its bounds and becomes the unlimited, undefined, and hence unassailable conspiracy in which each new insanity is fully explained by adding conspirators. Anyone who maintains this protean hypothesis, after giving it even trivial consideration, is mad, or conceals his real motives, or does not know his real motives.

At the other extreme of the scale, I can hypothesize another kind of conspiracy. Let me invent it. I shall begin with Oswald. I add another man, equally obscure, who is convinced of the total virtue of Castro and the Cuban Revolution, and further convinced that all American opposition to Castro is embodied in Kennedy. I add a man dedicated to communism, although not under communist discipline, who believes that the party he reveres would welcome the assassination of Kennedy; then another, with an obsessive hatred of Kennedy, as men once had obsessive hatreds for Roosevelt; perhaps still another, this one an adventurer, looking for action.

These men meet, sometimes alone, sometimes with others. They discuss the need to assassinate Kennedy. They canvass means. Perhaps in the end they lay plans, in which one of them will assassinate Kennedy, and another will draw off the chase, and a third will assure the assassin's getaway. Perhaps there is no such collusive effort; they merely draw lots and the short straw is assigned to be the assassin. Perhaps they only meet and disperse, with the effect that one of the four or five is now more determined than ever that Kennedy must be assassinated.

Basically, it is a conspiracy of this sort that Jim Garrison and others are trying to establish. The Warren Commission itself tried, by means of a searching investigation of Oswald's own life. So far, no one has succeeded. Yet, someone may. Garrison himself may, although as yet there are no real signs he can do so. Such a conspiracy is by no means to be ruled out. A reasonable man might even insist that it is quite probable and that some day it is bound to come to light.

But in what significant fashion does it alter the account of the Warren Commission to multiply Oswald by two or three or five? Now, instead of being assassinated by one trivial, insignificant man, the President was assassinated by the efforts, more or less concerted, of several trivial, insignificant men. There has been a conspiracy, it is true, but a conspiracy without real aim, without real purpose, and above all without any danger of consequences beyond the act itself.

The word *conspiracy* is a menacing word. But for a conspiracy itself to be menacing, it must embody some kind of broad consequences. It must itself be directly associated with government, or with the centers of power, or it must have some hopes of becoming so. Its acts must not be ends in themselves, but part of a design that is formed to some purpose, some large intent. The menace lies in the word because the word suggests great covert plots against some great institution, or large plans to reap large gains despite the best attempts of society to prevent them. But if the word is used, as it is often used, merely to state that a single disconnected offender must be multiplied by two, then its menacing overtones simply mislead. Two men who commit, for their own purposes, a crime however heinous are in no real manner different from one man committing the same crime.

If Jim Garrison can prove that a group of random malcontents in New Orleans, of whom Oswald was one, plotted the death of Kennedy, he will have provided the most powerful possible support for the Report of the Warren Commission, for he will have illuminated some of the obscurities of the Report, as the Commission itself was unable to do, and thus have brought the Report that much closer to its goal of representing in all its details the facts concerning the assassination. The central thesis of the Report, that the assassination was an isolated act and part of no grand design, will have merely been strongly substantiated with new evidence. Garrison, if he accomplishes this, will not have affected for one moment the formal soundness of the Warren Report, which itself refused to close the books on the possibility of such a conspiracy. He will, rather, have strengthened the Report by making available one more detail about the mechanics of the assassination. He will perhaps have added one small item to our knowledge—forever to be obscure—of Oswald's motivation. But this will not be the general view, for at this moment of great dissent any wound to the Warren Report is a grievous wound.

Every President knows the risk he runs, and knows too that it is an inescapable risk. Any man or small group of men who have no concern about the consequences can mount an attempt upon the life of the President, and now and then such an attempt will succeed, and the President will die for no reason other than the fact that he was President, and hence, target. By enormous efforts the risk can be minimized, but even so the dangers that remain are greater than the dangers that have been overcome. President Kennedy was aware of exactly that, and acknowledged it; so has President Johnson. Jim Garrison, or someone else, may some day tell us with far greater detail than we now possess just how, upon this particular occasion, the deed was effected. The deed itself, however, remains the same.

Jim Garrison, however, has indicated that he intends to do far more than that for which we have so far given him provisional credit. He has maintained specifically that he will show more than an idle plot; that he will show, in fact, a CIA connection which will indeed broaden the conspiracy to the point where an attribution of menace is reasonable. And the question of the CIA and the FBI is indeed troubling, for there is still another kind of conspiracy that must concern us.

It is not the question of a CIA or an FBI conspiracy which eventuated in the assassination of President Kennedy. We have in fact already disposed of any such question, for such a conspiracy would in fact be obliged to become open-ended, for exactly the reasons I have given earlier in this chapter.

It is quite natural that there should be doubts about both the CIA and the FBI, for both organizations possess by virtue of their missions some of the characteristics of a true conspiracy. Much of what they do is done secretly, they possess legal power to withhold certain kinds of information from certain people, and consequently some of the means to withhold almost any information from almost any people; they have at times shown the disposition to do so.

But at the same time, they act under important limitations. For one thing they have direct links to legitimate government, and could not exist without them. It is true that by statute the control exercised over them by Congress and by the executive may be lax and highly permissive, but it is always there, and if the CIA or FBI were ever tempted to act against that government, those links would have to be made secure before it dared make any attempt. At just that point, any CIA or FBI conspiracy would be forced to extend into normal governmental institutions. As the hypothesis is pursued, the dam once again breaks and such a conspiracy is seen to be unbounded, for it would have to include at the outset the government itself and the press, to go no further. It is important to realize that neither the CIA nor the FBI is a closed institution. Men pass in and out of both, and neither agency possesses the power of a true conspiracy, to assure its security by closing its gates and by murdering, if necessary, those who seek to pass through them. One does not simply opt out of the Mafia. Over time, no conspiracy can exist without that power. Whatever the powers of the CIA and the FBI (and whatever one's own attitude may be toward those powers) they are limited, and for purposes of conspiracy they are impossibly limited.

What is far more tempting to credit is the likelihood of what might be called a secondary conspiracy. Both the FBI and the CIA had knowledge of Oswald before the assassination. The CIA was well aware of his sojourn in Russia and his attempts to reach Cuba; the FBI of his association with Cuban activities. His notebook carried, at the time of his arrest, the name and telephone number of James Hosty, an FBI agent. It was explained that as a matter of routine surveillance the FBI had been in touch with Marina Oswald and with the Paines, in whose home she and Oswald had lived.

All this may indeed have been routine. It may also be, however, that Oswald was an informant for either the CIA, the FBI, or both; possible even that he was in Russia in the interests of the CIA, or was similarly bound for Cuba. There is no evidence for any of this, but here one should not necessarily be surprised. Neither the CIA nor the FBI could keep secret an attempt on the life of the President, but they are provided, legally, the means of keeping secret an association with an informer or an agent, and frequently do so. In principle at least one can imagine that after due consideration a high-level decision was made to retain those secrets even under the circumstances of the assassination, on the grounds that the secrecy was essential to the agency and the disclosure was not essential to the Warren investigation. Such a decision would be enormously high-handed, but we are all quite prepared to expect high-handedness from either agency.

What I am really touching upon here is the relationship, during the investigation, between the Warren Commission and the two agencies. I can more appropriately consider that relationship in another context and a later chapter. I can say here, however, that any secondary secrecy of the sort we are now considering, although perhaps highly deplorable and indeed highly dangerous, is not directly consequential in the context of the Report.

It leaves shrouded in secrecy some of the details of Oswald's past, and perhaps deprives us of further insights into his character and his motives. But it alters no essential fact of the assassination.

This remains so even if the further extension is made, as Garrison occasionally implies he intends, to a "conspiracy" in New Orleans. Fanciful as it may be, it can not be ruled out that Oswald was engaged in meetings and discussions in New Orleans and elsewhere as part of an FBI or CIA assignment. This would make Oswald an even more complicated character than we know him to be, but it is still not sufficient to show, or even to hint at FBI or CIA complicity in the assassination. It would indicate instead that either agency or both were incredibly inept in their choice of informants, which may very well be so: Every double agent who turns up is evidence to that fact. Informants being recruited as they are, it is not simple to be sure of their dependability.

None of this is intended as an apology for what I have called secondary conspiracy. It may be that the power of the FBI or the CIA, if it can be shown they possess such power, is a real threat to our government, greater by far than any threat Oswald could have mounted. But that is truly another question. It is wholly independent of the assassination, except to the extent that the assassination may in the end bring it into the light and invite a public revulsion. It was, in fact, this very state of affairs that constituted a problem for the Warren Commission when it was forced to deal with these matters. I shall, as I have said, consider this later.

For the moment I can sum up by saying that conspiracy does not enter fundamentally into the assassination. The menacing conspiracy can not survive as a hypothesis. The remaining kinds of conspiracy do not affect the Commission's conclusions in any real way. On the other side of that same coin there is simply not yet any hard evidence to indicate a conspiracy, either in Oswald's life, as the Commission scrupulously and diligently exposed it, or in the circumstances surrounding the assassination, and those who stubbornly insist on a theory of conspiracy are forced to invent evidence as they go along.

I can not say with absolute finality, any more than the Commission could say, that Oswald acted alone. I can say that if he acted with others, they were merely more of the same. The law would make all of them assassins, whether they handled rifles or not, and it is conceivable, though dubious, that someone may yet be imprisoned or executed for the assassination. It will be a fascinating outcome, in the fashion that the last chapter of any great detective story can be fascinating, but it will not alter the nature of the crime or the conclusions concerning the crime that the Warren Commission has drawn.

THE OPERATION OF
THE COMMISSION

I think the villain was the desire of government officials to be nice, to see to it that nothing would upset the American people. . . . The American people would have been upset surely if they were told there was a conspiracy which took the life of your President.   —Mark Lane

The first great question posed at the beginning of this book was the question of the accuracy of the Warren Report. We have seen that in its fundamentals the Report stands firm against any rational attack. It may be that it will be necessary in the future to modify details. CBS News believes its own investigation accomplished some of this, and I will readily concede that more is likely to follow; in particular it may well turn out that Oswald did not act entirely alone, but that others more or less like him had some part, if only a hortatory part, in the assassination.

The second great question is that of the operation of the Commission itself. As I sought to make clear, that question is independent of the accuracy of the Report itself. Abstractly one might be tempted to say that if the Commission ended with an irrefutable position, it is irrelevant how it managed to do so. But since the Commission was under the obligation not only to assess but to persuade, its own organization and functioning is an important part of the whole story. One looks into that organization and functioning, moreover, in the knowledge that the Warren Report did not in fact persuade; that Mark Lane, whose position crumbles to ashes under even casual examination, has succeeded where seven distinguished Americans and a report that is logically and practically very nearly impregnable have failed. How much has that failure come about because of deficiencies in the Commission?

The membership of the Commission is of itself interesting. Earl Warren, Chief Justice of the United States, was its chairman. With him were two members of the Senate and two of the House, in each case representing the two major parties. Finally, Allen W. Dulles and John J. McCloy made up the complement of seven. Now, looking no further than addresses and occupation, this is a most peculiar group. Six of the seven make their homes in Washington, and the seventh has spent a good share of his time there. All seven have made all or the major portion of their careers in government, four as elected officials, the chairman as both an elected and an appointed offical, and Mr. Dulles and Mr. McCloy entirely as appointed officials. Five of the seven were trained as lawyers.

The Commission was, in short, unabashedly a political Commission. In the fact is reflected more than anything else the personal style of President Johnson. One can almost be certain, for example, that had Eisenhower appointed a Commission to fulfill such a task as that which faced the Warren Commission, he would have managed somehow or other to include a general or two, just as Hoover might have found room for engineers and tycoons, Coolidge for merchant princes, and Wilson for a college professor or a university president. President Johnson chose the kind of men with whom he had lived his life, and whom he respected most and understood best.

It is not difficult to understand what impelled him to such a choice, but a good deal more difficult to justify it. As we have seen, in many of its most important aspects the Commission was asked to scrutinize the activities of the government itself. The result of its deliberations might well affect the stability of the government. Its judgments could conceivably shake important institutions of government. Yet the men who were to assume responsibility for all this were themselves important parts of the very government that was so intimately involved.

Here at the outset President Johnson created difficulties for his own Commission. It was not only that it made it possible for those anxious to dispute the Report to question the integrity of the Commission, as interested parties. The matter was somewhat more subtle.

One can dispose at once of the matter of the integrity of the seven men who sat in judgment. In the final CBS News broadcast, Eric Sevareid put the matter as cogently as it could be stated:

> **Sevareid:** Nearly three years after the Warren inquiry finished its painful and onerous work, there are not only the serious critics who point to the various mistakes of commission or omission, mistakes of a consequence one can only guess at, and of a kind that has probably plagued every lengthy, voluminous official investigation ever staged—there are also people who think the Commission itself was a conspiracy to cover up something.
>
> In the first place, it would be utterly impossible in the American arena of a fierce and free press and politics to conceal a conspiracy among so many individuals who live in the public eye. In the second place, the deepest allegiance of men like Chief Justice Earl Warren, or of John McCloy, does not lie with any President, political party, or current cause—it lies with history, their name and place in history. That is all they live for in their later years. If they knowingly suppressed or distorted decisive evidence about such an event as a Presidential murder, their descendants would bear accursed names forever. The notion they would do such a thing is idiotic.

One might ask, in passing, exactly how the President of the United States would go about asking the Chief Justice or the House Minority Leader to join a conspiracy. In a week there would not be much time to explore the matter tenderly. They would have to be asked outright, with the knowledge that total disaster would be the immediate outcome if either one of them refused. But even to consider the matter further is merely frivolous.

The point that might more reasonably be made, however, is that it would not be necessary to make any conspiracy explicit to men of that particular background. Themselves creatures of the government, they could be trusted to act of their own volition in a manner that would best serve the selfish interest of the government. They could be trusted to betray without ever suspecting that they were engaged in betrayal. Whatever one may think of the validity of such a charge, the mere fact that the charge could be made represented an important weakness. And in fact, as we shall see, the charge can be made, although it is only in matters peripheral to the main issue that it was of any significance.

In still another respect the makeup of the Commission might be brought into question. The Warren Commission was made up exclusively of extremely busy men, who could not under any circumstances drop all their other affairs in order to concentrate upon this one. The business of the Supreme Court, always taxing, would have to go on uninterrupted, whatever outside obligations its Chief Justice might assume. The four men chosen from the Senate and the House were chosen precisely because they were men of importance in Congress, and it was only to be expected that the principal burden of their thoughts and their activities would be Congress and not the Commission. In short, it was obvious from the outset that for every commissioner the work of the Warren Commission would be undertaken as a part-time job.

The naive view of such an arrangement is bound to be unfavorable. But the arrangement itself must be considered in the light of the actual operation of such commissions, which is not entirely what it seems to the uninitiated. The primary function of a commission, superseding all its other functions, is to sign a report. Their signatures give the report validity. They signify to the community at large that a group of men, selected explicitly because their own reputations carry weight, have come to agreement upon a statement. That statement thereupon carries the combined weight of all the reputations that lie behind it. The actual makeup of any commission reflects the judgment of those who appointed it with respect to the subgroups within the population at large whom it is important to convince. President Johnson's judgment, for example, was that the need to convince those who are of influence in partisan politics demanded the appointment of Gerald Ford. The ideal commission would be one which contained for every American at least one member of whom that citizen would freely say, "If he believes it, I believe it." No such commission has ever been appointed, but ideally one hopes to come as close as one can.

If the commisioners themselves are men of integrity, no one of them will sign a report which does not represent fairly his own views. How the commissioners manage to be sure that those views represent, in each case, the commissioner's own best judgment is likely to vary from commission to commission. A commission of experts, dealing with a subject in which they have special qualifications, will usually work very nearly full time at their problems and stand in an extremely intimate acquaintance with them; their report will carry maximum weight with other experts. A commission of generalists, intended to convince other generalists (which is after all what most of us are), is likely to rely more heavily on staff. In such a case, it is the role of the staff to convince the commission, both in matters of fact and of policy; it is the role of the commission to force the staff to its maximum efforts before it will be convinced. In the end the commission must know what it believes and why it believes it. It is the obligation of staff to bring the commission to that point, the obligation of the commission to come to it only reluctantly.

The Warren Commission was clearly intended to rely heavily upon the work of its staff. Measured in that light, the amount of effort exerted by the commissioners themselves composes a record which is in part completely acceptable, and in part highly questionable. It is clear from the record that while the Commission remained in being, most of its members were diligent. In any such commission, the brunt of the work falls upon the chairman, and Justice Warren gave a substantial part of his time to the task. The record shows also that the Commission members in general were available when they were needed, and that they saw to it individually and collectively that their staff hewed to the line.

The more questionable part of the record relates, not to the intensity with which the commissioners worked, but the duration of the Commission. There was great pressure upon the Commission to get out its Report. The Commission itself has denied that the pressure was applied from any specific source (except, perhaps, the press) but it was nevertheless latent in the situation. Uncertainty about the assassination and what it might signify was widely spread, and while it existed, it was unsettling: To some extent it left in abeyance the legitimacy of the government in office. It was not necessary for the Commission to respond to a sense of urgency that originated outside the Commission itself, for that sense of urgency was to be found among the members. Consequently the Commission imposed harsh deadlines on its staff and rushed its report to completion.

The Commission denies that it was rushed, and may not even have realized how it was racing toward completion of its work. Yet the Report shows signs of haste, and Mr. Epstein has reported haste in its preparation. No deliberations can go on forever, but when a deadline is issued for a chapter or for a memorandum, those responsible for the work itself are being told to stop working on the problem and to begin working on the statement of the problem. The deadlines issued to the staff of the Warren Report were, by any standards, deadlines that revealed a sense of urgency.

The worst of it was that the purpose haste was intended to serve was thus disserved. The uncertainty and the sense of unsettlement that were to be resolved by an early report were only heightened by the consequences of that haste. For the Commission, having issued its Report, now had no choice but to dissolve and to scatter its staff. When the Report itself came under fire, as it was almost certain it would, it was without official defenders and without the means to support a defense. When points of substance were brought up, or (far more often) points that could be shrewdly distorted to appear substantial, there was no means of holding a reasonable official discussion of them, for the commissioners, having said their final say, had no choice but to be silent.

It is clear today, in hindsight at least, that the Report issued in September, 1964, a bare ten months after the assassination, should have been a preliminary report, and that the Commission should have remained in existence with at least a modest staff. There would then have been no reason whatsoever to hurry, and the staff could have devoted two years or more to learning the areas in which the preliminary report was inadequate, or did not put its best foot forward, or might be greatly improved by additional efforts brought to the attention of Commission staff by responsible critics. There might even have been time to tie up the loose ends represented by such as Mrs. Walther and Mr. Holland, or to respond in one way or another to the great doubts that have arisen by reason of the withheld color pictures and X-rays. The demands of the commissioners themselves during the extended period need not have been great, but they would have continued to stand as surrogates for the accuracy and the integrity of the Report. To a large extent their decision to terminate left a void into which Mark Lane and others were only too eager to rush, and so it is Mr. Lane who is now popularly seen as the authority on the assassination, and not Justice Warren. Mr. Lane can at least maintain that he has worked hard on it longer.

I have spoken of the manner in which the Commission was constituted, and found it readily explicable but still somewhat odd. When we come to the constitution of the staff, one might be forgiven for finding it odder still.

The staff was made up exclusively of lawyers. It was headed by J. Lee Rankin, a lawyer (and again with strong government ties) and from top to bottom, from its principal personnel to its most lowly juniors, was composed of lawyers, many of whom in turn were normally employed by federal, state, or local government. Into this legal preserve not one foot from the outside world was permitted to enter. The investigation was planned by lawyers, executed by lawyers, and reported by lawyers.

Lawyers may be quite estimable people, and from all appearances the lawyers who served the Warren Commission were exactly that. There has been no reason to question their integrity, their diligence, or their shrewdness. But they are, in general, likely to share certain characteristics, and it is reasonable to wonder whether those characteristics are just those which would contribute most to the work of such a group as the Warren Commission.

To begin with, lawyers customarily serve clients. They represent the interests of others, and their principal activity is to assure that those interests are served as well as it is within the power of man to serve them. They do not normally take a disinterested attitude toward any activity in which they are engaged; their search is not for the truth but for advantage. If they seek expert opinion (and in any matter but those which deal with the law itself, they *must* seek expert opinion), they seek it first of all to buttress their case, and not to elicit any abstract truth.

In another jargon one might say that they are mission-oriented rather than problem-oriented. They operate with an end in view, and what does not serve that end is discarded as irrelevant. This, when there is a clear end in view, is certainly the most efficient of all operating principles. It fails as an exclusive mode of operation when the end is not clear, or when one is simply trying to find out.

It is interesting to speculate on how the Warren investigation might have differed if it had been turned over, for example, to a corps drawn from the President's Science Advisory Committee rather than from the Department of Justice. Where the lawyers concentrated their attention on the evidence they discovered that bore upon, for example, the number of shots fired at the President, and sought to establish methods of discriminating between "good" and "bad" evidence, the scientists would have been far more likely to embark upon a study of techniques by which the number of shots could be determined. (This, in essence, is what Professor Alvarez did.) The lawyers would devote their major effort to sifting what lay before them; the scientists to generating knowledge where it had not theretofore existed. Because the assassination was in fact a clearcut event, the outcome would not have been substantively much different, but to at least one group of citizens it might have been more persuasive.

To have turned the investigation over *in toto* to the Science Advisory Committee would, of course, have been impractical and indeed irresponsible. To turn it over to lawyers was indeed practical, but one might ask whether it was not quite as irresponsible. It predetermined in some ways the form that the investigation and the Report would take. And it assured that to many the Report would be unpersuasive. A good deal more would have been accomplished if the staff had included, in positions of authority and of responsibility, such men as pathologists, scientists, police officers, and the like. The staff used such men, of course, but there is a difference between a visiting expert who answers questions and a participant who is entitled to pose them. It might be suggested, too, that a journalist would have had public reaction in mind when the Report was being prepared, and would have attempted to cope with it.

That the Report bears much of the air of an *ex parte* document can be traced to the manner in which lawyers, despite themselves, are likely to operate, rather than to any explicit decision on their part. Deny it as the Commission may, the report reads as if it might be entitled "The Case Against Lee Harvey Oswald." One does not perceive, in the Report, any attempt to get at the truth, but rather an attempt to convince the reader of Oswald's guilt. That the two are certainly one and the same in their outcomes does not alter the fact that they differ in their spirit. It is simply because the Report bears so much of the marks of a legalistic indictment that attacks on it, also frequently legalistic in that they attempt to destroy credibility rather than provide an alternative account, have been so generally effective.

The hard truth is that a matter of consuming interest to all the American people was turned over for disposition to an essentially closed group of lawyers and government officials. As much as anything else, that is the state of affairs that has proved so damaging to the Commission. Only in a narrow sense was the Commission itself representative of the society it was intended to serve, and its staff could not possibly have been more unwisely chosen. It managed its easy task—the task of determining just what it was that happened—quite well. The harder task of persuading the American people escaped it entirely. What comments there have been from the staff since the Report was issued indicate that it escapes them still.

The legalistic attitude was most clearly, and most damagingly, seen in the manner in which the Commission and its staff treated the matter of the autopsy. From the point of view of a lawyer engaged in the prosecution of Oswald, the case was airtight. An autopsy had been conducted under circumstances that lay beyond criticism. The pathologist was available, with his notes and diagrams, to appear in "court" and to give his testimony under oath; no credible countertestimony was even conceivable, and any other testimony bearing on the autopsy could be refuted out of hand. From the point of view of the lawyer, the X-rays and color pictures were simply not needed; at most they would be corroborative in a situation where corroboration was unnecessary. If some members of the staff, diligent as ever, were troubled by the fact that any useful evidence was being withheld, they were unable to make any real issue of what must have appeared to most of their fellows as a trivial matter.

Even the Commission did not see the pictures and the X-rays. Justice Warren, as Commissioner John J. McCloy made clear in an interview with CBS News, was a little less than completely open about his role in the matter. Justice Warren, like all of those involved, respected the desire of the Kennedys to escape gruesome disclosure of the color pictures. Without ever quite stating it, he carefully gave the impression that he had personally examined the pictures and the X-rays, and the Commission willingly permitted what they understood to have been his examination to stand as an examination by the Commission. In fact, Justice Warren himself did not see that evidence; it was seen by no member of the Commission or of its staff. Looking back, Mr. McCloy is dubious about the propriety of that course of action.

In a court of law the effect of all this would have been insignificant. In the court of public opinion it has been immense. So long as any element of the evidence remains locked away, there is an area of doubt which can be exploited, and it is today being exploited to the full. There is no need to expose the pictures and the X-rays to public scrutiny. But if the Warren Commission and its staff had at any time been able to say: "We have examined that evidence, assisted by experts not otherwise involved in the events surrounding the assassination. They contain no surprises. Nothing has been concealed. They bear out in all respects the testimony brought before the Commission by Commander Humes." If any such statement had been made when the Report was issued, or made later when the question came to the fore, then the power to exploit those sequestered pictures and X-rays would have diminished to almost nothing. The autopsy is only the most awkward of the lapses committed by the Commission and its staff. There are others of the same kind, and taken altogether they make of the Report a document that falls far short of its purposes.

As serious as any cloud that hangs over the Commission is that associated with the treatment of the Federal Bureau of Investigation and the Central Intelligence Agency. In all fairness, it must be conceded that it is also the cloud most difficult to disperse. The Commission faced a dilemma from which there was no escape.

As we have seen, to suspect either agency or both of some association with Oswald was not only natural but almost inescapable. Any failure of the CIA to have sought to make some use of Oswald would have been (given the peculiar nature of the whole institution) somewhat more culpable than one expects an agency of that kind to be. Similarly, suspicions that the FBI too might have made use of Oswald, in one way or another, was natural enough, and in this case heightened by the appearance of the name and telephone number of an FBI agent in Oswald's notebook.

The Commission itself fell foul of these suspicions almost before it was fully organized. Rumors of an FBI association with Oswald were spreading in Dallas almost from the moment of the assassination. They were brought to the attention of the Commission by Waggoner Carr, attorney general of Texas and for a few brief days a man encouraged by President Johnson to believe that the conduct of an investigation of the assassination might fall to his office. The involvement of Mr. Carr has been exploited by some dissenters to give official status to the FBI rumors, but as Mr. Carr himself makes clear neither he nor his office ever pretended to possess any evidence.

Mr. Carr reported to CBS News that in the days that immediately followed the assassination, there were, as we have stated, rumors in circulation that the FBI was involved. He himself had no evidence at all of any such involvement, nor did his office. In his interview for CBS News he made that fact completely clear. He passed the information on to the Warren Commission in exactly that spirit: There were rumors, and they had an obligation to be aware that there were rumors. It is difficult to see how very much can be erected upon that.

Thus the Commission was forced at the very outset to provide its own answer to a critical question: What was to be the status of the FBI (and by extension the CIA) in the investigation that was to take place? The alternatives were not as simple as one might initially believe.

If the rumor had linked Oswald not with the FBI but with (let us say) the League of Women Voters—to be quite deliberately banal in my choice of coconspirators—there would have been no problem. The Commission and its staff, using its powers of subpoena if need be, would have turned the League upside down if it had found it necessary to do so, in order to get at the truth. It would have sought out the officers, the staff, the minor employees, and even those who provide services for the League.

In the end it would have been able to say, without hesitation or doubt, that Oswald was or was not a member of the League. If instead of the League an alleged association had involved a somewhat more conspiratorial organization—the Ku Klux Klan, let us say, or the Communist party—the task might have been messier and the outcome less clear, but the procedure quite as ruthless.

It is certainly questionable whether the Commission (or any other body that is not directly appointed for the purpose by the President of the United States) has any power to carry out such an investigation in regard to either the FBI or the CIA, both of them agencies of the executive. Certainly any attempt to do so would have been appealed by the agency directly to the President. But the heart of the matter does not lie there, but in the very nature of the two organizations. To investigate the CIA is to destroy it, and the FBI, rightly or wrongly, appears to take much the same view of its own vulnerability. The CIA certainly, and the FBI in its own attitudes, are secret organizations to the fullest extent consistent with democracy (and there are those who say that they are secret far beyond any extent consistent with democracy). Breach that secrecy, for whatever purpose, and the organizations cease to exist in their present forms.

Pressed to the issue, the Commission had but two alternatives. One of them was to spare the two agencies any investigation, and merely to go to them for any information they might be willing to give, fully cognizant that no corroboration would be forthcoming, or indeed would be sought. The other was to announce, indirectly it is true but nevertheless forcefully, that a full investigation was impossible so long as those two agencies existed, and that the American people would have to choose between full knowledge of the assassination and the continuance within the society of two government-associated secret agencies. Whether it intended to do so or not, the Commission would thus be thrusting itself into an immensely sensitive area, and would have extended its area of impact from the facts of the assassination of the President to the structure of the executive branch of the United States Government. Like a runaway grand jury, it might have effects that it neither intended nor wished to intend.

There are in this country pockets of great opposition to both the FBI and the CIA, and that opposition is frequently voiced by men and women who command respect. They are, moreover, just those persons who now dissent to the Warren Report. Without doubt, a general attack on the concept of secret executive agencies would have been welcomed in many quarters, and might have made the Warren Commission a good deal more popular than it is. But the Commission itself, constituted as it was of men closely associated with the government, could not have been expected to respond to any inclinations that would bring it head to head with the FBI or the CIA. Indeed, it is difficult to believe that any commission, however constituted, would have chosen to do so.

The whole matter must be firmly kept in context. No great acumen was necessary to realize that what was being brought to issue was the question of a CIA or FBI involvement with Oswald, and not any involvement with the assassination. As I have already sought to point out, a CIA or FBI conspiracy, against the life of the President or intended to transfer power by means other than the ordinary channels, would have necessarily involved so many persons that in all likelihood it would have been exposed long before it acted, and would in any case have been immediately exposed upon action. (The Bay of Pigs *was* in a sense a CIA conspiracy, but it was a badly kept secret before it occurred and became open to the world once it took place.) It would be misleading merely to say that the Commission had no reason to believe the CIA or FBI were involved in the assassination. The accurate statement is that the Commission had every reason to believe the CIA or FBI were *not* involved. Any inability to explore the relationships between Oswald and those agencies would consequently be of only trivial significance to the Commission's task of ascertaining the facts. A detail of no great moment in Oswald's biography would be lost, and perhaps some further insight into the manner in which the crime took shape in Oswald's mind.

So the Commission took the only responsible course that was open to it. It asked questions of the two agencies, and accepted their answers. It asked the FBI if Oswald had ever enjoyed any formal connection with that agency, and was told there was no record of such an association. The Commission set this down in its records and went on to the next matter.

By the rules of the game there is no means of pressing the FBI for corroboration. The answer may represent the truth—and in all likelihood it does—or it may be an evasion (what records have been destroyed?), or it may be a lie. At the moment, we do not know and there is no way of getting the FBI to tell, for anything further that the FBI may choose to say may again be either the truth, an evasion, or an outright lie.

It is quite possible that either an FBI or a CIA connection will come to light: Indeed, if one existed, one may be certain that at one time or another it *will* come to light. If it does, the entire structure of the Warren Report will tremble, and without any good reason. The lie such a revelation will give to certain trivial portions of the Report will spread its influence over the entire Report. There will be little that can be done about it. That is the corner into which the situation drove the Commission and from which there is no escape unless after twenty or thirty years one can begin to say with confidence that it now appears the FBI and CIA did *not* lie.

Meanwhile, the simple possibility that new evidence will come to light is enough to cast doubt upon the Report. There are statements in the Report that can not be accepted at their face value. They are the statements which emanate from the FBI and the CIA. If the reasonable doubt that necessarily follows could in some way be limited to those statements, the damage would be negligible, for the statements themselves are negligible. But doubt is infectious. One can sum it all up by saying that it is not the Warren Commission itself, but the mere existence of the FBI and the CIA that has robbed the Report of some portion of the credibility to which it is entitled. But that statement, in the end, becomes trivial, for it only asserts that no society is a fully open society if its governmental structure includes secret agencies. The writer, when he comes to deal with the matter, is forced into the very corner that the Commission occupies. He is dealing no longer with the assassination, but with the shape and form of the American society. It is just as well to leave the matter there.

I can sum it up by expressing the opinion that the Warren Commission was unwisely constituted, unwisely staffed, its efforts subordinated to a sense of urgency that was not wisely handled, and inescapably affected by at least one insoluble problem. It was, at the same time, made up as Commission and staff of honest, diligent, public-spirited men—there can not ever be found any suggestion of a taint of evil in any of its acts or in any of its Report.

To the easier of its tasks, it was completely adequate. It did not turn out to be at all difficult to ascertain what happened that day in Dallas, and the Commission has nailed it all down as tightly as anyone could have hoped to see it done. The more difficult task, that of persuading the American people, escaped it, for the American people are not all convinced. A part of that failure can fairly be laid to the Commission itself, but we must also ask how great a part lies on the Commission's doorstep. Would any commission, however constituted and however managed, have been substantially more successful? I have come to the last of the three major questions: Could this Commission— could *any* commission—have reasonably hoped to convince the overwhelming majority that its account could be trusted? We are done, now, with looking at the assassination and at the Warren Report. We must begin to look at ourselves.

14

THE RESPONSE TO
THE BROADCASTS

*There's the credulity of people generally. This is pretty spicy,
pretty scandalous. . . . There have been an enormous amount
of books written now . . . with the most shocking and distorted
statements in regard to the evidence. There are other things
I suppose you can talk about: strange attitudes. The people
associate their politics with their belief, or their disbelief, in
the report.* —John J. McCloy

It is by now apparent how much this book owes to the four
television broadcasts *A CBS News Inquiry; The Warren Report.*
Much of the information contained here was gathered by the
staff of CBS News, or developed upon the initiative of CBS
News. The concepts represented were in some degree worked
out in association with all of those who shared in the making of
the programs.

The broadcasts, however, are germane in still another way.
They themselves have become part of the data thrown up by the
Warren Report. They have become, for example, targets of the
more free-swinging critics in exactly the manner that the Report
itself is a target. They have attracted criticism of a more sober
kind that in some degree reflects the general malaise which any
account of the assassination seems to generate. They stimulated
mail from viewers which also revealed the deep uncertainties felt
by so many ordinary American citizens—men and women who
have in fact taken no fixed position on the events that led up to
and followed the assassination, and who are in some degree
distressed by their inability to find a position that satisfies them.

In the two weeks that followed the broadcasts, CBS News
received 1,465 letters from viewers commenting upon them.
Since the programs were each seen by 30,000,000 viewers or
more, the numbers hardly appear impressive at first sight: a
return of .005 per cent would not keep a mail-order house in

business very long. In television, however, it is more than respectable. That nearly 1,500 people should move of their own initiative from television set to writing desk is in itself out of the ordinary, and the total does not take into account the number of people who wrote to their local station instead of to the network, which is what most viewers tend to do.

The letters were analyzed by a member of the staff of CBS News who had not had any connection with the preparation of the Warren Report Inquiry. He reported that of the 1,465 letters, 1,136 expressed rational opinions concerning the programs, and that these opinions ran considerably better than 2-1 (the figures were 811-325) favorable. His tabulation, in his own words, follows:

Generally pro	811
Generally con	325
Weirdos, flying- saucer types	70
Assassination buffs	123
Hard to classify	136

This would not be likely to satisfy a graduate department of sociology, but it can stand as a fair statement of the response of those who wrote.

To those within the industry the 811 favorable comments are noteworthy. What stimulates letters to the producer or the network is generally anger, aroused by something within a program that strikes at one or another of the emotions. Anything that appears to a viewer as salacious, for example—and it is extraordinary how quickly some viewers will detect salaciousness—is likely to arouse a flood of letters. Anything that can be interpreted as an attack on a public personality will do much the same. If stimuli such as those are applied, the volume of mail can be startling. Favorable letters are a good deal harder to come by—a viewer must be pleased indeed to be inspired to dash off a friendly note.

All this was rewarding, but it was the critical letters that were most instructive. It was remarkable that the most serious slip that had been made in the preparation of the broadcast series was noted by so many viewers, and disturbed them so. The slip in question occurred in the account of experiments in which test bullets had been fired through gelatin blocks. Having in mind the fact that the bullet fired through the President and the Governor—the famous "single-bullet"—was later recovered almost unmarked (as the account I have given here tells the story) CBS News was asked by viewers to divulge the condition of the test bullets after they emerged from the gelatin blocks. That is, CBS News was asked by some viewers. Others simply accused CBS News of having concealed the fact that the test bullets, emerging totally deformed, clearly rebutted the single-bullet theory. I have already stated in an earlier chapter that the test bullets, like the "single bullet," were not significantly deformed—a picture of test bullets after firing through the blocks appears in the photograph section. But the broadcast neglected to make that simple statement and to show that unarguable picture, for no reason except carelessness. The staff was too close to its story.

Many other comments were entirely fair criticisms, applying less to the productions themselves than to inherent limitations of television. (A great many viewers objected to intrusive commercials.) All those criticisms are covered in full in earlier parts of this book. Others were frivolous.

Leafing through the critical letters, one is most forcefully struck by the persistence of legends concerning the assassination. In almost every case the basis for those legends can be traced. But the legends themselves do not survive simply because there is some rational means of accounting for them. They survive, rather, because the critical literature concerning the Warren Report has made a business out of publicizing the legend and suppressing the fact.

This can be clarified by accounting for one such criticism which recurs in letters from viewers. In a typical letter, the viewer refers to the single-bullet theory and continues ". . . the fact that the bullet emerged intact, with less particles missing from it than were in the entire wrist of Governor Connally makes this theory completely untenable. Yet you didn't mention that the bullet particles in the Governor's wrist *outweighed* the particles missing from the bullet."

The reason CBS News failed to mention the alleged discrepancy is, of course, because no such discrepancy exists. As an earlier chapter makes clear, the mass of the bullet, before firing, was in the neighborhood of 160-161 grains; the recovered bullet was 158.6 grains; the fragments recovered from the Governor's wrist together with those seen on X-ray but allowed to remain in the wrist were well within the difference, and were stated to be so by the doctor who treated Governor Connally. There is simply no contradictory evidence that can be detected in the examination of the bullet and of the Governor's wounds.

What did happen, however, is that Colonel Pierre Finck, the forensic pathologist who assisted in the autopsy of the President, testified that on the basis of what he had heard, he believed the fragments outweighed the missing portions of the bullet. Colonel Finck never saw the bullet, never saw the Governor, made no examination of any kind, and did not state where he got his information. No doubt what he testified was completely accurate: From *what he had heard* he *believed* such and such was so. In the absence of any other evidence, one would take Colonel Finck's evidence for no better than what he maintained it was: a conclusion drawn from unspecified hearsay. In the presence of hard physical evidence Colonel Finck's testimony becomes nothing more than idle gossip—and the Colonel would no doubt be the first to concede as much.

On the Mark Lane theory, the critic of the Commission has no obligation to state the facts. He performs his mission when he simply points out that Colonel Finck rules out the single-bullet theory by testifying that the fragments could not have been left by the bullet later recovered at Parkland Hospital. No doubt a critic who acts in this fashion scores a legalistic point for the length of time it takes before the opposing lawyer makes hash of it (and perhaps longer still if one juryman or another stubbornly remembers only the point and not the refutation). In the absence of an opposing lawyer to provide the direct refutation, the critic who publishes findings in this fashion is simply guilty of spreading a lie. No kinder statement is justified.

This kind of established misconception is by no means limited to the uninstructed viewer. It appears wherever the Warren Report is discussed. Thus the *Variety* report of the four broadcasts includes the following: "It may be remembered, for instance, that Richard Dudman of the St. Louis *Post-Dispatch,* for one, observed that the Kennedy windshield had been shattered. . . ." Whatever Mr. Dudman believed he observed, the windshield in question is in the National Archives, available for anyone who wishes to look at it. It is anything but shattered—there is a single hole in it which is seen under even casual examination to have been produced by the impact of something from the rear. Closer examination shows lead residues on the inside surface, and a pattern of cracking on the outside that unambiguously defines the direction of the impact. It is the clearest possible mute testimony to the fact that a fragment of a bullet struck the windshield from *inside the car* with a velocity high enough to punch a hole in the glass but not high enough to pass through the glass. None of this is secret; it is all as publicly available as it can be. But here again, the misapprehension has been disseminated by those who believe it to be their obligation to reproduce only Mr. Dudman's error, made in the frenzy of the assassination scene, and not the facts that were later elicited.

From the point of view of the television news technician—the producer, the director, the writer, the reporter—the criticisms expressed in the unfavorable letters and in some of the published reviews can be accepted with equanimity. CBS News *did* fail to show the undeformed bullets, which was careless but hardly a central matter. CBS News failed to cover every issue which a dozen critics have managed to raise, but it could not have done that in four hours or two hours or twenty hours, and in any case it was not worth doing. Every important issue was covered, and most of the rest are merely frivolous.

There was indeed another kind of failure. Earlier this book took into consideration the conflicting testimony of Mrs. John Connally, and stated reasons for dismissing it. Those reasons are, in fact, spread in general form throughout the early portions of this book, where the whole question of eyewitness testimony, and the role of testimony in reaching a conclusion, and allied matters are considered at some length.

That kind of presentation is very difficult for television. It is essentially an appeal to the reader's intellectual processes, and the reader, as distinct from the viewer, is usually willing and accustomed to provide the requisite effort of intellectualization. Television, it seems to me, does not know how to handle an appeal to intellectual processes, and when it tries to do so, as on educational television, the viewer tunes out the program. It is something television must learn, sooner or later, to accomplish. Each network tries. Year by year, they all get better at it. Sooner or later they will know how. Viewers who protested that CBS News did not give reasons for discounting the testimony of Mrs. Connally are in a sense correct—they were given, in general form, when Walter Cronkite discussed briefly the problems of the eyewitness, but the best that treatment can be called is an easy once-over. This is not an apology—merely a statement that the best of television broadcasts, if it deals with any subject of intellectual significance, is likely to require a book to complement it, *pace* McLuhan. Someday, perhaps, networks will know their business well enough to dispense with the book. Or perhaps television sets will come equipped with small copying devices, and the necessary printed matter will issue, line-by-line, from a slot under the vertical and horizontal controls. Until one or another of those days arrive, one can only continue to do the best one can.

Yet all the specific criticisms, whether made amiably or hostilely in those 1,465 letters, were less significant than the prevailing atmosphere that the mail more subtly indicated. Many of the correspondents displayed a will to disbelieve that was clearly more powerful than anything we could bring to bear out of the evidence. Others manifested almost an eagerness to believe, and at the same time a helpless inability to do so. Among those letters there was almost an undercurrent of desperation, as if nothing would be more to their liking than to dismiss the debate about the Warren Report once and for all.

One need not look far for reasons for such anxieties. Whether they so intend it or not, the attacks upon the Warren Report made by many—although not all—of the more virulent critics are in fact direct attacks upon the manner in which the United States Government operates. Once a widespread official conspiracy is stipulated, which came into being and continues in being merely to conceal important information from the American people, the form of our government is declared to be fundamentally altered. Just that charge has been repeatedly made, knowingly by some and perhaps without clear appreciation of the fact by others. Most Americans are reasonably content with our form of govern-

ment; certainly few of us would wish to believe that it has been
metamorphosed, without our knowledge, into government by
conspiracy and cabal.

The widespread uneasiness about the Warren Report is in
some degree notice of the fear that such a metamorphosis may in
fact have taken place; only, of course, in some degree. It is possible to be doubtful about a great deal that is to be found within
the Warren Report, or within the CBS News programs, merely
upon the basis that "those people haven't got it right." But to be
doubtful upon the basis of a feared concealment of evidence, or
upon the basis of doubts concerning the integrity of the seven
commissioners and their staff, or upon the even more monstrous
fears that are expressed from time to time, is to hold fundamental
misgivings about the entire American enterprise. Few people
truly want to hold any such misgivings; it is hardly surprising
that they are anxious about their own attitudes.

It is the thesis of this book that any such misgivings, once
they are exposed to any kind of reasonable scrutiny, are unwarranted at least by the facts of the assassination and the Warren investigation. I am led directly, to the third of the major
questions with which the programs were intended to deal: Is
there an element, or are there elements, within our own environment that make it inevitable that doubts concerning the Warren
Report would prevail generally over a belief? I have asked, so
far, whether Americans *should* have put full faith in the Warren
Report, and I have answered that they should have; that the
imperfections in the Warren Report were those one must expect
from any such document. Now I must ask whether the American
people *would* have believed in *any* report, regardless of its imperfections or the absence (if that can be imagined) of imperfections. I have pointed out respects in which the Report could have
been substantially improved, involving the manner of the organization of the Commission, the manner of its operation, and the
credibility of some of the data themselves. But was there in fact
any hope at any time that a report on the assassination of President Kennedy would have been greeted by something better than
general incredulity? That is the matter that must concern us next.

15 THE MAN ON THE STREET

Well, I don't think that all the facts were brought out. I think something was held back. —Interview

An observer leaves the realm of hard evidence when he begins to look into men's minds. Pertinacious examination of the facts will no longer be of much use, for if there are facts, they are buried deep within each one of us, and there is no certain manner of eliciting them and holding them up to light. And if he manages to reach conclusions, he can not safely ascribe any kind of certainty to them. He can say only that somewhere in the neighborhood will be found his best guesses, which in a sense are not likely to be any better than another man's best guesses.

One does begin with a hard fact—or at least, he does so if he reposes any confidence in public opinion polls. A great number of Americans do not place great faith in the Warren Report: That seems to be the fact. The Harris poll has revealed that seven out of ten Americans are convinced that there remain "many important unanswered questions"—that the whole truth has not been told. Perhaps more to the point, a Gallup poll taken in early 1967 showed that more than six out of every ten Americans doubt that there was a lone assassin and consequently are persuaded of some kind of conspiracy theory.

A private poll is likely to be even more definitive. By mid-1967, when the four broadcasts were produced, any inquisitive American could have set a roomful of his acquaintances off on a discussion of the assassination and its aftermath by the mere act of dropping a comment on Oswald or Mark Lane into a general conversation. He would discover quickly that few people were truly easy in their minds about the Warren Report, and that only those who held positive doubts about the Report really had true conviction in their own opinions. No one was so aware of this phenomenon as those of us who were working on the CBS News programs. The presumption that we possessed inside knowledge was enough to make us centers of interest at cocktail parties and other social gatherings.

If one went beyond the discussion itself and began to probe for the background to the general skepticism and disbelief, certain patterns emerged from the answers. There was, to begin with, an appalling amount of misinformation of the kind mentioned so often in this book. There was further a widespread familiarity with the weaknesses of the Warren Report, of which there are admittedly many, and an equally widespread unfamiliarity with its strengths, of which there are a great many more. It was everywhere known, for example, that certain persuasive witnesses insisted that shots had been fired from the grassy knoll; it was not known that police had examined that area immediately after the assassination and had found nothing, and that furthermore there were even more persuasive witnesses whose testimony ruled out the grassy knoll entirely.

This signifies most obviously that the assailants of the Warren Report had attracted more publicity than its supporters. That is to be expected—it is not a state of affairs peculiar to the Warren Report, but an inevitable consequence of the manner in which the news media interact with the news. Conflict is the heart of a good news story (or catastrophe, which is conflict with nature), and it is the dissenters who create the conflict. But this is only the superficial aspect of the matter, for it leaves unanswered the two real questions: What has kept this atmosphere of conflict in being for four years and more? Why do the dissenters gain in strength with the passage of time? That kind of explanation, in short, does not answer any of the truly troubling questions. It merely allows us to phrase them in another way.

To answer them, one must discover what goes on in men's minds. There is no easy way to go about this. In television it is conventionally done (as the first of the four CBS News programs did it) by the man-on-the-street interview, which makes good television but not very good sense. In a book like this, perhaps I may be permitted to borrow that technique and to alter it in a strange way, for I will borrow from fiction as well, and my man-on-the-street will be wholly imaginary.

·   ·   ·   ·   ·

The man in Dallas never really liked John F. Kennedy. The style of the man was strange to him: the Eastern intellectual, product of private schools and Harvard, tolerant of avant-garde artists and new-wave novelists, at home in the world of academics, vaguely supercilious in his attitude toward the man who lacked his own advantages. He had the stigmata of the man of thought rather than the man of action. The man in Dallas, riding to work each morning over superhighways in his air-conditioned Buick, shuffling papers in his fifteenth-floor office, returning each evening to his split-level home, thought of himself none the less as somehow a man of the frontier. Involved in the Bay of Pigs, he would have seen it through to the end. Faced with Russian missiles in Cuba, he would not have devoted his greatest efforts to providing a face-saving way out for Khrushchev.

The man in Dallas looked forward to 1964, when he would have the opportunity, along with his fellow Americans, to make good sense once again prevail and vote Kennedy out of office. Some of his friends or acquaintances thought otherwise. Some spoke of impeachment, some would mutter that it might be well if the man died in an airplane accident, or even if he were to be assassinated. Some joined groups in which they replaced individual distaste with collective fury. There were even a few who stored arms in their basements and planned for the glorious revolution. The man in Dallas did not agree with any of these extremists—at least, most of the time—but he conceded that on occasion they made good sense, and in any case they remained his friends and his acquaintances, which Kennedy certainly was not.

He was truly horrified by the assassination. He may have wondered at the beginning whether some of his friends and acquaintances had a direct hand in it. But more profoundly, perhaps unconsciously, he may have wondered too whether *he* had a hand in it. For if he had not contributed directly to the atmosphere of hate, he had certainly tolerated it. Perhaps on occasion he had even fed it. Had that atmosphere of hate, impressed upon a weak-minded book-clerk day after day after day, insidiously tipped that book-clerk toward direct action of the most hateful sort? Was he, the good citizen of Dallas, in a way as guilty as Oswald?

That was a thought to put out of mind. Far better to believe that the assassination had little or nothing to do with Oswald; that it was part of a general plot that would have come into being whether or not the friends and the acquaintances of the man in Dallas hated the President. Whatever the implications of such a plot, it would allow the man in Dallas to sleep each night with a clear conscience.

· · · · ·

This particular man-in-the-street has been placed in Dallas, for obvious reasons. But he exists everywhere in the United States, although his local characteristics may differ from place to place.

Nor is it necessary to sketch him in such sharp lines. Being what we are, there is a little of the man in Dallas in every one of us. To some extent, we all have dark thoughts about men in power, and give ourselves over to them now and then. To that extent, there is at least some feeling of guilt in all of us, so far as the assassination is concerned. This kind of statement verges, perhaps, upon parlor psychoanalysis and is fairly suspect. But there is now offered for sale in most major cities a lapel button, of the sort used at political conventions and elsewhere when one is encouraged to substitute slogans for direct thought. The button reads "Where is Lee Harvey Oswald Now That We Need Him?" A few people buy those buttons and presumably wear them. If they did not, the buttons would not be manufactured and offered for sale. A great many others see them on display— or even on lapels—and are amused. Among every one of those men and women there will be at least a small residual feeling of guilt if another Lee Harvey Oswald does appear. And a great many of them will go to extreme lengths to persuade themselves at the very least that appearances are deceptive, and that the new assassination was not in fact the work of another Lee Harvey Oswald.

· · · · ·

The man in Butte does not think of himself as a religious man. He goes to church now and then, to please his wife as much as for any other reason; she herself attends primarily for social reasons.

Yet there is a deep feeling of religious belief that has possessed them since they were very young, even though some of its doctrinal appurtenances may have worn away with time. The man in Butte believes that there is some kind of divine purpose that animates his life and the life of all of us. He can not look upon himself as nothing more than an array of amino acids, cast haphazardly upon an unthinking world and bound in time to dissolution and decay. To him and to others his life may appear to be bounded by uncertainties and chance, but in his heart he trusts that it is nothing of the kind; high in the heavens there is a plan.

Now, suddenly the futility and the capriciousness of the human existence is thrust upon him. The most powerful single man in the United States, a man moreover who is young, handsome, wealthy, at the height of what are clearly great capacities, has been struck down, for no assignable reason, as a consequence of an endless series of implausible chance occurrences, by an assassin whose own insignificance is manifest. What becomes now of the divine purpose? How strongly can he still maintain that his own life—that of an unimportant citizen of Butte—is part of a large, meaningful scheme, somewhere divinely planned and divinely overseen?

It is more consoling to look elsewhere for explanation. It is not the divine plan that has somehow failed. It is the human ability to explain. It is better to be certain that a better commission than the Warren Commission would have found somewhere and somehow the real truth that would reveal the major cause behind so major an effect, and thus reduce the horrifying capriciousness of the assassination. By reducing the significance of a great life, the assassination as it is officially recounted reduces the significance of all life, and hence the significance of the life of the man in Butte. Better look for a different explanation.

·   ·   ·   ·   ·

It was to this kind of response—an essentially religious response—that Seymour M. Lipset, professor of sociology at Harvard University, referred when CBS News asked his comments on the general attitudes toward the Warren Report.

> I think one reason why a lot of people find it difficult to believe one man, particularly one mentally disturbed man, assassinated the President, rather than a conspiracy, is that it's much more irrational if it's one man. A conspiracy by a political group, whether left or right, is a rational act which you can understand. It flows from a certain kind of concern of individuals which you may not agree with—but at least it makes sense. If people get killed by an irrational screwball, then anything can happen to you, too. You're living in an unpredictable world—a completely uncontrolled world.
>
> We're terribly bothered by murders—the kind of Jack the Ripper thing, or this fellow in Texas who shot people down. If someone is killed for his money, if someone is kidnapped for money—that is OK. You know we don't want this, but we can understand what happened. If there is an assassination that is the consequence of a plot, it's like a murder in the context of a crime for money. But if someone is just shot down in the street by some fellow who just picked up a gun and shot him, then if it happened to him, it can happen to you. If the President was assassinated not because of a rational plot but because of just a nut who had a gun, then not only any President can be assassinated this way (which he can) but anyone else can. It becomes a much less controlled world.

Such a response is perhaps more likely from the dimly religious than from the deeply religious. The latter, more firm in their faith, will concede easily that the ways of God are inscrutable to man; that what appears to them to be capricious is more truly to be seen as part of a plan that God alone in all his majesty knows. And perhaps it is because the American people are no longer a deeply religious people that this resentment against the capriciousness of the act has led so many to deny it credence.

·   ·   ·   ·   ·

The man in St. Louis is nobody's fool. He has been around. He knows what people are really like. Others may be taken in by official explanations. He knows that the real truth is to be found elsewhere, and he resents anyone's attempts to convince him otherwise.

He knows how it is in his own affairs. He runs a fairly large office, with thirty men and women working under him, and you may be certain that he doesn't tell them all he knows. In fact, from time to time he is obliged to deceive them, for their own good or for the good of the business. He knew for four months, for example, that the company had lost the Bulge account, but he was careful not to let it get around until the Mank account came in and everything was on an even keel again.

Other people may believe what they read in the papers. He doesn't. The stock market page, for example—there are people in New York who run the market, for their own private purposes, and what gets into the paper is what they want in the paper. He subscribes to an insider's newsletter, straight from Wall Street, and gets the real story long before it becomes officially known. The same with politics. There is one crowd running the country, and another crowd that wants to run it, and neither one is telling all they know.

Whatever happened that day in Dallas, says the man in St. Louis, you won't find out from any official report. If it ever comes out, it won't be because the government let it. It will be because the government wasn't able to keep it hidden. Some of it has leaked out already, in the books by that fellow Lane and all the others. In time, the man in St. Louis will know all about it. Meanwhile, no one is taking him in with the Warren Report—or with those CBS programs, either.

·   ·   ·   ·   ·

The hard-headed man from Missouri is in the good American tradition. He has been with us always. His touching faith in the existence of "inside knowledge" from which the ordinary citizen is by definition barred keeps gossip columnists, newsletters, and race-track touts in existence. Frequently he comes as a surprise to the insider himself, as Eric Sevareid commented during the fourth program:

When this reporter returned home after the first few years of World War II in Europe, I made a few speeches to American groups: intelligent, middle-class, Town Hall kind of audience. But almost invariably some man, or group of men, would get me aside after the speech and say in effect, "Now tell us the real lowdown."

This was my first adult encounter with that strain of permanent skepticism about what they read or hear that runs through so much of the American people. This distrust governs people's feelings toward government and public events more than their feelings toward one another in their daily life. Part of the impulse is simply that traditional Yankee horse-trader desire not to be taken in. Part is the wish to be personally in the know—one up on the other fellow.

The belief in a constant pattern of concealment is of course one form of a conspiracy theory. The world is divided into "them" and "us," and we may be certain that "they" are not going to tell "us" what they are up to. And that general belief in conspiracy, as Sevareid, Professor Lipset, and others were at pains to state in the last of the four programs, has a history as old as the nation itself. Professor Lipset commented:

If one goes back and looks at nineteenth century America, you find that at one time or another there was the belief that there was a hidden conspiracy consciously running the country or plotting to take over the country that had to be combatted. It was very strong, for example, all during the nineteenth century. Anti-Catholic nativism was a very dominant movement in the United States. The Know-Nothing party, which was also known as the American party, got as much as a quarter of the vote in the 1850's, and this propagated the notion of a Catholic conspiracy operating behind the scenes, seeking to take over the country.

This clear idea of a Catholic conspiracy was very strong after the Civil War. In fact, one of the great dominant rumors was that Lincoln was killed by Catholics. Many of the Republicans—not Lincoln himself but many of the people prominent in the party—had been Know-Nothing, and it is fairly clear from the electoral analysis that most of the Know-Nothings became Republicans. These people *preferred* to believe that Lincoln was killed by Catholics.

Ulysses S. Grant at one point suggested there was a real possibility of a new civil war in the United States if these conspirators, by whom he meant the Catholics, continued their activities. In effect he, as President, threatened a civil war to suppress what was clearly a nonexistent Catholic conspiracy. . . .

The Ku Klux Klan, which had many millions of members and which had crucial influence in the early 'twenties in both the Democratic and Republican parties, believed in both a Catholic and Jewish conspiracy which was taking over the country. Henry Ford published the Protocols of the Elders of Zion in his newspaper, the Dearborn *Independent,* in the early 'twenties and it's clear that Ford, one of the major industrialists in the United States, actually believed there was a Jewish plot to run the United States and that the Jews were running the economic market place on Wall Street and the like.

On the other side, you find a belief in big business-banker conspiracy, in the Populist movement of the 1890's, going back to the Greenback and other movements. They believed in the existence of conspiracies of bankers and industrialists and business men who were dominating the country for their own interests, doing all sorts of Machiavellian and evil things. There was the assumption of a conscious conspiracy of bankers and the business elite which was symbolized by people in high places to decide what ought to be done, and tricking us.

This has continued down to the present so that you can find the assumption of conspiracy or at least of deliberate plots to violate the rights of people in various prominent civil liberties and civil rights cases. There is a whole history of cases in which people believe that the police system and the courts deliberately sent innocent men to jail. There was the Mooney case in California when Mooney was convicted of bombing a Preparedness parade in San Francisco at the time of World War I. There was the Sacco-Vanzetti case in Massachusetts and a variety of others. During the time such cases were issues, many Americans were convinced that the police and courts, even the Supreme Court, were involved in a conspiracy to send innocent men to the chair.

The propensity to believe in these plots is a very old and continuing American trait. It covers both the Left and the Right; Protestants, and Catholics, and Jews.

The movements with which Professor Lipset dealt in his comments go far beyond anything we have attributed here to the mythical man from St. Louis. His reactions, at least under normal conditions, are somewhat less vivid than those of the Know-Nothings. Yet they stem from the same general attitude. And it may be that the general attitude is stimulated, for a variety of reasons, by an event such as the assassination. It is not a healthy attitude, for it makes its holder peculiarly resistant to fact and peculiarly vulnerable to rumor. (It is an odd fact, and odder

still that it comes as a paradox, that the man who believes everything he is told is less often deceived than his totally skeptical
fellow. Most people tell the truth, out of laziness if for no better
reason.)

．　　．　　．　　．　　．

The man in Cambridge, although it happens he has no profound knowledge of mathematics, or science, or engineering, is
none the less very much a child of the Age of Technology. The
artifacts with which he surrounds himself, the books and magazines and newspapers that he reads; the general atmosphere of
his environment, have combined to convince him that science
is the thing.

And science is marked by proof. When something is known in
science, it is known because A causes B, and B causes C, and C
causes D, all the way down to Z. What is more, A and B and C
and all the rest are good hard facts, which you can observe and
measure and define, and more often than not, you can hold them
in your hands. That is Proof. It works, and it brings in its train
Vitamins and Television and Moon Rockets. Anything short of
Proof is simply nothing at all, and as a man of the twentieth
century he will not be tricked into taking it seriously.

The Warren Commission did not provide Proof. It was de-
plorably short of hard facts, and even when it tried to link
together A and B and C and all the rest, it had to confess that
F or J was missing. It was full of hypotheses and suppositions
and arguments from probability, none of which are entitled to
be a part of Proof.

But somewhere in the universe, says the man in Cambridge,
the Proof exists. Someday somehow it will be discovered, and put
down on paper in canonical form, with all the capital letters of
the alphabet present and accounted for in their proper order.
Until then, the man from Cambridge intends to withhold his
opinion. Any man of science would do the same.

．　　．　　．　　．　　．

The faith of the man in Cambridge is a touching thing, which
loses none of its charm simply because it refers to nothing known

by man or beast. The proof he seeks does not exist, and never has existed, in science or anywhere else. It is the latest of the fantasies man has created for himself, and all the more persuasive because the evidence for that fantasy is extremely good, provided you do not look too carefully.

There are indeed procedures in the various sciences which the practitioners of each science might agree (for the time being, at least) to call proof. By *proof* they would mean, more or less, that they followed a set of rules generally accepted by their colleagues, and that by doing so they arrived in the end where any of their colleagues would have arrived. Of course, what a biologist would call *proof* is not necessarily what a physicist would call *proof*, and is quite unlikely to be what a mathematician would call *proof*. (And what any one of them calls *proof* he might not have accepted a generation back, and probably would not accept a generation hence.)

The scientist knows, too, that he can push the matter of proof just so far and no farther. At some point or another it begins to fade away until he has nothing left but vague beliefs, and general faiths, and a sense of origins about which he is helpless. The physicist who makes a measurement today can not prove it would come out the same tomorrow. He can only hypothesize that it will and go on about his business. Once in a while he is wrong.

Most of all, every scientist knows that his own science is full of things he should be able to prove, that may even be provable in principle, but that he simply cannot prove for reasons that escape him at the moment and may escape science forever, for all he knows. The mathematicians, being always a step ahead of the natural scientists, have even managed to prove that some things which appear quite provable can not in principle ever be proved, which is highly confusing, but which is nonetheless a relatively recent theorem of which the profession is quite proud. And the physicists, never too far behind, have elevated Uncertainty to the eminence of a Principle.

And finally, the scientist is always aware that the domain in which he can even hope to grapple for a proof is an extremely limited domain, in which most of the matters that concern him in his nonprofessional life are not to be found. He has means of discovering why an electron behaves as it does, but limited access to information on why his wife behaves as she does and perhaps an intuition that the information is not available at all. The domain of all the sciences may be an extremely interesting domain, and an extremely productive domain, and an extremely tidy domain, but it is not a very inclusive domain. Into it may be crammed Oswald's metabolism, but not Oswald. Not yet, anyway—and perhaps not ever.

In a sense a good deal more refined than the sense in which the matter is understood by the man in Cambridge, the Warren Report *does* contain a good deal of "proof," and it is highly probable that a good deal of "proof" escaped the Warren Commission and will ultimately be discovered. But there is no science, or body of sciences, that can or could offer a tidy package, with no loose edges, no hypotheses that had to be accepted merely for the purpose of going ahead with the proof, no assumptions, no arbitrary definitions, and above all no gaping holes. If you are dealing with a hydrogen atom, you can safely pretend that such a package is available and proceed upon that assumption. But with a helium atom it is already difficult, and with the world of human beings and human events it is entirely out of the question.

•   •   •   •   •

The man in Berkeley is a young man. He is of the new generation, committed and concerned, inclined to be something of an activist. He is by no means enamored of the world he will inherit from the generation that came before him, and he is anxious to undertake at once the process of making it a better world. He does not begin to have the appropriate amount of doubt concerning his capacity to make a better world—that will come when he is older.

A few years ago, in college, he belonged to student organizations that dealt with matters he found of interest. Some of those organizations were fairly well heeled. When he or others asked where the money came from, private foundations were named. A good deal later he discovered that the answers were half-truths; that the foundations in turn received their money from the CIA. He recalls now that at the time any CIA connection had been explicitly denied.

He is concerned about Vietnam. He is aware that over the years flat lies have been told by his government concerning Vietnam, and that upon occasion those flat lies have been blandly replaced, as their utility has diminished, by still other flat lies. He is aware that even within the government itself the integrity of the President, the Defense establishment, and members of the Congress has been questioned. In his eyes, the rebuttals have not always been convincing.

He can say much the same about other issues that trouble him: issues of free speech (usually also concerned with Vietnam), of civil rights, or civil liberties, of academic freedom. In all these cases, he is convinced (and he has some evidence, although perhaps not nearly as much as he thinks) that his government is engaged in a consistent and a calculated attempt to deceive him, and that his government is not always as scrupulous as it might be in choosing its weapons.

He finds it reasonable to place the Warren Report in the category of official deceit. At the very least it rounds out the charges he wishes to make against the government. It is one more area in which it can not be trusted. That attitude fits neatly with all the other attitudes that have been engendered in him, and makes for a tidy outlook. As he trots off to see "MacBird" for the third or fourth time, that is all he needs.

•   •   •   •   •

This is, of course, the general question of the "credibility gap." Its connection with the general reaction to the Warren Report was suggested by Professor Lipset:

> If the political division in the country that stems from the Vietnam war were not in the picture, the discussion about the assassination would go on, but it wouldn't be very important in long-term implications. What I think has happened, however, is that there is a kind of congruence between opposition to the war and opposition to the Warren Commission. On the whole, with the exception of the extreme Right, I would guess that if you analyzed people's belief in the Warren Commission Report as to whether they believed Oswald committed

the assassination alone or as part of a conspiracy, you would find that the more Liberal Left they are the more likely they are to believe this was a conspiracy.

When you get these two views going together—the belief that the Administration has concealed an assassination plot and that it is involved in an evil and immoral war—these reinforce each other and many people come to the conclusion that this is an immoral, corrupt society. And this is particularly true among young people who are opposed to the war, and whose opposition to society, if you will, is largely derivative from their opposition to the war. Their coming to a general conclusion that this is a corrupt society where you can't trust anything that anybody says is reinforced by the Kennedy assassination and its aftermath.

Professor Lipset was not alone in making the linkage. Henry Steele Commager, an elder statesman among American historians, was asked about the general atmosphere of suspicion.

Well, I'm inclined to· think the suspicion is justified. I think the question we have to ask here is, how the government has allowed itself to drift into this, or to be maneuvered into this position, where its credibility is so widely suspected; and to my mind, again and again, justly suspected.

I think this is to be explained . . . by the growing feeling that you can create an image, that you can manipulate news, that you can manipulate people's thinking and people's minds. To some extent, I think this administration—it is not unprecedented, to be sure—has surrendered to the Madison Avenue image makers. They seem to think that if something is going wrong, or if a man is unpopular, or people don't trust the Army or the State Department or something, instead of finding out what's wrong you call in experts on image-making and say "Fix up the image."

Even so otherwise sensible a man as Vice President Humphrey came back from Europe and said "We have all the wrong image in Europe. Every paper is filled with the fact that there are demonstrations in the streets, there's crime in the streets, there's discontent among the Negroes, there's hostility to Vietnam." Of course the papers are filled with this, because it is the truth about the United States. But Vice President Humphrey seemed to think if we could just change the image somehow. . . .

There is involved here a serious exacerbation of a conflict between the generations that is no doubt as old as man. The mature man is a hypocrite. He is not necessarily willingly so, but a hypocrite he is likely to be nonetheless. He finds it progressively more desirable, as he grows older, to say things he does not entirely believe, and to act in a manner that does not accord with his own statements.

It sounds worse than it really is. A man may learn that in an imperfect world of imperfect communications, life is made easier by a willingness to tell an occasional slight lie. When he, in turn, impresses upon his son or daughter the necessity for absolute and uncomprising truthfulness, he is being hypocritical, but he is also making a last attempt to make the world somewhat more perfect. He may be servile in the presence of the boss, but in asserting to others the importance of individual independence he is at least confessing that he, too, thinks more highly of the independent spirit. Hypocrisy, as someone once said, is the homage vice pays to virtue.

But the young accept no such rationalization. To them hypocrisy signifies a concession of defeat (when it is not sheer trickery). It means that the hypocrite has not the courage to say what he believes, or to act as he believes. The young—and we should all be grateful—have no patience with defeat, or with strategic withdrawal. Hypocrisy is an affront, which they are committed to attack and to expose. It is a gauge of battle, and at once their banners fly.

And when it appears that such hypocrisy has been institutionalized within their own government, the affront goes beyond bounds, and the banners fly higher than ever. It is this undifferentiated rage that the young man in Berkeley feels—a generalized sense of universal betrayal. To this feeling of rage he has assimilated the Warren Report—it is merely one more act of the hypocrites.

This is no trivial matter. I have earlier dealt with its consequences, drawing upon Professor Lipset for his own insights. For the moment I note only that it represents another stimulus for the denial of the integrity of the Warren Report.

I chose our imaginary men-on-the-street with some care, excluding the lunatic, and the scavenger, and the man who would indeed topple the government, and the publicity seeker. They are in permanent dissent, and can be permitted to remain so.

But they are not without significance. In what they say, the man from Dallas finds evidence of a plot, the man in Butte is encouraged to hope for a more consoling explanation, the man in St. Louis painfully puts together what he fondly believes to be inside knowledge, the man from Cambridge detects the absence of Proof in the Warren Report, and the young man from Berkeley finds amassed the evidence of official hypocrisy. It is not one or the other of these forces, but all of them in combination that have led to the general dissent. Without support from the general fabric of society, the fringes would ravel away. Unsustained by the barrage of dissent, the man-on-the-street would sooner or later turn his attention to matters nearer his heart.

So I come at last to the question: Given both these batteries of forces, could any official report have won a better response from the American people than the Warren Report won? The programs did not answer that question, nor shall this book. It is a question each man must answer for himself.

To some degree, we are all of us represented in two or three or more of the five imaginary citizens this chapter has conjured. We are most or all of us conscious of some personal guilt, resentful of the capriciousness of the President's death, hardheaded and skeptical, children of the technological age, dubious of the good faith of our own government in some greater or lesser degree. We can not escape any of these characterizations, nor indeed should we wish entirely to do so.

It is not some alien "they" that refuses to accept the Warren Report. It is we who must, each of us, ask ourselves whether we really mean to do so, and what it all signifies. Those are by no means easy questions.

16 THE CASE FOR A NEW INVESTIGATION

I see no value, really, in another investigation. The conspiracy theory, the conspiracy mentality, will not accept ordinary evidence. —Professor Henry Steele Commager

One further matter remains, to which the four television broadcasts paid only cursory attention. In view of all the considerations that were raised in the four programs, and that have been raised again in somewhat different form in the earlier chapters of this book, should a new investigation into the assassination be embarked upon—a new investigation which would once again have official status on the very highest level, together with the power to subpoena witnesses and records?

If the question is to be put at all, it must be put in that extended form, for the question does not ask merely if there should be a new investigation. The investigation into the facts surrounding the assassination of President John F. Kennedy began even before the Warren Commission was constituted, and has continued unabated since the Commission dissolved. It will continue throughout the lifetimes of all of us, and long after that. Many Presidents will have come and gone before historians give over rummaging in this particular corner of the past. Jim Garrison will go on about his work, and when he has finished with it, there will arise from time to time others to carry it on, as long as the subject is politically alive. In that sense, it is meaningless to ask if there should be further investigation into the death of the President, for no force on earth can put a stop to it, without at the same time putting a stop to the whole society in which we live.

We must consider rather a new Warren Commission, necessarily under the direction of another chairman, and certainly with an entirely new or at least a predominantly new membership and staff. Such a commission would not necessarily be a disavowal of the Warren Commission. It would simply take note that the Warren Commission acted under certain very real disadvantages, such as the time pressure that was exerted upon it, and would take note further that the passage of four years and the current status of all the central questions have created an entirely new situation, which did not exist when the Warren Commission did its work.

Any such new commission would labor under certain very real disadvantages. It is only four years, more or less, and most of the central witnesses are still on hand to give testimony. But as I have already said the reliance that can be placed on certain kinds of witnesses gains in significance as the events to which they testify recede into the past. The witnesses and their recollections now have a long history of their own, which may not affect in the least their integrity, but surely affects the credence that can be reasonably granted their accounts.

Still, eyewitness testimony is the least important aspect of an investigation, and the more useful evidence is still in being, laboriously collected in the National Archives. So far as feasibility is concerned, there appears to be no compelling reason to rule out a new investigation. A straightforward decision by the President or by Congress could bring it into being, and its activities would be at once well defined.

I have already expressed, in several places and in several fashions, a viewpoint on the manner in which a new commission should operate. Like the first Commission, it should be constituted of men of unquestioned integrity and of eminence, with a chairman who would be in both those respects *primus inter pares*. But unlike the first, there should be diversity among its members. They should be identified with a variety of institutions and not merely with government; they should bring to the commission a variety of qualifications and a variety of interests. They should be a representative body not in the political sense but in the social sense. And roughly equivalent remarks might be made about their staff. It should possess within itself all the special knowledges that are relevant to the investigation, and not merely the special knowledge that is concerned with the management of an investigation.

The attitudes of such a commission, conscious and subconscious, would protect it from some of the major weaknesses of the Warren Commission. It would not set out to make a case against Lee Harvey Oswald, although unquestionably an irrefutable case against Oswald would emerge. It would set out instead to elucidate, as well as the nature of the task permitted, the facts concerning the assassination.

The television programs and this book only begin to suggest some of the things that might be done. CBS News's own firing tests and camera tests are persuasive, but in any absolute sense they are lamentably inadequate, simply because CBS News was never able to obtain Oswald's rifle or Zapruder's camera. Simple and straightforward tests that might be made upon the bullets and bullet fragments were precluded altogether. And it must be forthrightly conceded that my own criticism of a staff composed entirely of lawyers can fairly be turned upon myself; a staff composed entirely of journalists is not that much better.

From such a commission two major outcomes might be expected. It must be granted, as an item of faith and as an unarguable lesson from experience, that there is no knowing what one will find until the search is undertaken. But having made that concession, and in the light of that concession, it is reasonable to express also an enormously high degree of confidence that the account of the assassination provided by the new commission would be identical in all its essential details with the account provided by the Warren Commission. It would no doubt be more ample. It would be better buttoned up, in part because more work would have been accomplished, and in part because four years have told us just where buttoning is most urgently needed. But it would not be very much different, any more than the CBS account has been very much different, or than Jim Garrison has produced or promised to produce anything very much different. There is simply no good reason to believe that anything much different from the account already given will ever be brought to light.

It would, on the other hand, be enormously more persuasive.

The temper of the people performing the investigation, together with the assurance of their integrity and their skills, would go a part of the way toward persuasiveness. The rest would follow from an unavoidable awareness on the part of all concerned of the vital need to convince a skeptical (and rightly so) general public. All the internal evidence of the Warren Report itself, as well as the manner in which it came into being, indicates that such an awareness came hard to the Warren Commission and its staff. To put it brutally and no doubt a bit hyperbolically, there appeared instead to be an attitude that if the staff convinced the Commission, the task was done. The society in general would accept it for no reason other than that the Commission did so. Given the right commission, their own acceptance does indeed do a large part of the job—but not all of it. We are not that kind of people. There is far too much of our imaginary "man from St. Louis" in all of us.

In the end, how many minds would be changed? I can begin by asserting with complete confidence that a great many minds would hold firm in dissent. "I see no reason," Dr. Commager told us, "to suppose that anyone who doesn't believe the first [investigation] will believe the second, or a third, or a fourth." This appears to be a blanket condemnation of a further investigation, but Dr. Commager continued directly in a fashion that made it clear that he had in mind not the general public but a small subsection of the general public:

> The conspiracy theory, the conspiracy mentality will not accept ordinary evidence, any more than the conspiracy mentality accepts the ordinary explanation of the assassination of Lincoln and the death of Booth.

> It has—there's some psychological requirement that forces them to reject the ordinary and find refuge in the extraordinary. If another investigation were to be held, and came to the same conclusion, as I'm inclined to think it would, I think it would be found just as unsatisfactory, and the critics would say "Well, of course, this too is part of the Establishment, the Establishment appointed this, they want this kind of explanation, and we don't believe any of it because we *know* there's dirty work at the crossroads somewhere and they're covering things up."

In his remarks Dr. Commager lays bare a dilemma brought about by what can be predicted with some confidence to be the third outcome of a new investigation. The dilemma is embodied, in a considerably less troublesome form, by this very book.

The book has been written by a quite fallible human being, assisted before and after the fact by other human beings more or less as fallible. It can be asserted with considerable assurance that it contains errors: errors of fact, errors of statement. Anyone well informed about the assassination will be able to find one or two; anyone fanatically well informed will find more than one or two. No amount of effort—and there has been much effort—can rid this book or any other of such error.

The book, moreover, is riddled with phrases and clauses and sentences which can be ripped out of context to prove whatever one might wish to prove. It is not necessary to look very far for them. Consider the last sentence in the quotation from Dr. Commager, a few paragraphs back. Strictly speaking, anyone would be quite correct in reporting that "in this book, Dr. Commager is quoted as saying "There's dirty work at the crossroads somewhere and they're covering up." Quite correct—and at the same time a savage lie. There is no recourse against such attacks—they can be made, to no less effect, on the Sermon on the Mount.

Thus this very book, or any book like it, whatever the intent that animates the writer and the publisher serves the lunatic fringe. Its very existence stimulates their virulence; to each of them it is a personal affront and their eyes redden. What is worse, it provides raw material for their lunacies, for they find it in new conspiracies to battle, new evidence for their own irrational constructs, new statements to wrest out of context, provocation to new fantasies, innocent errors here and there that can be gleefully employed to bring the entire book into question. For that lunatic fringe, the Warren Report has provided a whole new way of life, and this book willy-nilly is a modest further contribution.

What this book does on a small scale, a new investigation and a new official report would do on an enormous scale. What is worse, it would have a further effect that this book is not likely to have. The extremely high visibility of an official report

would assure an equally high visibility for those who would
launch violent attacks upon it. Only a few lunatics are likely
to make anything significant of a minor misstatement in this
book, and they will be able to talk about it only to each other.
The same misstatement in an official report might make front-
page news.

Thus in a very real sense a new investigation might stimulate
the very behavior it was intended to discourage. It would not be
merely a new and perhaps highly persuasive official account that
would reach the general public, but a new and in its own fren-
zied way persuasive barrage of dissent, rising perhaps to new
heights of violence and dishonesty. This may sound at first hearing like an argument that the public must be protected because
it can not be trusted ultimately to find the truth, but it is nothing
of the kind; it is an argument, rather, that a new official report
might have the paradoxical effect of hindering the public recognition of the truth, and hence of delaying it.

There is still another consequence of a new investigation
which should not be ignored or deprecated. For a great many
people it would revive in all their horror the memories they
would prefer to have lie as quiet as they might. It is not only the
Kennedy family of which this is true, although it is of course
most applicable to Jacqueline Kennedy and her children, to the
Kennedy parents, and the Kennedy brothers and sisters. But it
applies as well to hundreds of men and women who enjoyed
some intimacy with John F. Kennedy, or who had dedicated
themselves in some intimate way to his career and his purposes.
It is no small matter to force those people to relive the last days
of November, 1963—one should think hard before the demand
is made.

It is obvious that if all that is said above is granted, any
decision to reopen the investigation will be made on the basis
of an estimate of the considerations put forward in the preceding
chapter. Is the present division of opinion over the Warren
Report, of itself or in conjunction with a largely parallel division
of opinion over the Vietnam War, a matter of some danger to the
stability of our political processes? Are we likely to have over the
next thirty or forty years a generation alienated in some degree
from normal democratic processes, largely or partially as a con-

sequence of the dissent to the Warren Report? And finally, is a new investigation likely to take the sting from that dissent?

There are no firm answers available to any of those questions. It may well be that relative to the alienation that is being brought about by the Vietnam war, any dissent stemming from the Warren Report or any incremental dissent arising out of the Warren Report is too insignificant to warrant consideration. If that is true, or if anything that leads to an equivalent conclusion is true, then a new investigation can not reasonably be sought on grounds that it will create unity where unity does not now exist. The case for a new investigation becomes a pure case, resting entirely upon the belief that addition to our knowledge of any human event, however small the addition may be, is worth while on its own merits alone. And that, by the way, is no ignominious case.

Yet it does not appear to be enough of a case. However much human curiosity may be valued, there is more at issue here. Unless there are real injuries that flow from the inadequacies of the Warren Report, it seems most reasonable to propose that the matter be left where it is, and that time be relied upon to correct the record insofar as it needs correction and to persuade those who are now in doubt.

The question of a new investigation is in the end one that the reader can answer far better than the author of what he reads. There is in existence an official account of the assassination, and there are at hand certain small modifications of that account which have been arrived at by essentially the same procedures as those adopted by the Warren Commission. There is of course some chance that a new investigation would overturn the present account—some chance, but so close to zero that it takes an incredibly fine eye to detect the difference. It is almost as certain as mortality itself that a new investigation at its best would present a slightly modified version of the old account, although it would also be certain to present it far more persuasively.

The reader who has read this far and who still entertains grave doubts about the Warren Report must answer on his own the question of a new investigation. He must ask himself first whether he still doubts, and ask himself further where any investigation that did not coincide with his dissent could possibly affect him. In short, *can* his mind be changed, under any circumstances? If the answer is *yes*, he has every right to clamor for a new investigation. If the answer is *no*, he should be silent. He can wait, with all the rest of the world, for time to make the final case. If minds are hardened, a new investigation will not hasten the process—it can only retard it.

This is not a particularly decisive way to leave the matter, but this book will go no further. The deterrent is not a lack of will, but a lack of data, and an indisposition, on this question at least, to guess.

The twenty-seven blue volumes that issued from the Warren Commission now go back to the shelves. The notes and memoranda and transcripts go into the files. This has not been the first time they were put to use, but perhaps it will be the last.

At CBS News there is a small group of men and women who have devoted a good deal of their lives since 1963 to these matters. Some of us were occupied with them almost without remission from November 22, 1963, until September 24, 1964; from time to time between then and late 1966, and then once again without remission until the time of the broadcasts in June, 1967—and for this writer and others, for several months thereafter.

It has not been the kind of work in which one takes pleasure or from which one derives elation. There are sometimes flashes of magnificence in tragedy, but the death of John F. Kennedy was a tragedy of another sort, unrelieved except by the unbelievable courage displayed by Jacqueline Kennedy during the days of mourning that followed the assassination. But aside from Mrs. Kennedy, herself more a shattered witness to the events than a participant, there were no heroes. For the most part, it is an ugly story, from which few emerged with high marks.

But the tragedy itself was real. We who worked on it at CBS News were not uniformly enthusiasts for John F. Kennedy; he had among us his supporters and his adversaries. Nor were we, as individuals, of one mind about Kennedy—we were most of us quite capable of feeling about him in one month somewhat otherwise from the way we felt a month before. Yet all of us recognized that he was a man with a difference. And all of us recognized that he had affected changes in American society and in American politics and in American government that had nothing at all to do with the success or failure of his legislative program, or the impact of his confrontation with Khrushchev. There is a coincidence here that one does not always find between the cold fact and the impression: The fact tells us that John F. Kennedy, born in 1917, was the first President to be wholly of the twentieth century (his predecessor was twenty-seven years his senior). He was the youngest man ever to be elected to the Presidency, and he died youngest.

For him or against him, we mourned the man. And mourning him, it was not pleasant to force ourselves, day after day, to the recontemplation of his assassination. To many of us he was no abstraction but flesh and blood—we had shaken his hand, stood chatting with him, shared a drink or two with him at the end of the day. It was never without pain to turn away from those recollections and write or speak hard-headedly of the bullet that smashed into the President's skull at frame 313. Perhaps that leads some of us to think a little more harshly than we should of Mark Lane, Harold Weisberg, Sylvia Meagher.

One kind of hatred almost certainly contributed to the assassination of President Kennedy. Another, more generalized kind of hatred, represented by so many of those who have risen in dissent against the Warren Commission, keeps the memory of that assassination in the foreground of our attention. In the end, somewhere there the tragedy lies.

17 THE SUMMING-UP

Measured against the alternatives, the Warren Commission Report is the easiest to believe, and that is all the Report claims. —Walter Cronkite

Writer and reader have been standing close to the events of the assassination and its aftermath, looking at their details and trying to recreate them while they are still reasonably fresh in our minds. In all probability, almost all that will ever be known about the assassination is already known. Details may be filled in, with the passage of time, but there is little reason to believe that they will amount to a great deal. Jim Garrison may or may not be able to show that some kind of gossip went on in New Orleans before the crime was committed. If he does so, he will enjoy his thirty-day sensation and perhaps build upon it to enter the Louisiana State House or the Senate. But none of these eventualities is really likely, and he seems to be coming no closer with the passage of time.

In a few years material that is now being withheld may be available for students of the assassination. There can be no surprises in the color pictures and the X-rays. They have already been studied with extreme care, and studied in the full knowledge that in a relatively short time, well within the lifetime of those directly concerned, any dissimulation or prevarication would be laid open to the public gaze. Nothing of any significance has been destroyed that could have been retained. Dr. Humes burned the first draft of his report, and Governor Connally's coat was sent to the cleansers. The President and his assassin, and the assassin's assassin, rest in their graves.

The passage of time bleaches the bright colors of events, and in the same process makes it possible to see them in another perspective. No one yet has that perspective, and it is impossible to look upon the assassination and all that followed as a historian fifty or a hundred years hence will look upon them. We can only speculate, always certain that it will not appear to our grandchildren as it now appears to us.

It is enlightening to consider, as we speculate, the assassination that took place almost exactly a century earlier. Lincoln, too, had been recognized by his contemporaries as a great President. The crisis through which he led the country was a hot war and not merely a cold war, and the stakes were no less in the 1860's than the 1960's. There was an official account of his assassination, and there were multitudes at the time who refused to accept that account. Time has added little to what was learned during the first few weeks after the assassination of Lincoln.

What impresses the student today is not the fact of the assassination, nor the detail of the assassination, but the political consequences of the assassination. Lincoln faced the task of binding up a nation's wounds. The South had been routed in open warfare. Most of its leaders had engaged in a rebellion against the government of the United States. To punish them for their misdeeds would be to leave a large part of the country leaderless; to permit them to continue as political powers might in some fashion undo the victory. Millions of slaves had been set free. To deny them political and economic power would be to make a mockery of that freedom and to establish dishonesty as a cardinal American political principle; to grant them those powers would be to impose upon the South a social revolution for which there was no precedent anywhere in history, and would almost inevitably turn the South over to the rabble that would move into the vacuum created by the Negro's ignorance and poverty.

What John Wilkes Booth accomplished assured that those enormous tasks would be assumed not by Lincoln but by others. In the outcome, Lincoln's successor was unable to prevail over a dissenting wing of his own party, lost the factional struggle to a headstrong Congress and let fall the resolution of the issues to those whose motivation was largely vindictiveness. All these events created in the post-bellum South a certain kind of political and social structure—whether better or worse than the structure to which Lincoln would have contributed, no man can say with assurance.

When the historian studies the events of 1865 and the years that followed, it is not the assassination which occupies his attention. His interest is rather the Reconstruction period, and the effect of the assassination on the development of events during the Reconstruction. Booth's motives for killing Lincoln are of limited interest—what is important is that Booth *did* kill Lincoln, and certain important consequences flowed from that act.

It can be concluded that the assassination of Kennedy will take on in time the same general aspect. Decisions that would normally have been taken by John F. Kennedy, or guided by John F. Kennedy, must now be taken in another manner. It is possible to argue that no real difference ensues, and that the flow of history is not for long affected by the will and the acts of a single individual. It is far more likely that there is a real difference, and that much that is happening today might be happening otherwise if the last of Oswald's three shots had missed its mark.

In the current flow of history, caught up in that flow and unable to stand outside it and study it from neutral ground, great issues seem to hammer at us: the war in Vetnam and all that it carries in its wake; the Negro revolution; the development of relationships with Russia, with China, with Western Europe; the plight of the cities. Out of all this some coherence will emerge for the student of the future. He will see connections where a contemporary does not; find great issues that we are too near to recognize; dismiss some of our current preoccupations as trivial. The transition from Kennedy to Johnson may become a single element in his account. The manner in which that transition was effected may be simply an interesting singularity in the history of the times. In that event the analogy between the assassination of Lincoln and the assassination of Kennedy will be more nearly complete.

Yet it is also possible that the assassination will have a significance that is separate from other issues, or that it will be seen in the future to be compounded with other issues. I have already quoted Professor Lipset and Walter Cronkite. Professor Lipset's conclusion bears repeating here: "To some extent the question of what the potential is relates to how long the war goes on. The longer the war goes on, the more possibility there is for producing a very bitter, fairly large group who would then remain a potential source of support for radical extremism much of their lives."

And at the close of his remarks, Mr. Cronkite added: "The damage Lee Harvey Oswald did the United States of America . . . did not end when the shots were fired from the Texas School Book Depository. The most grievous wounds persist, and there is little reason to believe they will soon be healed."

It is difficult to say how real are the fears expressed by Professor Lipset and Walter Cronkite, and others as well. To evaluate them properly, one would want to know just what is likely to happen over the next weeks and months and years in Vietnam and in China, how the next election will turn out and the election after that, how many Americans the New Left will be able to carry with it, how the American right and the American ultraright will develop as the years pass. All these are matters hidden in the womb of time. All that we know surely is that they will not develop as we expect they will. And we are far too close to see other matters that are developing along with them, and that may alter the history of our times far beyond our present recognition.

Proximity in time complicates an account of the assassination in other ways as well. This book is about the assassination of a President, but the man who was assassinated was also a son, a husband, a father, and a brother. It is possible to write dispassionately about "the bullet that passed through the President's throat," but no such sentence can be read or heard dispassionately by those to whom John F. Kennedy was no awesome figure at 1600 Pennsylvania Avenue but a creature of flesh and blood who is held in memory as a child, a high-school student, a young man, a naval officer, an ardent and ambitious comrade and collaborator.

The world would know more about the assassination itself (although not significantly more) and certainly much more about the events that followed the assassination if the Kennedy

family were willing. That is far more than we have any right
to ask. As time passes and the event recedes into distance, their
reticence will surely diminish. We will learn a little more than
we now know.

At the same time it is useful to recognize that their very
silence is evidence that the story, as we now have it, is in all
essential respects the story that will stand in history. It is hard
to conceive that the Kennedy family would detect any purpose
in permitting the circulation of deceits about an event that plays
so central a role in their lives. It is impossible to believe that the
Kennedys have knowledge of a conspiracy, and that they have
chosen to be silent about it.

Robert Kennedy in particular plays a unique part in the
assassination. He was the brother of the murdered man. But
he was also the man ultimately responsible for the nation's
largest and most powerful investigatory agency, for as Attorney
General of the United States, his was the jurisdiction under
which the FBI fell.

It is true that the FBI under J. Edgar Hoover has led a life
of its own, and that the degree to which it has in practice been
answerable to any man who happened to be Attorney General
is at least open to question. To an overwhelming degree that has
been true because no Attorney General has ever been willing
to run, for small gains, the political risk of challenging Mr.
Hoover, whose allies in Congress are staunch and not entirely
rational where Mr. Hoover is concerned.

Yet even the barest knowledge of Robert Kennedy, and of
his devotion to his brother, makes it obvious that in the days
and weeks that followed the assassination no considerations of
political expediency would have persuaded him to look aside if
there had been any reason in the world to question the role the
FBI played either in events that preceded or events that followed
the assassination. That the FBI blundered repeatedly, before the
assassination and after it, is distressingly clear. The Warren
Report went to some pains to point out those blunders. But
Robert Kennedy himself is warrant enough for the assurance
that the FBI did nothing more than blunder, that it played no
substantive part in the assassination, and that it devoted its very

best efforts, for whatever they may have been worth, to the investigation that followed.

Robert Kennedy's own future will certainly be powerfully affected by the assassination. Although it is not as yet certain he will be the next Democratic presidential candidate, it is a reasonably safe assumption. If so, the odds are inordinately favorable that he will be elected—more favorable, at this writing, than the odds for any other living man. It is at least questionable whether such would have been the case if John F. Kennedy had survived to run for reelection. There is, among most Americans, something faintly disagreeable in the notion of electing brothers only a few years apart to the Presidency: It smacks somewhat of dynastic rule. Then too, Robert Kennedy's light would have dimmed in the brighter light of the President or the ex-President; he would never have emerged so strongly as a person in his own right. It is a cold, inhuman thing to consider, but nevertheless it is probably true that Robert Kennedy, most of all men, is likely to benefit personally from the assassination. It can be added quickly that no one can believe the fact is any comfort to him.

Setting down in order of greatness the roster of Presidents of the United States, more people than not would put Abraham Lincoln in the highest place. Yet the four years in the Presidency that he never lived to serve would have been more trying by far than the four he served, and no one can say how well he would have survived them. He is today among the most loved, it is not beyond the bounds of credibility to believe that he might, save for Booth, have lived to become one of the most reviled.

In that roster of greatness John F. Kennedy will also be high —perhaps one day among the highest of them all. (Our descendants must make that decision. We can not.) To some degree, he may hold that position precisely because he was assassinated. He was not, in November of 1963, at the peak of his popularity. Many were becoming disillusioned with him. They sensed in him, late in 1963, more of the politician than of the statesman. His legislative program was stalled in Congress, and there were more than a few who believed he was making no real effort to get it started again. He had, for example, made little real progress in civil rights; the war in Vietnam hung over him like the sword of Damocles; Cuba and the Russian confrontation constituted a crisis that was far from resolved.

Yet Americans were most of us aware that whatever the setbacks of the moment—even if in time they proved to be more lasting than the moment—John F. Kennedy had brought to the Presidency a style, a spirit, a flavor which had never before been associated with the Presidency. He was young, high-spirited, alert. He looked forward into the years that were ahead, not back to the years that had passed. He brought in his train other young men and women, and made of Washington again the city of high excitement it had been briefly during the early years of Franklin D. Roosevelt. A true poet read at his inauguration, and the chef at the White House was something of an artist. There was life where Kennedy trod. The White House, for a time, became the center of the nation's vigor, the touchstone of the nation's quality—blood flowed within it.

Events might have tarnished all that. The assassination made it certain they would not. Brutally, the glow vanished, but the very brutality, the outrageous incongruity of the act made it certain that the memory of the glow would endure. In the shock of the assassination, the momentum of the Kennedy legislation program was miraculously restored, and most of it flashed through Congress. Oswald destroyed the man, but he may have helped elevate the image. It is a superb image. We are better that we have it.

Dallas goes about its business. The Texas School Book Depository is unchanged, so far as the eye can see. Men move among its somber floors, taking textbooks from cartons and forwarding them to this school or that school. Passers-by turn to look curiously at the window on the sixth floor and stroll away. Amos Ewing, the child who looked up and saw a gun protruding from that window, is a young man now. Marina Oswald has remarried and left Dallas, the cab driver who took Oswald to Oak Cliff is dead, Ruth Paine remains in Irving and wonders about the two wanderers to whom she once offered her hospitality.

Elm Street bends and drops gently as it approaches the triple underpass, and cars race along it on their way out of the city. A street sign has been removed, since 1963, and a few other improvements made in the interests of highway efficiency, but to the casual eye the scene is exactly as it was in late November of 1963.

At the head of Dealey Plaza, behind the fountain, the city of Dallas has erected two tablets, to instruct the curious concerning the events that gave the Plaza its ignominious place in history. There is usually someone or another reading the tablets, and turning to relate the geography of the Plaza with the graven words. The density of cameras is high, as it was on that day.

On the sunny Saturday in June, 1967, when CBS News had its cameras in Dealey Plaza and was completing work on the programs, an event was in progress at the fountains, a few feet from the tablets. Half a dozen young men, dressed in brown military uniforms, were stationed as a sort of guard of honor to still another young man, who stood rigidly at attention and addressed a small gathering seated by the twin pools of water. The men wore swastika armbands, and their banners identified them as the Nazi Party of America. The speaker had much to say, all of it quite familiar, about the Communists, the Liberals, the Jews. It was all orderly, and if one did not listen closely to the words it was quite peaceful. In a way, it was difficult to realize that an assassination had taken place a few yards away. In another way, it was not difficult at all.

EPILOGUE: June 6, 1968

Today the news comes that another assassin has accomplished his end, and another Kennedy has paid with his life for his devotion to our country. And this morning there came also comments from a Mideast newspaper that Robert Kennedy had been killed to prevent him from reaching the White House where he would inevitably have discovered the "truth" about the death of his brother. So, perhaps, it begins again, with new fantasies about the events that led to the death of John F. Kennedy, compounded now with detailed accounts of this conspiracy or that conspiracy out of which emerged the plot and the act directed against Robert Kennedy.

A few hours after the death of Robert Kennedy, a few weeks after the death of Martin Luther King, there is almost an urge to discover plots of some kind to explain these acts. A plot, after all, has at least shreds of logic attached to it, even though the premises of that logic are likely to be insane or very nearly so. But our society becomes somewhat less than human when we must face the fact that these repeated acts of violence are senseless, maniac, irrational, and that at the whim of an insignificant madman the course of history can be changed. A movement of the trigger finger and all that Robert Kennedy might have done for his country and his world is irretrievably lost. A world in which such things can happen—in which causes are so trivial, effects so great—is a hard world to live in. And so it is.

Robert Kennedy, like his brother, knew that fact bitterly and well. That knowledge did not prevent him from offering himself to danger so that he might leave society a little better than he found it. It is a knowledge we must all face, although few of us have the strength to face it as bravely as the Kennedys did.

—STEPHEN WHITE

Artist's model of Dealey Plaza indicates more clearly than actual photographs of the scene the small area of the Plaza and the close proximity of points involved in the assassination.

Eddie Barker, News Director of KRLD, Dallas, stands on white marble perch from which Abraham Zapruder filmed the assassination. To the right and ahead of the car is the grassy knoll.

This would have been a gunman's view of the presidential car if he had been hidden behind the fence at the top of the grassy knoll. One witness is certain that a second gunman was stationed here and that he actually did fire at the President from this spot.

CBS Newsman Dan Rather sits at the window from which the fatal shots were possibly fired. He holds a Mannlicher-Carcano rifle similar to the one believed to have been used by Oswald.

A gap in the foliage of an oak tree on Elm Street would have provided the gunman with a fleeting glimpse of the President.

Rifleman's view of Elm Street from the sixth-floor window of the Texas School Book Depository. The car, fixed in the telescopic sight of the rifle, has reached approximately the point on Elm Street where President Kennedy received the fatal shot.

Dan Rather makes his way through stacks of book cartons on the sixth floor of the Texas School Book Depository. Oswald is believed to have crossed the floor to the back stairs carrying the assassination rifle, which was found hidden behind cartons near the stairs.

Stairway from the sixth floor of the Depository down which Oswald is thought to have made his escape after the assassination.

Dan Rather stops in the second floor lunchroom of the School Book Depository where Oswald is thought to have paused to buy a Coke before fleeing the building.

CBS News test firings of Mannlicher-Carcano rifles at Bel Air, Maryland. Specially constructed tower simulated elevation of sixth-floor window of the Texas School Book Depository from Elm Street.

Bullets fired in the CBS News tests simulating the path which the Commission felt one bullet had taken—through President Kennedy's neck, then through Governor Connally's chest, wrist, and into his thigh. These bullets, photographed after tests more painstaking than the ones on which the Commission based its conclusions, are even less deformed than the famous "single bullet."

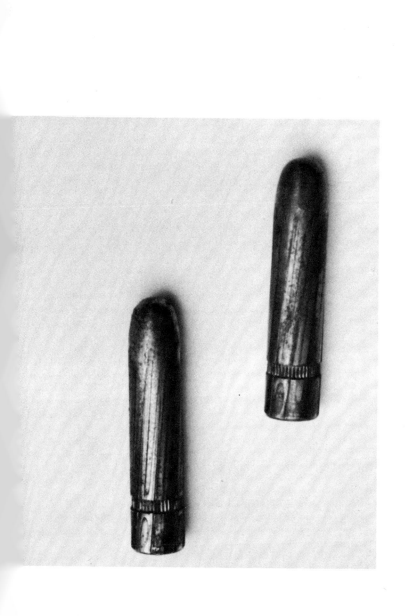

Ruth Paine befriended Lee and Marina Oswald when they moved to Dallas. Marina Oswald lived at the Paine nouse while her husband worked and boarded in a room closer to downtown Dallas. The night before the assassination Oswald arrived unexpectedly to visit Marina and, so the Commission believes, to pick up the rifle that he had stored, among his other belongings, in the Paine's garage.

Linnie Mae Randle saw Oswald leave the Paine's house the morning of November 22 carrying a long, narrow brown paper package. The Commission's investigation indicated that it was in a package such as this that Oswald carried his rifle into the Texas School Book Depository.

Charles Givens, who returned to the sixth floor of the Texas School Book Depository shortly after noon on Nov. 22, is believed to have been the last person to see Oswald before the assassination.

Bonnie Ray Williams, Hank Norman, and James Jarman, Jr. watched the motorcade from the fifth floor of the Texas School Book Depository, directly under the window from which Oswald is believed to have fired at the President. They told the Commission they heard the rifle bolt being drawn back and the sound of the ejected shells hitting the floor above them.

S. M. "Skinny" Holland, Dallas railroad supervisor who was watching the motorcade approach from the overpass, thought he saw a puff of gunsmoke under the branches of a tree on the grassy knoll. He is convinced that a second gunman was firing at the President from this area.

Governor John B. Connally of Texas adjusts microphone before interview in which he gave CBS News his account of what happened in the President's motorcade.

James Altgens,
AP photographer,
standing close to the
presidential car, took a
photograph that the Commission
later identified as having
been made about two seconds
after the President received
the shot that wounded him in
the neck. As he was preparing
to take his next picture, he
saw the fatal shot hit the
President, but was too
horrified to record the scene.

Orville Nix, Sr., one of several amateur cameramen to film parts of the assassination sequence.

Amos Euins, Jr., standing on the corner across the street from the Texas School Book Depository, looked up at the sixth-floor window and saw protruding what he thought was a piece of rusty pipe. Not until after he heard the sound of shots did he realize that it was the barrel of the assassin's rifle.

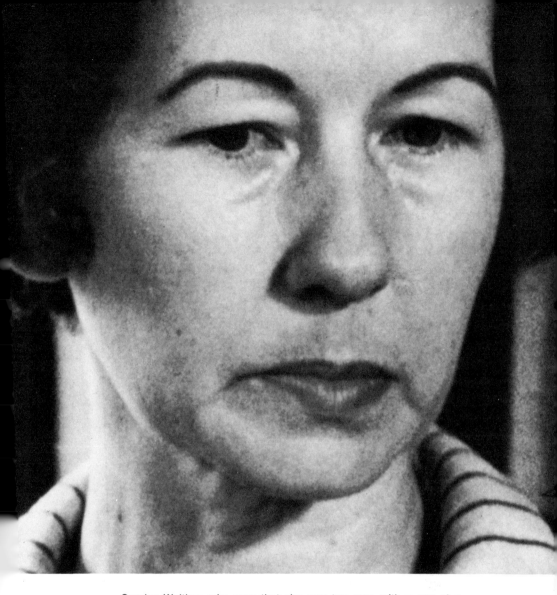

Carolyn Walther, who says that she saw two men with a gun at a window of the Texas School Book Depository, is the focal point of many criticisms of the Commission's report. Although she gave testimony to FBI and police investigators, Mrs. Walther was never called to give evidence to the Commission staff. Mrs. Walther's account differs directly and critically with the accounts of other witnesses—accounts supported by indisputable evidence—and her testimony was not supported by any of the "hard" physical evidence found at the scene.

Officer Murray Jackson,
Dallas police dispatcher who
assigned his friend, J. D. Tippit,
to patrol the area where
he was later murdered.

Domingo Benavides testified that he was driving his pickup truck
along Tenth Street in the Oak Cliff section of Dallas, when he saw
Officer Tippit get out of his patrol car to approach Oswald; seconds
later, he said, he saw Oswald shoot and kill Tippit.

Dallas Deputy Constable
Seymour Weitzman discovered
Oswald's rifle on the sixth
floor of the Texas School
Book Depository and erroneously
identified it for the press
as a Mauser. Although he now
has no doubt that the rifle
he saw was actually a
Mannlicher-Carcano, the
confusion created by his
error has persisted.

Sergio Arcacha Smith, Cuban
refugee now living in Dallas,
denied that he had anything to
do with a right-wing Cuban
conspiracy to assassinate
President Kennedy. District
Attorney Jim Garrison of New
Orleans tried unsuccessfully
to question him.

Appendix: THE MAKING OF THE BROADCASTS

by LESLIE MIDGLEY, *Executive Producer,* CBS NEWS

In addition to its principal job of covering news daily on television and radio, CBS News originates a wide variety of special broadcasts each year dealing with subjects ranging from painting and religion to wars and riots. Consideration of the Warren Report as a subject for one of these special broadcasts began early in the summer of 1966. Gordon Manning, Vice President for News, persistently proposed that CBS News conduct an independent investigation into charges being made in books and magazine articles that the Warren Commission's work was erroneous, or at least unsatisfactory. Most critics claimed another investigation would show that the murder of John F. Kennedy had not happened as the Report described it. Polls indicated that a great many Americans did not believe the basic conclusions of the Warren Report.

Richard S. Salant, President of CBS News, was skeptical that an organization lacking legal powers and resources for a really full-scale investigation into such a major and complicated event should undertake one. He felt that a mere recital of the arguments pro and con would only add to the confusion and that, lacking such powers and resources, CBS News could not shed new light on the controversy. But he was persuaded that the subject was at least worthy of preliminary examination.

The job was assigned to a Special Reports unit consisting of about a dozen people headed by myself. This group is a small part of a main news organization that consists of seven hundred people all over the world. The same Special Reports staff had been responsible for a two-hour broadcast the night the Warren Report was made public in 1964. The experience and background gained in that effort obviously would be extremely valuable in any new one.

There was, however, a basic difference between the projects. The 1964 effort was not an investigation of the circumstances of the assassination itself but solely an illustration, translated into a television broadcast, of the findings of the Report. The findings were not questioned; they were illustrated.

But now the suggestion was that an actual investigation be conducted centering around major questions raised by critics of the Warren Report.

CBS News is a reporting organization, not a scientific laboratory or a detective agency. It was apparent that it would not be possible to develop "proof" that would lead to drastic new insights into the conclusions of the Warren Report. In the fall of 1966, most objections to the Report were based on the stories of witnesses who believed they had heard more than three shots, or had seen evidence of firing from directions other than the School Book Depository building. The names of almost all of them had been provided by the Commission itself, in the 26 supplementary volumes of the Report. Some of their stories seemed worth following up.

The producers and reporters asked various experts if any tests might be made that would indicate the validity of the Warren Report conclusions. One test seemed obvious: The speed at which Oswald's rifle could be fired. But the rifle was in the National Archives and a routine request brought the expected answer: It could not be made available. Several rifle experts believed, however, that testing other Mannlicher-Carcano rifles might indicate if three shots could be fired in the 5.6 seconds the Commission believed Oswald had taken.

Such tests never could *prove* that Oswald had enough time or that he alone fired. But if they indicated strongly that he *did not* have enough time, they would certainly raise serious questions and might even be a form of *disproof* that he was the sole assassin.

And in this particular matter, the work of the FBI seemed grievously inadequate. Its tests of Oswald's rifle had been made by firing at a stationary target, from a shorter distance than that between Oswald's window and the President's car. CBS News believed it could set up a more valid test and it did so—a series of firings from a perch at the right height, distance and angle from a moving target. The results appear in this book.

It also became obvious that the matter of timing involved the Zapruder camera, since it had been used as the "clock" for the assassination from the time the Presidential limousine turned into Elm Street to the moment it sped off to Parkland Hospital. A routine check by CBS News disclosed that Mr. Zapruder's camera was in the hands of the Bell & Howell Company; they had given Mr. Zapruder a film projector for a charity in exchange for the camera. Company spokesmen advised Associate Producer Jane Bartels that they were "testing" the camera but were vague about why and how. And when she flew to Chicago and went to their offices, she was told that the company had donated the camera to the Archives *that very day*. Bell & Howell then issued a statement that its own tests showed the camera probably was running at 18.3 frames per second, a speed already decided upon by the FBI. Curiously, all the critical books and articles had accepted that figure without question.

During the fall, as the preliminary investigation progressed, it became more and more apparent that much useful work could be done in investigating many details of the assassination, and that tests and interviews could be translated into a meaningful television broadcast or series of broadcasts.

Then in November, 1966, *Life* magazine published a series of frames from the Zapruder film, along with an interview with Governor Connally, who examined prints of the film frames and reiterated his consistent opinion that he had not been hit by the same bullet which struck President Kennedy. *Life* called editorially for a reopening of the investigation.

After publication of these frames, Professor Luis Alvarez of the University of California, one of America's foremost physicists and a man of great curiosity and inventive turn of mind, began to study the *Life* pictures; he then obtained the 26 supplementary volumes of the Warren Report from the University library to examine the grainy reproductions of the Zapruder film. Dr. Alvarez thought that photo analysis might reveal evidence of shock waves reacting on the camera held in Mr. Zapruder's hands, which could determine the number and timing of the shots. Dr. Alvarez communicated his theory to Mr. Salant and Mr. Manning, and I went to talk to him at Berkeley. (As it turned out, Dr. Alvarez later decided that the shock waves could not be traced, but the suggestion opened up a train of inquiry that had much to do with the final form and content of the broadcasts.)

CBS News requested permission from *Life* magazine to study the original Zapruder film in its possession; the request was denied. John Watters, General Manager of *Life*, wrote Mr. Manning that the Zapruder film was an "invaluable asset of Time Inc."

But the general notion of submitting guns and cameras and film to at least some basic form of scientific checking seemed to be more and more valid. Both copies of the film and enlarged frames from it were in the Archives and could be examined, and various copies of the film existed in other hands around the country.

Mr. Salant, Mr. Manning and Bill Leonard, Vice President for Programming, agreed that the project should proceed, and on December 1, Mr. Salant formally proposed to Jack Schneider, President of the Broadcast Group of parent CBS, that a series of three one-hour broadcasts be developed, for use in prime time, at the same time on successive nights. The inquiry began in earnest.

Routine requests were made to the FBI and the CIA for cooperation. There appeared to be conflicts between the Kennedy autopsy report and summary reports by FBI agents. Replies from both organizations advised that no cooperation could be extended and no information was available beyond what was in the Archives and in the Warren Report.

Associate producers were assigned to set up the testing of guns and cameras. Bernard Birnbaum was assigned as Producer in Dallas, and Associate Producer Jane Bartels went there to find pertinent witnesses. Mayor Eric Jonnson, the City Manager of Dallas, Scott McDonald, and Police Chief Charles Batchelor, said that they could not give any additional information, but would not object if individuals cooperated. Mr. Birnbaum especially wanted to interview Police Captain Will Fritz, who had been Lee Oswald's principal interrogator. Captain Fritz declined. (He has yet to talk publicly about the matter.) But Officer Murray Jackson, who had been the dispatcher on duty and assigned Officer Tippit to the spot where he was murdered, did agree to talk and to appear in the broadcasts.

Weeks and months passed in seeking out witnesses and experts. Some, such as S. M. Holland, a railroad man widely quoted as saying he saw evidence of firing from in front of the Presidential limousine, readily agreed to be interviewed by Eddie Barker, News Director of the CBS affiliate KRLD-TV in Dallas.

Before the work was done, sixty-four people had been interviewed on camera and hundreds had been contacted in the background research effort. Reaction to requests for interviews was extremely varied. Governor Connally was a little reluctant but did agree. Domingo Benavides, a controversial witness to the shooting of Officer Tippit, had refused in 1964; he cooperated with reluctance in 1967. He just did not want to "get involved." Dr. Malcom Perry, who had tried to save President Kennedy's life immediately after the shooting, was very reluctant but finally said yes. Mrs. Sylvia Odio, who said she had been visited in Texas by fellow Cubans accompanied by a man who looked like Oswald, had gone to Puerto Rico. A CBS News correspondent found her there but she refused to talk on camera.

Dr. Cyril Wecht, a prominent and respected pathologist who is deeply critical of the autopsy and the Report, agreed readily to talk on camera. Constable Seymour Weitzman, who had mistakenly identified the Oswald rifle as a Mauser, was not happy to be seen on camera correcting himself, but he appeared. Critics such as Mark Lane, William Turner and Edward Epstein agreed readily enough. Commander James J. Humes, Chief Autopsy Surgeon, always had refused to talk publicly about the case, but he agreed after clearance had been obtained from Attorney General Ramsey Clark. Warren Commission member John J. McCloy was doubtful about participation, although he did, in the end, agree.

Most of the people whose stories and opinions were pertinent were not hard to locate physically. It was usually more difficult to obtain their cooperation.

In January, 1967, BBC produced in London a three-hour special broadcast about the Warren Report, which included films made by Mark Lane, a principal critic of the Report, and a debate between Mark Lane and Arlen Specter, who had been a key Commission staff member. I flew to London to observe the BBC effort and returned with a video tape of it that was interesting but yielded little except a determination that CBS' own broadcasts would not be in any such format or consist of debates between critics and defenders.

One of Associate Producer Robert Richter's assignments was to travel throughout the country and interview all of the principal critics of the Report whose opinions and conclusions seemed to have some validity or at least were not completely zany. (Like those who believe that John F. Kennedy is alive and was at Truman Capote's masked ball.) One of these sources hinted that the District Attorney of New Orleans was conducting an investigation and Richter telephoned Jim Garrison. Garrison suggested that Richter come to Louisiana; correspondent Mike Wallace happened to be there at that time and both men had long sessions with Garrison, who told them he had evidence that the President had been killed by plotters who had met in New Orleans.

This presented a problem. If Garrison's evidence turned out to be valid, his inquiry, not one by CBS News, would be the central story. And if Garrison got indictments the whole matter would be placed before the courts and it would be extremely difficult for CBS News to treat it, legally and ethically. Associate Producer Clint McCarty was assigned the Garrison section of the broadcasts, and in May Leonard and I met with Garrison in New Orleans for a final check on his information. On the basis of our judgment, Mr. Salant concluded that the Garrison material could be included in the CBS News investigation.

Most interviews were done on 16 mm color film, sometimes, as in the case of Mr. Holland, on the spot where the principals had been on the day of the assassination. The films were returned to New York for me and my assistants to process and evaluate. In work of this kind it is common to film ten times the amount of footage that is finally used; in this case the ratio was nearer twenty to one.

After the films were processed, transcripts were made and the uncut reels screened. In each case judgment was made by the producers as to what material was pertinent and what could be discarded. (In the case of Dr. Wecht, for example, the interview ran to more than an hour, yet only two minutes appeared in the final broadcasts.)

The editorial problem here was to arrange the material—the interviews, film of the tests, the bridging sentences that would be done later—in a logical sequence to make a coherent story line.

All the CBS News tests were originally made on film. So were most of the interviews, although some, such as those with Commander Humes and Mr. McCloy, were originally recorded on video tape using television cameras.

Correspondents Walter Cronkite and Dan Rather and News Director of KRLD, Dallas, Eddie Barker appeared in a studio set for bridging portions of the broadcasts. Their contributions were recorded on video tape from Studio 41 at the CBS Broadcast Center on the West Side of Manhattan, ten days preceding the first broadcast of the series. At the same time, the portions originally on film were transferred to video tape.

As the story line was developed in New York from the interviews shot all over the country, two things appeared vital to staging the broadcasts: first, to obtain permission from the owners of the Texas School Book Depository building to film from inside it, and second, to obtain permission from the Dallas police to reenact the motorcade, while cameras stationed in the building recorded it. After a great deal of negotiation by Mr. Barker and Mr. Birnbaum, both permissions were obtained for Saturday and Sunday, June 10 and 11. Six color cameras were placed in the building and around Dealey Plaza and Mr. Rather was recorded on video tape at the window where Oswald was believed to have crouched. At this point the series had been set at four one-hour broadcasts on successive nights beginning Sunday, June 25.

The end product of all the effort was about five hours of video tape, which was then spliced together in form following the script and then edited to time. Other production elements, such as rear-screen projection of the questions CBS News proposed to pose and answer, were worked into the final product by Director Vern Diamond. The editing was as complex as a news documentary can get, because of the diversity of materials involved. Finally, then, commercials were spliced into the reels.

As is often the case, the work proceeded up until the morning of the last broadcast, when the staff still was considering a change in wording of the final conclusion. (It was not changed.)

Because of the size of this effort and what is represented in terms of responsibility for CBS News, Messrs. Salant, Manning and Leonard were unusually concerned and involved. Mr. Salant took great pains to keep the staff on a straight line of clarity in what constantly turned out to be very muddy matters.

The reporters and editors who participated in this investigation represented, at the outset, a wide range of opinion about the Warren Report. Some of them, especially as they read more and more books and talked to authors and students of the assassination, tended to believe there was "something wrong" about the Report. One really believed the conspiracy theories and was persuaded that Jim Garrison "had something." Others dismissed the theories as silly and Garrison as unreliable.

As the CBS News project began, Mr. Salant determined that it would not be a documentary marshaling of facts. He said, long before the work was done, that CBS News would reach and state its own conclusions—no matter what they might be—about the Warren Report and its credibility. And the conclusions, at times critical but basically in agreement with the Warren Report, seemed to grow naturally out of the basic reportage. Each viewer of the broadcasts—or reader of this book—can judge the conclusion for himself.

Production of television broadcasts is perhaps the ultimate in group journalism. It is an immensely collaborative enterprise requiring not a single reporter to produce an interview, but a team of cameraman, reporter, sound man, assistant cameraman, director, and often researchers and others. These pages necessarily omit the names of dozens of people who made valuable contributions to this journalistic effort. A full list of the credits for the four broadcasts appears on page 304.

Perhaps it is necessary to set down here that these reports to the American people and the conclusions they contain were not dictated or suggested by anyone in the management of the Columbia Broadcasting System. But the avid critics and attackers thrive in a mental climate such that most of them undoubtedly believe CBS, its News Division, and its staff to be part of a vast conspiracy to conceal "the facts" about the assassination from the American people; and the broadcasts to be "proof" of it. They are wrong but nothing can be done about it.

The people who wrote, filmed, produced, and appeared on these broadcasts would have been the happiest journalists of this or almost any other century if they could have come up with a sensational "solution" to the Kennedy murder.

But it didn't happen.

CBS NEWS INQUIRY: "The Warren Report"

PART I   *As broadcast over the* CBS TELEVISION NETWORK *Sunday, June 25, 1967*

CRONKITE: This is what a rifleman would see from a sixth-floor window if he tracked an automobile down Elm Street in Dealey Plaza, Dallas, Texas.

This is a marksman firing three shots from a Mannlicher-Carcano rifle at a target below him and moving away. These two reenactments represent the heart of the Warren Report. In the view of the Warren Commission, they describe fully the circumstance of the assassination of President Kennedy.

But is there more to this story than the Warren Report ever discovered?

ANNOUNCER: This is a *CBS News Inquiry: The Warren Report.* Here is Walter Cronkite.

CRONKITE: On November 22, 1963, at precisely 12:30 P.M., John Fitzgerald Kennedy, the youthful thirty-fifth President of the United States drove triumphantly into this square, where hundreds waited to cheer him . . . and where another waited as well.

Seconds later a dying President sped away from Dealey Plaza—into history, into legend, into a national nightmare of suspicion that persists to this day.

In this country rumors spoke of left-wing plots, right-wing plots, Castro plots; even plots to elevate a Texan to the White House. Abroad, where the transfer of political power by violence is historically more familiar, no rumor was too extreme. Faced with this dangerous condition of rumor out of control, President Johnson quickly appointed a commission to discover the real facts of the assassination, a commission of seven Americans so distinguished that their conclusions must be above suspicion— or so it was thought.

As chairman, the new President literally drafted the Chief Justice of the United States, Earl Warren. The other commissioners: Allen W. Dulles, former head of the Central Intelligence Agency; Hale Boggs, Democratic Congressional whip from Louisiana; John Sherman Cooper, Republican senator from Kentucky; Richard B. Russell, Democratic senator from Georgia; John J. McCloy, lawyer, diplomat, and adviser to Presidents; and Gerald R. Ford, Republican representative from Michigan.

The Warren Commission had the mandates it needed to do the job. It could subpoena witnesses, could invoke the cooperation of any agency of the United States Government, could and did use the FBI and the Secret Service as its investigative arms.

This is the result. On September 24, 1964, the Commission presented its findings in the form of this 888-page report to the President. Two months later it published these twenty-six additional volumes, the exhibits and hearings on which the report was based.

Dan Rather at the scene of the assassination:

RATHER: The basic story pieced together by that Warren Commission Report on the assassination is this: A man named Lee Harvey Oswald crouched here in this dingy window of the Texas School Book Depository as the President passed below. Oswald, the Commission tells us, fired three shots. One missed. One struck both the President and Texas Governor John Connally, riding with him. The third killed the President. Oswald, the Report had it, hid his rifle over there, then ran down the stairs, left the building on foot, and hurried down Elm Street. He made his way to his rented room, picked up a revolver, and about twelve minutes later shot Police Officer J. D. Tippit.

Oswald was captured shortly after the Tippit murder, was questioned for two days in a madhouse atmosphere of confusion, and then, in a grizzly climax, was himself murdered right in the

Dallas police station, by a nightclub operator and police hanger-on named Jack Ruby.

CRONKITE: And that was to be that—an official version of the assassination, arrived at by men of unimpeachable credentials, after what the world was assured was the most searching investigation in history.

Yet in the two and a half years since the Warren Report, a steady and growing stream of books, magazine articles, even plays and a motion picture have challenged the Commission and its findings; have offered new theories, new assassins, and new reasons.

Only a few weeks ago, a Harris poll revealed that seven out of ten Americans are convinced that there remain many "important unanswered questions," that the whole truth has not been told.

A Gallup poll shows more than six of every ten Americans question that there was a lone assassin.

MAN: Well, I don't think that all the facts were brought out. I think something was held back.

WOMAN: I think there were more involved in it than just Oswald.

WOMAN: The only thing that disturbs me is the fact that they've sealed away some of the evidence, and I think that's rather disturbing to most people.

WOMAN: I've read the Warren Report, and as I say, I think those men are men of honesty and integrity. And I think they were asked to do a tremendous job within a very short period of time after the assassination, and I think they did the very best they could.

MAN: I think it's very accurate.

WOMAN: I don't know how in the world they could ever reach a conclusion that one person assassinated him. It's ridiculous. I saw the whole thing on television. I just happened to be home at that time and I don't think that Oswald . . . I think that he was working for the CIA myself.

CRONKITE: Screening out the absurd and the irrational, we are left with a series of real and critical questions about the assassination, questions which have not been answered to the satisfaction of the people of the United States.

In this series of broadcasts, CBS News will try to cast light on those questions. They fall under four headings, which we will examine on successive evenings at this same time.

Tonight's question: Did Lee Harvey Oswald shoot President Kennedy?

For the next two nights we will take up the question of conspiracy. Tomorrow night we will ask, was there more than one assassin firing in Dealey Plaza?

On Tuesday night we will ask whether, regardless of the actual number of gunmen, there was a conspiracy leading to the President's murder.

And on Wednesday night we will ask: Why doesn't America believe the Warren Report?

We will examine these questions here in our studios in New York, in libraries and laboratories from coast to coast, with KRLD News Director Eddie Barker at the assassination site in Dealey Plaza, and with CBS News Correspondent Dan Rather on the sixth floor of the Texas School Book Depository, as for the first time since the assassination, news cameras enter and explore the Depository building itself.

Tonight we ask if Lee Harvey Oswald shot the President. To help us answer that fundamental question we must resolve some lesser questions:

Did Oswald own a rifle?

Did Oswald take a rifle to the Book Depository building?

Where was Oswald when the shots were fired?

Was Oswald's rifle fired from the building?

How many shots were fired?

How fast could Oswald's rifle be fired?

What was the time span of the shots?

First: Did Oswald own a rifle? There is no reasonable doubt that Oswald owned a Mannlicher-Carcano rifle No. C2766. This is the coupon with which he ordered the rifle, by mail, from Klein's Sporting Goods Company, of Chicago. Hidell is one of several aliases Oswald used from time to time. Oswald paid for the rifle with this money order. Here is the application for the post office box to which the rifle was sent—all these documents in Oswald's handwriting.

This photograph, traced to Oswald's own camera, shows him with an identical rifle. This photograph has been widely challenged by Mark Lane and other critics of the Warren Report. During his interrogation, Oswald himself said that his head had been superimposed on someone else's body. Several publications later admitted that they had retouched it and in so doing may have altered the rifle and other details. Lawrence Schiller, of Los Angeles, a professional photographer and photo analyst, made an independent study of the original picture and negative.

SCHILLER: This photograph of Lee Harvey Oswald, which was found the day he was captured and disclaimed by him, has been used by numerous critics of the Report. They say that the disparity of shadows, a straight nose shadow from the nose, and an angle body shadow proves without a doubt that this head was superimposed on this body. To properly re-create the picture to see if the straight nose shadow does correspond to the body shadow, you would have to go to the same address, at the same day of the year and at the same time. We did that. This picture was taken on March 31, 1967, at 214 Neeley Street. And it shows without a doubt that a straight nose shadow corresponds with an angular body shadow; and that the fact that there is a disparity of shadows, that fact cannot be used to discredit the photograph.

CRONKITE: Marina Oswald told the Warren Commission that her husband had posed and she had taken the picture. She also said he had owned a rifle.

BARKER: Did you ever see the rifle?

MARINA: Yes. But you know, I fear to take this rifle. I just saw it, you know, in the corner. I never touched it, his rifle.

CRONKITE: It seems reasonable to accept the conclusion of the Warren Commission Report that Oswald did indeed own a Mannlicher-Carcano 6.5 mm rifle No. C2766. The answer is *yes.*

CRONKITE: Our next question is: Did Oswald take his rifle to the Book Depository building?

At the time of the assassination Lee and Marina Oswald were together only on weekends. He lived in a rooming house not far from his job, and she lived with a friend, Mrs. Ruth Paine, in the suburb of Irving. Mrs. Oswald said her husband kept his rifle wrapped in a blanket in Mrs. Paine's garage. Oswald usually went to Irving on Friday nights with a fellow worker, Buell Wesley Frazier, but the day before the assassination his routine changed.

FRAZIER: Well, he come to me the Thursday, November twenty-first, and asked me could he ride on with me that afternoon, and I said *yes*. And I said, "Why, are you going home this afternoon?" and he replied that he wanted to go home and pick up some curtain rods, so he could put some curtains up in his apartment.

RATHER: Oswald got a lift to the School Book Depository that Friday morning from coworker Frazier. Frazier's sister, Mrs. Linnie Mae Randle, lived across the street from the Paine house.

MRS. RANDLE: I was preparing lunches for my brother there at my sink, and I looked out the window and saw Mr. Oswald cross the street and come up cross my driveway and he had a brown paper bag in his right hand. It was about twenty-seven inches long. It was made out of a heavy brown paper with heavy-looking tape on it.

RATHER: Incidentally, the search of the Book Depository building made after the assassination failed to turn up any curtain rods. And the furnished room which Oswald was then occupying was equipped with curtain rods.

So Oswald made an uncharacteristic trip to the Paine home Thursday night, returning to the Book Depository on the morning of the assassination with a heavy-looking package that could pass for curtain rods. Was it the rifle? A difference of about eight inches has made this one of the most contentious points for the critics. Within this package I have a disassembled Mann-licher-Carcano rifle identical to Oswald's. Before I tell you the dimensions, you might want to try to estimate them, as Mrs. Randle and Wesley Frazier did, from memory. Mrs. Randle variously estimated Oswald's package of "curtain rods" as twenty-seven or twenty-eight inches long; her brother, Wesley Frazier, said about two feet, "give or take a few inches." As a matter of fact, the disassembled Mannlicher is 34 and 8/10 inches long. Furthermore, Frazier said Oswald, preceding him into the Depository building, carried the "curtain rods" under his armpit with his hand around the bottom. Now obviously, you can't carry this package that way.

Oswald had gotten out of the car first, and was then walking away from Frazier. The Commission decided that Frazier easily could have been mistaken about Oswald carrying the package. You can decide whether Frazier, walking some fifty feet behind, and in his own words, not paying much attention, might have missed the few inches of the narrow end of such a package sticking up past Oswald's shoulder.

CRONKITE: Despite the dispute about just how he carried the package, the reasonable answer to this question is that he did take a rifle to the Book Depository building.

Our next question concerns Oswald's whereabouts at the time of the murder: Where was Oswald when the shots were fired?

These men have just witnessed the assassination of the President. They are coworkers of Oswald, photographed by Tom Dillard, The Dallas *Morning News* photographer, in fifth-floor windows within a minute after the shots were heard.

RATHER: Walter, here in Dallas, Eddie Barker has reinterviewed those men who watched the tragedy from the window just below me. Later on, we will be hearing their own story of the assassination itself. But for now, we wanted to know just what Oswald was doing, and where he was doing it, through the morning of November 22, 1963. We spoke first to this man, Harold Norman.

NORMAN: That particular morning three or four of us were standing by the window, and Oswald came over, and he said, "What's everybody looking at, and what's everybody excited about?" So I told him we was waiting on the President. So he just snudged up and walked away.

RATHER: Our next witness from the fifth floor window, James Jarman, Jr.

JARMAN: I was talking to him around about ten o'clock. On the outside of the building some people had gathered. And he asked me what was they gathering around out there for, and I told him that the President was supposed to come by there that morning. And he asked me what time, and I didn't know what time it would be, but some of the people had started gathering around. And he asked me which way would the President be coming, and I told him. And so he said, "Oh, yeah?" And I said, "Yeah." Then he turned and walked off.

RATHER: The last man known to have seen Lee Harvey Oswald before the assassination was another co-worker, Charles Givens. Mr. Givens saw Oswald here, on the sixth floor.

GIVENS: Well, he was standing about middle ways of the building on the sixth floor.

BARKER: What was he doing there?

GIVENS: Well, he was just standing there looking with his orders in his hand.

BARKER: And what did you say to him?

GIVENS: I just said, "Fellow, it's lunch time, you going downstairs?" And he said, "No." He said, "Close the gates on the elevator when you get out." Well I, you know, kind of excited, wanted to see the parade, so when I got downstairs, I really forgot it. I just rushed off and went out to lunch.

BARKER: This would be about what time?

GIVENS: Well about one or two minutes after twelve.

RATHER: So the testimony from those who saw Oswald inside the Book Depository is consistent. The testimony from eyewitnesses in the Plaza below is not. The Warren Commission had to choose between seriously conflicting accounts, and many of the critics think it chose badly.

Down in the Plaza Eddie Barker can show us where those witnesses stood and what they were in a position to see, as they tell their own stories.

BARKER: Dan, Arnold Rowland was here with his wife on Houston Street in the crowd waiting for the motorcade. A few minutes before it arrived, Rowland told the Warren Commission, he noticed an elderly Negro man up in the window where you are now, where Oswald is supposed to have fired from. But he told the Commission, and a few days ago repeated his story for us here, of seeing a gunman lurking in another window entirely:

ROWLAND: And I just lookin' around and we noticed a man up in the window and I remarked to my wife, tried to point him out. And remarked that he must be a security guard or a Secret Service agent.

BARKER: So, the window, then, that you're referring to is on the opposite end of the building from where the main entrance to the building is?

ROWLAND: Yes, it is on the other side of the building. And he had a rifle. It looked like a high-powered rifle because it had a scope which looked, in relation to the size of the rifle, to be a big scope.

BARKER: Now over here, Dan, still on Houston Street and not very far from the Rowlands, was Mrs. Carolyn Walther. Mrs. Walther says she saw *two* men with a gun in the Book Depository.

MRS. WALTHER: I looked at this building, and I saw this man with a gun, and there was another man standing to his right. And I could not see all of this man, and I couldn't see his face. And the other man was holding a short gun. It wasn't as long as a rifle. And he was holding it pointed down, and he was kneeling in the window, or sitting. His arms were on the window. And he was holding the gun in a downward position, and he was looking downward.

BARKER: About what floor would you say these two men were on that you saw in the window?

MRS. WALTHER: The first statement that I made, I said the man was on the fourth or fifth floor, and I still feel the same way. He was about—in a window that was just about even with the top of that tree. I saw the man had light hair, or brown, and was wearing a white shirt. That—I explained to the FBI agents that I wasn't sure about that. That was my impression on thinking about it later. That I thought that was the way the man was dressed.

BARKER: Now, what about this other man who was in the window?

MRS. WALTHER: This other man was wearing a brown suit. And that was all I could see, was half of this man's body, from his shoulders to his hips.

BARKER: Now over here, on the corner opposite the Book Depository, stood a fifteen-year old boy named Amos Euins. A few days ago Amos Euins came back here with us and gave a vivid account of the assassination itself and of a "piece of pipe" he saw poking out of a window—your window, Dan.

EUINS: When he come around, and when I was standin' here, I happened to look up, and I seen a pipe, you know. So I never did paid no attention thinking it might be a pipe, you know, just a pipe stickin' out. So it was stickin' out about a foot, about that high, you know.

BARKER: Point out for me, Mr. Euins, the window where you saw the pipe.

EUINS: It was about on the sixth floor, right below the banister.

BARKER: Among the witnesses here in the plaza, the Commission relied heavily on the testimony of Howard Brennan, who, watching from just about here, said that he actually saw the assassin firing.

HOWARD BRENNAN: I looked directly across and up, possibility of a forty-five-degree angle. And this man, same man I had saw prior to the President's arrival, was in the window and taking aim for his last shot. After he fired the last or the third shot he didn't seem to be in a great rush, hurry. He seemed to pause for a moment to see if for sure he accomplished his purpose, and he brought the gun back to rest in upright position, as though he was satisfied.

CRONKITE: It should be noted here that the Commission failed to follow up Mrs. Walther's story. She was interviewed briefly by FBI agents but never called before the Commission or its staff, who accumulated vast minutiae on the relatives of Lee Harvey Oswald.

Despite these discrepancies, his co-workers knew and certainly saw Oswald. The CBS News answer: Oswald was in the Book Depository building when the shots were fired, most probably on the sixth floor.

We come now to our fourth question for tonight: Was Oswald's rifle fired from the building? To answer this one the Commission placed major reliance on physical evidence found within the building. Three shells, later identified as fired from Oswald's rifle, were found forty-two minutes after the shots. Ten minutes later a rifle was discovered.

RATHER: The rifle was found on the sixth floor, back near the stairway between some cartons, by Deputy Constable Seymour Weitzman. And from that episode came a description that has plagued the Warren Commission account for years: the identification of it as a German Mauser.

Eddie Barker asked Constable Weitzman what happened.

WEITZMAN: I'll be very frank with you. I stumbled over it two times, not knowing it was there.

BARKER: Just went right by it.

WEITZMAN: Went right by it. And Mr. Bone was climbing on top, and I was down on my knees looking, and I moved a box, and he moved a carton, and there it was. And he in turn hollered that we had found a rifle.

BARKER: Well, when did you first get a full view of the gun?

WEITZMAN: When the crime lab brought the gun out, after they had gone over it. I could see portions of the gun while they were doing partial investigation of it here in the building.

BARKER: What kind of gun did you think it was?

WEITZMAN: To my sorrow, I looked at it, and it looked like a Mauser, which I said it was. But I said the wrong one because just at a glance I saw the Mauser action, and—I don't know—it just came out words, it's a German Mauser. Which it wasn't. It's an Italian-type gun. But from a glance it's hard to describe, and that's all I saw it was at a glance. I was mistaken, and it was proven that my statement was a mistake, but it was an honest mistake.

RATHER: So Mr. Weitzman now seems sure that the rifle was indeed Oswald's Mannlicher-Carcano, and that his identification was simply a mistake.

The most important ballistic evidence in the case is a spent bullet, two bullet fragments, and three empty shells, or hulls, as they are sometimes described. The nearly whole bullet was found in Parkland Hospital under circumstances we'll consider in detail tomorrow night. The two fragments were found in the Presidential limousine. The shells were found here on the sixth floor, below the windows here, by Patrolman Gerald L. Hill, who told Eddie Barker about it.

GERALD L. HILL: We saw a barricade, a sort of three-sided barricade of boxes that would have shielded anyone between the boxes and the window from general view, from the rest of the floor. And then immediately under the window that was later determined to be the actual spot that the shots were fired from, there were three rifle bullet hulls, right against the baseboard of the building, where the floor and the wall come together.

CRONKITE: One of the experts who made the ballistic examination for the Warren Commission was Dr. Joseph D. Nicol, superintendent of the Bureau of Criminal Investigation for the State of Illinois. Walter Lister asked about his conclusions.

NICOL: It is my feeling that both the fragments, as well as the one relatively whole bullet, had been fired in the same gun. And then based upon the comparison of the tests which were available to me, it was my opinion that the same weapon which fired the tests also fired the—the three evidence specimens.

LISTER: In the case of the virtually intact bullet that was found on a stretcher in Parkland Hospital, and the two fairly sizable fragments found in the front of the Presidential limousine, you felt that those were definitely fired from Oswald's rifle?

NICOL: Yes, sir.

LISTER: To the exclusion of all others?

NICOL: To the exclusion of all others, right.

CRONKITE: From the ballistic evidence it seems that the answer to the question of whether Oswald's rifle was fired from the building is *yes*.

To this point the Warren Commission's case appears strong; despite minor discrepancies it appears that Oswald had the opportunity and the murder weapon.

And now we come to one of the most telling arguments that has been raised against the Warren Report in these past two and a half years, a point which we now know seriously disturbed members of the Commission itself. For the critics argue that Lee Harvey Oswald could not have fired his rifle fast enough and accurately enough to be the sole assassin. The critics argue therefore either that Oswald was not the gunman at all, or that there was more than one gunman. Well now, here we have twin questions. How many shots were fired in Dealey Plaza that day? And how long did it take to fire them?

First, how many shots were fired?

RATHER: Walter, the obvious way to answer those questions seemed to be to talk to our eyewitnesses in Dealey Plaza, ask them how many shots they heard, and in what kind of sequence. That's what we tried first.

MRS. WALTHER: I'm sure there were four shots.

BARKER: How many shots did you hear?

WILLIAMS: I heard three. The first and second was further apart than the second and third. In other words, there was a bang— and a bang-bang right thereto.

BARKER: How many shots did you hear?

NORMAN: Three.

BARKER: In how long a period of time?

NORMAN: Oh, I'd say just about like this, you know—boom (clicking sound)—boom (clicking sound) boom. Something similar to that.

NIX: I would say—bang—bang—bang.

HOLLAND: There were definitely four shots.

WEITZMAN: Well, just three quick bursts, like bang-bang-bang.

CRONKITE: There is an old axiom among lawyers that nothing carries more weight with a jury, or is less reliable, than eyewitness testimony. In this case we have just learned that the testimony of assassination earwitnesses also is unreliable. In a moment of utter horror and confusion, in a bowl certain to start echoes, it's too much to expect that human ears will register and correctly recall the number and sequence of a series of quick shots.

But we have heard Mr. Hill describe how he found three shells, and Mr. Nicol state that they were fired from Oswald's rifle. Many critics maintain that additional shots were fired; but no physical evidence ever has been produced. The most reasonable answer to this question seems to be: three shots.

But it is only barely possible that three shots could have been fired by Oswald alone. The most dramatic and most important single piece of evidence of the assassination was provided by Mr. Abraham Zapruder, who, on November 22, 1963, stationed himself with an amateur movie camera right here.

On one roll of 8 mm color film, Mr. Zapruder had the astonishing luck to capture the entire assassination. We cannot show you that film on television. It was purchased from Mr. Zapruder by *Life* magazine. That film, though, serves as a clock. If we know the exact speed the camera was running, and can see in the film where the bullets struck, it should be possible to determine not only how many shots were fired, but the amount of time between them. This is critical to the question of whether Oswald could have physically accomplished the murder.

If the time between shots was less than the time necessary to operate Oswald's cheap bolt-action rifle, a rifle like this one, then obviously he was not the sole assassin. A test of time between shots could not prove that he did fire the shots. It might prove that he did not.

RATHER: Here is how the Warren Commission reconstructed a

time sequence from the film. Now Mr. Zapruder was filming the motorcade from the grassy knoll. At the very moment the gunman must have been tracking it from up here.

Using the critical frames of the Zapruder film as a guide, the Warren Commission, and now we, can reconstruct exactly what the gunman must have been seeing at every moment.

We know that the President had not yet been hit when the car slipped beneath this oak tree. The President would have come into the gunman's sights, in the Report's words, "for a fleeting instant through an opening in the leaves, just as frame number 186 went through Mr. Zapruder's camera." Remember that frame, 186.

We stop the car at frame 186 to show you what a gunman would have seen in that instant, except for the fact that the tree has grown since 1963. There's more foliage on it now. And the overhead highway signs were not there then.

The Commission did not think the shot was fired here. Now the President is again concealed by the leaves, emerging just as the Zapruder camera, over on the grassy knoll, is shooting its 210th frame. The gunman can now see the President again, but Mr. Zapruder's view was blocked by a ground level sign, and his film didn't show what was happening in frame 210, which the Commission decided was the first moment that President Kennedy could have been hit.

The Zapruder film did not show the President again until frame number 225, where we stopped the car once more. Here the Zapruder film seemed to show the President already hit; so that hit must have occurred somewhere between frames 210 and 225 of the Zapruder film. As to just where, we'll have some intriguing new evidence in a few moments.

Along here the Commission said a second shot was fired, probably a miss. But at this point the third shot, the fatal one, destroyed the President's head. That moment is clearly shown in Mr. Zapruder's film, at frame 313.

Could Oswald really have done this? Marine Corps records show Oswald had attained the rank of sharpshooter; but he was not a genuine expert, according to his fellow servicemen. One of his fellow Marines claimed that Oswald was actually a very poor shot, and simply was not interested in marksmanship activities.

CRONKITE: It seemed evident that we should try to establish the ease or difficulty of that rapid-fire performance. Hence, our next question: How fast could that rifle be fired?

Oswald's rifle was test-fired for the Warren Commission by FBI and military marksmen. The rate of fire for this bolt-action rifle and its accuracy against a moving target were critical to the Commission's case against Oswald. And yet, incredibly, all tests for the Commission were fired at stationary targets. The FBI won't comment on why.

Based more on testimony than on firing tests, the Commission concluded it was an easy shot for Oswald to hit the President at that range. From its tests the main conclusion drawn was that this Mannlicher-Carcano could not be fired three times in a span of less than 4.6 seconds, because it took about 2.3 seconds to operate the bolt mechanism between shots.

To explore glaring omissions in the tests fired for the Commission, CBS News decided to conduct its own tests with the Mannlicher-Carcano.

RATHER: A moving target is harder to hit than a stationary one, and the elevation of the sixth-floor window might make a difference. The only elevation for the Warren Commission firing tests were the thirty-foot tower, less than half the height of the Book Depository's sixth floor above Elm Street.

So CBS News had a tower and target track constructed to match exactly the heights and distances in Dealey Plaza. The target track was angled to match precisely the angle of Elm Street. The target, a standard FBI silhouette, moved by electric motor at eleven miles an hour, approximately the speed of the Presidential limousine. A rifle of the same make and age as Oswald's was fitted with the same four-power telescopic sight found on his rifle. These CBS News tests were conducted on different days at the range of the H. P. White Ballistics Laboratory, in rolling farmland, north of Bel Air, Maryland. Eleven volunteer marksmen took turns firing clips of three bullets each at the moving target. None of the men had much familiarity with the Italian Mannlicher-Carcano, although each was given time to practice at a nearby indoor range; and most of the volunteers were experienced with bolt-action rifles.

In each case the first shot was fired at a point approximating the point at which the Warren Commission deduced the first shot was fired. Distance, about 175 feet. In six seconds the distance grows to 270 feet.

Results varied. A Maryland state trooper made two hits in the silhouette, one near miss—in slightly less than five seconds. Another state trooper's best time was 5.4 seconds. One hit, two near misses.

A weapons engineer had the best score. Three hits in 5.2 seconds. A technician at the H. P. White Ballistics Laboratory managed three shots in the fastest time, 4.1 seconds, half a second faster than the fastest time turned in for the Warren Commission, but only one hit.

Altogether the eleven volunteer marksmen made thirty-seven attempts to fire three shots at the moving target. Seventeen of those attempts had to be called no time, because of trouble with the rifle. In the twenty attempts where time could be recorded, the average was 5.6 seconds.

CRONKITE: From our own tests we were convinced that a rifle like Oswald's could be fired in 5.6 seconds or less, and with reasonable accuracy, at a target moving much the same as the Presidential limousine was traveling away from the Book Depository's sixth-floor window.

So, clearly, there is no pat answer to the question of how fast Oswald's rifle could be fired. In the first place we did not test his own rifle. It seemed reasonable to say that an expert could fire that rifle in five seconds. It seems equally reasonable to say that Oswald, under normal circumstances, would take longer. But the circumstances were not normal. He was shooting at a President. So our answer is: probably fast enough.

In addition to the number of shots, and the capability of the rifle, it is important to know the time span between shots—since, as we pointed out previously, if the shots were closer together than the rifle could be fired, two rifles must have been involved.

So, our next question: What was the time span of the shots?

The answer might lie in Mr. Zapruder's film of the assassination. You'll recall that the Commission decided that the first shot was fired at frame 210 on the Zapruder film, and the last shot at frame 313.

Tests of the camera made by the FBI reported that it was running at a speed of 18.3 frames a second. Divide 103 frames by 18.3 frames a second, and you get 5.6 seconds—which is the time the Commission reported Oswald probably had to take.

It's a point upon which the critics have seized. Could Oswald have fired three shots in 5.6 seconds? Well, then new evidence made its appearance.

It was at first called to our attention by a distinguished physicist, Dr. Luis Alvarez, of the University of California at Berkeley.

BILL STOUT: What was it that made you interested enough to dip into the Warren Report to begin analyzing the photos of that day?

ALVAREZ: Well, I think it was probably that I had lunch every day with a bunch of my graduate students who were keenly interested in the controversy that was going on at the time. For a while I couldn't get very interested in it. But then when *Life* Magazine republished the frames from the Zapruder movie, I spent an evening looking at them—and I found something that excited my interest.

STOUT: What first caught your eye, Dr. Alvarez?

ALVAREZ: Well, it's right here in the picture. At frame 227, the highlights on the windshield of the car are all drawn out into rather pronounced streaks. And you can see that in the frame ahead the highlights are individual dots. And again in the frame beyond them are individual dots.

So something rather violent happened to the line of direction of Mr. Zapruder's camera in frame 227. It swung violently.

CRONKITE: If Dr. Alvarez were right, the Zapruder film might contain a record of the number of shots fired. If blurs, which could be accepted as evidence of gunshots, occurred in a certain time span—then the shots themselves would be in the same span.

We remind you again that the film is owned by *Life* magazine, and is not available for broadcast. So, CBS News commissioned an expert photo analyst, Charles Wyckoff, of the

Massachusetts firm of Edgerton, Germeshausen and Grier, to make an analysis of the Zapruder film frames.

Dan Rather interviewed Mr. Wyckoff.

RATHER: Mr. Wyckoff, the entire Zapruder film shows the whole assassination?

WYCKOFF: Yes, it does, Dan. The—the film was an 8 mm motion picture film, and the entire record, in which the President was in view, was represented on a film about this long—which only took about ten seconds. And all of the records of interest were on this small piece of film. We actually looked at all the frames, but we only studied certain frames in detail. And the reason for studying those frames in detail was the fact that there were certain little things in there that looked blurred at first. And we were quite interested in why they looked blurred.

For instance, on frame 190 here, or rather, let's start with frame 189—there's a wall in the background with little—little holes, that you can see a white building through those holes.

RATHER: Now, that's a tiled . . .

WYCKOFF: That's a tiled wall. And you can see the little holes, if you look at it with a magnifying glass. Here, you see those that are nice and round, and fairly sharp. And, yet, in frame 190, right next to it, you can no longer tell that those holes are circular. They're blurred out.

RATHER: Now, why is that?

WYCKOFF: Something must have happened to Mr. Zapruder when he was—something must have startled him when he was holding his camera. He had a—a camera very much like this model right here, which is an 8 mm camera. And as he held it up to his eye, focusing—concentrating on the President, something startled him —and he jumped a little bit with the camera.

RATHER: Not nearly that much?

WYCKOFF: Not anything like that at all. Just a very subtle jump. But that was just enough to cause a blur of these little holes in here. And also a blur of highlights on the car.

RATHER: All right, now, you see that very clearly in frame 190, and that frame does look distorted—and you can't see the white holes in the wall across the street clearly at all. Now, how many times does that occur in this ten-second stretch of 8 mm film?

WYCKOFF: Now, that—that occurs several times, as we've represented up here on the—on this film on the wall. It occurs at frame 190, it occurs again at frame 227. Frame 227 was the next evidence that I had of Mr. Zapruder moving his camera. And it occurs at frame 318.

Now, this is interesting, because we all know that at frame 313 the President received the fatal shot. We have a natural reaction time—that—that he heard the sound at about the same time that the—that something happened to President Kennedy, when he was fatally wounded here. We can apply this same correction, of about four or five frames, to each one of these frames where I noted motion.

In other words, I am saying that it was possible that there could have been a shot fired here, another one fired in this area of 222, 223, and another one in the area of 313—noticeable now in 318.

I think the important thing is the fact that we have found an indication some twenty frames prior to the time the Warren Commission thought that the first shot was fired. Now, whether or not this was a shot, we cannot say. But certainly Mr. Zapruder, the photographer, was disturbed at that point.

STOUT: What does this finding mean to those of us who simply have followed the controversy over the assassination, and are not physicists?

ALVAREZ: Well, to me, it means that there were indeed three shots fired, as the Commission said; that the one that apparently didn't hit anyone in the car was fired before the one that hit the President, and not between the two shots that obviously hit the President.

CRONKITE: Just as a rough check on this theory, we decided to try it ourselves, using other cameramen holding similar cameras, standing on a rifle range, filming an automobile while a rifleman fired over their heads.

These two volunteers are aiming their cameras at a parked

limousine. Their instructions: "Hold the cameras as steady as possible, and keep filming no matter what happens." The shots will come between them and the car. The cameramen are as far from the firing platform as Mr. Zapruder was from the sixth floor of the Book Depository. (Sound of gunfire in background.)

The reaction was obvious. The film taken by these cameramen showed the effect of the shots, despite instructions to hold steady. Even in steadier hands, motion was always noticeable. This frame shows highlight dots around the car's windshield. In reaction to a shot, the dots changed to crescents. And in the following frame they become streaks, comparable to streaks found on some frames from Mr. Zapruder's film.

Incidentally, Dr. Alvarez also suggested that the first shot might still be lodged in the tree. We checked it with a metal detector. But, unfortunately, it did not reveal any presence of a bullet. Perhaps more sophisticated equipment will be developed in the future to X-ray the tree.

Perhaps the most intriguing feature of the entire Alvarez-Wyckoff experiment is this: At the time he undertook to study the film for us, Charles Wyckoff was unaware that there was anything unusual about frame 186 of the Zapruder film. He tentatively placed one shot there, only because of Mr. Zapruder's slight jiggle at frame 190. Yet, in the Warren Commission Report we learn that, to a gunman tracking from the Book Depository the President's head would have come into view for an instant through a hole in the foliage, just at frame 186—where it now appears something startled Abraham Zapruder.

If a shot had been squeezed off there, a shot which missed, the length of time available to Oswald begins to stretch, even if the Commission's clock is right for the Warren Report placed the first shot at frame 210.

But, now, that brings up a second question. Was the clock right? You'll recall that the Zapruder film is the basic clock for all of these events. Now tests of the camera, made by the FBI— a camera like this one—reported that it was running at an average speed of eighteen point three frames per second. The camera had been obtained from the Bell and Howell Company, the manufacturers.

During our CBS investigation we asked the company if they

had tested the camera's speed. The result was a public announcement that they had tested it, and the result was the same as the FBI test. And the announcement continued that they had that day donated the camera to the National Archives—and this is it.

But if the clock was not exactly right, then the whole sequence of events—from the number of shots, to the time span of the shots, and many other things—would be affected.

Curiously, most of the critics themselves accepted the 18.3 speed without a question—except one, who insists it was running at twenty-four frames, as could have happened if the control had been depressed.

Now, we decided to see if we could clock the clock. We turned again to photo expert Charles Wyckoff.

WYCKOFF: They have a clock over here with a sweep second hand. And if we photograph that clock with each one of these cameras, we're—we will be able to measure the time that it takes to run through the few hundred frames, as we've shown here. And I'll—I'm—I will try this for you right now. What I'll do is to turn a light on and illuminate the clock dial, start the camera, and then start the clock and let it run for about a ten or fifteen second period.

RATHER: And you do that with each camera?

WYCKOFF: We do that with each camera. And then we take the film out, process it from each record—and we end up with a result very similar to what you see on this chart right here.

This corresponds to the first camera. This is the second, the third, the fourth, and the fifth. We started each frame here—we edited until we got the frame corresponding to zero time on each one of the cameras. Then we counted off the same number of frames on each camera record that corresponded to frames 190 to 318 in the Zapruder record.

RATHER: And there was this much difference in the cameras, although they were the same kind of cameras?

WYCKOFF: Same kind of cameras. There was this much difference in time. The first camera read 6.90 seconds; the second camera, 7.30 seconds; the third, 6.70; the fourth, 8.35; and the last, 6.16 seconds.

RATHER: So, under this theory, the shooter, or shooters, of the shots could have had up to how many seconds to fire?

WYCKOFF: They could have had, according to this, up to as much as eight and thirty-five hundredths of a second—which is a pretty long time.

CRONKITE: In this hour we have been considering the relationship between Oswald and the assassination. To the account given in the Warren Report we have made three additions, each of which rests on evidence at least as persuasive as any provided by the Commission.

Our analysis of the Zapruder film suggests strongly that the first shot was fired at frame 186. The Commission said only that the first shot to hit came between frames 210 and 225.

Something startled Mr. Zapruder earlier. And the evidence is that a rifle shot was what startled him.

We have shown that the Zapruder camera was quite possibly running slower than the Commission thought. The earlier shot and the slow camera together mean that the rifleman may have had additional time to get off three shots.

We have shown by carefully controlled experiments that a Mannlicher-Carcano rifle can be fired more rapidly and accurately than the Commission believed.

Now, these points strengthen the Warren Report's basic finding. They make it more likely that Oswald shot the President. They significantly weaken a central contention of the critics—their contention that Oswald could not have done it because he did not have enough time to fire.

It is now reasonable to assume that the first shot fired through a tree missed its mark, and that it was this shot that Governor Connally heard. The Governor's insisted all along that he was not struck by the first shot. It now appears he was correct.

Now we can answer all our secondary questions.

Did Oswald own a rifle? He did.

Did Oswald take a rifle to the Book Depository building? He did.

Where was Oswald when the shots were fired? In the building, on the sixth floor.

Was Oswald's rifle fired from the building? It was.

How many shots were fired? Three.

How fast could Oswald's rifle be fired? Fast enough.

What was the time span of the shots? Seven or eight seconds.

Did Lee Harvey Oswald shoot President Kennedy? CBS News concludes that he did.

Yet this is only the beginning of our inquiry. We drew the distinction between Oswald as *a* killer, and Oswald as *the* killer.

The Warren Commission, despite the most widely accepted and often restated capsule version of its findings, did not state that Oswald was the only killer. It did state that it could not find any evidence that others had conspired with him.

Yet it is on precisely this point that most Americans question the Commission's conclusion most strongly. Almost two out of three Americans seem to feel that behind such a monstrous deed there must have been a conspiracy.

CBS NEWS INQUIRY: "The Warren Report"

PART II *As broadcast over the* CBS TELEVISION NETWORK *Monday, June 26, 1967*

CRONKITE: Last night, in the first of this series of four broadcasts about the Warren Report, CBS News considered and tried to give reasonable answers to some major questions about the Report.

Did Lee Harvey Oswald take a rifle to the Book Depository building? Our answer was *yes*.

Where was Oswald on the day President Kennedy was shot? In the building on the sixth floor.

Was Oswald's rifle fired from the building? *Yes.*

How many shots were fired? Most likely three.

How fast could Oswald's rifle be fired? Fast enough.

What was the time span of the shots? At least as large as the Warren Commission reported? Most likely the assassin had more time, not less.

These, CBS News concluded, added up to the answer to last night's central question: Did Lee Harvey Oswald shoot President Kennedy? Our conclusion was that he did. Beyond reasonable doubt, the chronic misfit and malcontent was at least one of the men who fired on President Kennedy. But was he *the* killer or *a* killer? A lone madman or the agent to the monstrous and successful conspiracy? Tonight's central question: Was there a conspiracy to assassinate President Kennedy?

In the 888 pages of the Warren Commission Report on the assassination, these are certainly among the most significant words: "The Commission has found no evidence that either Lee Harvey Oswald or Jack Ruby was part of any conspiracy, domestic or foreign, to assassinate President Kennedy." And the Report also states: "The Commission has found no evidence that anyone assisted Oswald in planning or carrying out the assassination."

Let's stop a moment to examine just what that says, and more important, what it does not say. Note that, contrary to the popular impression, the Commission, by these words, left the door open on the question of conspiracy just a crack. The words do not preclude the possibility of a conspiracy. They don't say that the Commission concluded that there was no conspiracy, or that Oswald was the sole assassin. They only say that the Commission could find no evidence that others were involved, no evidence that there was a conspiracy.

If there was a conspiracy, it could have taken one of two forms: Either Oswald was a sole triggerman for behind-the-scenes manipulators, or there were one or more additional gunmen firing at the President. Most of the critics of the Report insist there were other gunmen.

Within the broad matter of conspiracy, our basic questions for tonight are: Where did the shots come from? If the shots did not all come from the Book Depository window, then there was most likely some form of conspiracy. Could a single bullet have wounded both President Kennedy and Governor Connally? The single-bullet theory has become perhaps the most controversial aspect of the report. The Commission said it was not essential to its conclusions. But, to make those conclusions square with the facts, either three groups of wounds were caused by two bullets, which is the single-bullet theory, or all three bullets from Oswald's rifle struck President Kennedy and Governor Connally, which the Commission rejected in the belief that one bullet missed completely.

The only other alternative is a second assassin. Let's look first at the scene of the assassination in Dealey Plaza, Dallas, Texas. Correspondent Dan Rather.

RATHER: First, Walter, here's the part of the story that is not in dispute, and that any theory of the assassination must explain.

The Presidential motorcade entered the plaza in a sharp right turn off Main and onto Houston. It ran slowly along the eastern edge of Dealey Plaza. Then the motorcade slowed even more, for the extremely sharp left, more than ninety degrees, onto Elm Street, which runs directly under the windows of the Texas School Book Depository. It's a perfect place for an ambush. And as the limousine drifted into the odd S curve, shots began to rain on it.

CRONKITE: Here is our first basic question for tonight: Where did the shots come from?

RATHER: We decided on last night's program that some of the shots came from up here, Lee Harvey Oswald's nest in the sixth-floor window. But, there are persistent reports of other virtually simultaneous shots, which would admit more than one assassin and therefore a conspiracy. Most often the other shots are reported from over there, the famous grassy knoll, ahead of, to the right of, and slightly above the President's car. The witnesses for both sets of shots are generally positive and persuasive.

This photograph, taken only seconds after the assassination, shows one group of those witnesses, Oswald's co-workers, who perched themselves in fifth-floor windows to watch a parade and instead saw a murder.

BONNIE RAY WILLIAMS: So, when the President came around, we remember seeing him standing up and waving. And as he's turning to go down Elm Street, we heard a shot, and we saw the President slump. Well, be—prior to that, though, we decided there was some fireworks and everything, you know? And then after we saw him slump, we said—I think one guy, I don't remember which one he was, say that I believe they're shooting at the President, and I believe it came from right up over us.

HAROLD D. NORMAN: Then I think, about that time, well, Jarman says, somebody's shooting at the President. And I told Jarman, I said, I said, I know it is because I could hear—they are above me, and I could hear the shots and everything, and I could even hear the empty cartridges hitting the floor. I mean, after the shots had been fired.

And so, after the shots were fired, well, all the officers and everyone else seemed to think they came from by the track over by the underpass, because that's where everyone ran, over that-a-way. But, I—just like I said, I've been hunting enough to know the sound of a rifle from—from a backfire or a firecracker or anything like—especially that close to me.

RATHER: The witnesses in the fifth-floor windows say they heard the shots right overhead. But other observers below thought they heard firing from other directions. This is the view of Elm Street from the grassy knoll, up behind the picket fence where some critics claim another gunman lay concealed. We're looking through the trees at the spot where the final shot took effect, the shot that killed the President.

At this point, the President would have presented as good a target from here as from the School Book Depository. Some think that right here is where the fatal shot came from.

EDDIE BARKER: Now, railroad man, S. M. Holland, was up on this overpass when the firing started. From here you can see the Book Depository and the grassy knoll. Mr. Holland came back up here with us a short while ago, and his is perhaps the most telling account in favor of the grassy knoll theory, not only because of what he saw and heard during the assassination, but what he says he found on that grassy knoll immediately afterward.

S. M. HOLLAND: Just about the time that the parade turned on Elm Street, about where that truck is—that bus is now, there was a shot came from up—the upper end of the street. I couldn't say then, at that time, that it came from the Book Depository book store. But I knew that it came from the other end of the street, and the President slumped over forward like that and tried to raise his hand up. And Governor Connally, sitting in front of him on the right side of the car, tried to turn to his right and he was sitting so close to the door that he couldn't make it that-a-way, and he turned back like that with his arm out to the left. And about that time, the second shot was fired and it knocked him over forward and he slumped to the right, and I guess his wife pulled him over in her lap because he fell over in her lap.

And about that time, there was a third report that wasn't

nearly as loud as the two previous reports. It came from that picket fence, and then there was a fourth report. The third and the fourth reports was almost simultaneously. But, the third report wasn't nearly as loud as the two previous reports or the fourth report. And I glanced over underneath that green tree and you see a—a little puff of smoke. It looked like a puff of steam or cigarette smoke. And the smoke was about—oh, eight or ten feet off the ground, and about fifteen feet this side of that tree.

And I immediately ran around to the spot that this shot came from. Of course, there was no one there because it took us quite a little while to thread our way through the cars—there's so many parked there—and they parked at every angle, that when I got over there, I did find where a man had been standing and walking from one end of the bumper to the other, and I guess if you could have counted the footsteps there'd a been two hundred or more on the muddy spots—footprints. And there were two mud spots on the bumper of this station wagon.

BARKER: Would you take me over there and show me this place you're talking about?

HOLLAND: Yes, I will.

BARKER: All right, let's go. Well now, Mr. Holland, where would the person have to be standing to have fired that shot that you heard that came from up here?

HOLLAND: From the footprints and all indications, he was standing right here.

BARKER: Were they fresh footprints?

HOLLAND: They were fresh. It had been raining that morning. There was footprints—mud on these two-by-fours—there was mud on the bumper of the station wagon, and they was only two sets of footprints that I could find that left this station wagon and they went behind a white Chevrolet car that was settin' over there.

BARKER: Abraham Zapruder, whose film of the assassination was studied at length on last night's program, was standing up on this little wall right at the edge of the grassy knoll. Now, shots from behind that picket fence over there would have almost had to whistle by his ear.

Mr. Zapruder, when we interviewed him here, tended to agree that the knoll was not involved.

ABRAHAM ZAPRUDER: I'm not a ballistics expert, but I believe that if there were shots that come from my right ear, I would hear a different sound. I heard shots coming from—I wouldn't know which direction to say—but they was driven from the Texas Book Depository and they all sounded alike. There was no difference in sound at all.

BARKER: Associated Press Photographer James Altgens was actually looking toward the Book Depository.

JAMES ALTGENS: As I was getting ready to make some pictures, why, I heard this noise. I thought it was a firecracker explosion. So, I just went ahead and made the picture, which shows the President right after he was struck by a bullet, struck in the neck, the first shot. And this was a picture that the Warren Report later fixed as being made two seconds after the shot was fired. And as they got in close to me, and I was prepared to make the picture, I had my camera almost at eye level; that's when the President was shot in the head. And I do know that the President was still in an upright position, tilted, favoring Mrs. Kennedy. And at the time that he was struck by this blow to the head, it was so obvious that it came from behind. It had to come from behind because it caused him to bolt forward, dislodging him from this depression in the seat cushion, and already favoring Mrs. Kennedy, he automatically fell in that direction.

The one thing that did seem to be a little bit strange, immediately after the car proceeded on to Parkland Hospital, men with drawn guns ran up the terrace of this plaza, up into what is considered to be and referred to as the knoll area. And, thinking that they had the assassin cornered up in this knoll area—and it seemed rather strange, as I say, because knowing that the shot came from behind, this fellow had to really move in order to get over into the knoll area.

BARKER: You had no thoughts about another assassin behind the fence or on the knoll?

ALTGENS: I've had a lot of people to contact me in that they felt there was another person involved, and trying to get me to verify either photographs they had or to work out some information they felt they had come across to substantiate the evidence of— substantiate the fact that there was another assassin. But at no time has any of this evidence proved to me beyond a shadow of a doubt that there was another assassin.

OFFICER JACKS: The car in which I was driving, which occupied the Vice President, was—had just completed its turn, and I felt a blast which appeared to be a rifle shot come from behind me. I turned and looked up to the School Book Depository.

BARKER: Well now, what about these people who say shots came from this fence area up here? Would you agree with that at all, or not?

JACKS: No, sir. I—I—I don't think there was. I heard three shots, and I could feel the concussion from all three.

CRONKITE: Eddie Barker went to Austin to ask the same question of Governor and Mrs. Connally, who were in the best possible position to know the direction from which the shots came.

GOVERNOR CONNALLY: All of the shots came from the same place, from back over my right shoulder. They weren't in front of us, or they weren't at the side of us. There were no sounds like that emanating from those directions.

BARKER: Was there any doubt in your mind, the direction that those shots came from?

MRS. CONNALLY: No. They all came from the same direction.

BARKER: Which was?

MRS. CONNALLY: It was behind us, over my right shoulder. You see, the first one—the first sound, the first shot, I heard and turned and looked right into the President's face. So, the sound drew me to that direction and had a definite reaction.

CRONKITE: In Abraham Zapruder's film of the assassination, the fatal shot appears to move the President's head back. The critics contend this can only mean the shot came, not from the Book

Depository, but from somewhere in front. Not for the first time, nor for the last in these reports, we find equally qualified experts in disagreement.

We put the question of the President's head movement to an experienced photo analyst and two expert pathologists.

RATHER: From a physicist's point of view, from a photographic analysis point of view, what can you tell about the direction of the bullet?

CHARLES WYCKOFF: Well, the—in frame 313, the—there was an apparent explosion at this point, which would be on the front side of—of—the head. Now, characteristically, this would indicate to me that the bullet came from behind, and this is what's called spalling. It's a minor explosion where pieces of material have—have left and go generally in the direction of the bullet.

RATHER: But now, the explosion, this minor explosion, occurs forward of the President. Now, wouldn't that indicate the bullet coming from the front?

WYCKOFF: No, quite contrary. It does indicate that the bullet was coming from behind.

RATHER: Well, you're aware that some critics say that by the very fact that in the picture you can clearly see the explosion of the bullet on the front side of the President, that that certainly indicates the bullet came from the front.

WYCKOFF: Well, I don't believe any physicist has ever said that. This picture might explain the principle that we've been talking about just a little bit more clearly. It's a picture taken in a millionth of a second, of a thirty calibre bullet being shot through an electric lightbulb. The bullet was traveling from this direction, entered the lightbulb here, passed through and caused a rather violent explosion to occur on the exiting side, and it's very similar to the situation in the Zapruder Kennedy assassination films.

CRONKITE: That is one explanation from a physicist as to how a head could move backward after being struck from behind, which seems to many laymen not possible. Forensic pathologists are experts in the examination of victims of violent death, both medically and legally qualified. Dan Rather put the matter to one of them, Dr. Cyril W. Wecht, professor at Duquesne University.

CYRIL W. WECHT: I have seen too many biological and physical variations occur in forensic pathology to say that it would have been impossible. I say that it is quite unlikely. I say that it is difficult for me to accept, but I would have to admit that it is a possibility that his body could have moved in that direction after having been struck by a bullet that hit him in the back of the head.

CRONKITE: Eyewitnesses, and even film analysts often produce as many problems as they solve. In this case, the physical evidence would seem to be more reliable, and that evidence came first to the attention of the doctors at Parkland Hospital, who were the first to look closely at both the massive head wound and the less critical neck wound.

At Parkland, Dr. Malcolm Perry, attending surgeon, tried desperately to keep the President alive. But the very urgency of that problem prevented him from examining the two wounds, as he now explains in his first public statement since the Report was published.

DR. MALCOLM PERRY: I noted a wound when I came into the room, which was of the right posterior portion of the head. Of course, I did not examine it. Again, there was no time for cursory examination. And if a patent airway cannot be secured, and the bleeding cannot be controlled—it really made very little difference. Some things must take precedence and priority, and in this instance the airway and the bleeding must be controlled initially.

BARKER: What about this wound that you observed in the—in the front of the President's neck? Would you tell me about that?

PERRY: Yes, of course. It was a very cursory examination. The emergency proceedings at hand necessitated immediate action. There was not time to do more than an extremely light examination.

BARKER: There's been a lot said and written about was this an exit wound or an entry wound? Would you discuss that with me, sir?

PERRY: Well, this is a difficult problem. The determination of entrance or exit frequently requires the ascertation of trajectory. And, of course, this I did not do. None of us did at the time. There was no time for such things.

The differentiation between an entrance and exit wound is often made on a disparity in sizes, the exit wound generally being larger, in the case of an expanding bullet. If, however, the bullet does not expand—if it is a full jacketed bullet, for example, such as used commonly in the military, the caliber of the bullet on entrance and exit will frequently be the same. And without deformation of the bullet, and without tumbling, the wounds would be very similar—and in many instances, even a trained observer could not distinguish between the two.

BARKER: Did it occur to you at the time, or did you think, was this an entry wound, or was this an exit wound?

PERRY: Actually, I didn't really give it much thought. And I realize that perhaps it would have been better had I done so. But I actually applied my energies, and those of us there all did, to the problem at hand, and I didn't really concern myself too much with how it happened, or why. And for that reason, of course, I didn't think about cutting through the wound—which, of course, rendered it invalid as regards further examination and inspection. But it didn't even occur to me. I did what was expedient and what was necessary, and I didn't think much about it.

BARKER: You did not turn the President over?

PERRY: No, there was no reason to. There was not time at that problem, and there was really no reason to. It made very little difference to me, since my immediate concern was with an attempted resuscitation.

CRONKITE: The nature of the throat wound can no longer be verified, for no records were made and no pictures taken before Dr. Perry cut through it in an attempt to relieve his patient's breathing. The doctors at Parkland were engaged in a desperate struggle to keep the President alive; all else was secondary. But their task was impossible. One of the shots had virtually destroyed the President's head. Even as the doctors worked, the President died.

At the hospital the scene was turbulent and disordered. The press and public were clamoring for news. Dr. Perry was rushed from the emergency room to a news conference, where he was badgered into giving a description of the wounds.

The neck wound, he told the press, looked like an entry wound, and he pointed to the front of his neck. In the transcript of that news conference there's no doubt that Dr. Perry made it sound as if he had a firm opinion. Well, the reporters flashed the news, and in that moment of confusion and misunderstanding established once and for all in the minds of a great many people a conviction that at least one bullet had been fired from the front to the motorcade.

Legally, the dead President was now just another part of the evidence in a Texas homicide case. The murder had been committed in that state, and there were no laws which gave the federal government jurisdiction.

In his book, *The Death of a President,* William Manchester describes a scene of almost horrifying confusion, in which the Dallas County Medical Examiner tried to prevent the removal of the President, and Kennedy aides almost literally bulldozed his coffin out of Parkland Hospital.

During the flight to Washington it was agreed that an autopsy had to be performed, and Manchester writes Mrs. Kennedy chose Bethesda Naval Hospital because her husband had been a naval officer.

The autopsy was performed by the chief of Pathology, Commander—now Captain James J. Humes; Dr. J. Thornton Boswell; an Army Lieutenant Colonel, Pierre Finck, a forensic pathologist. They reported in a document reproduced in the supplementary volumes of the Warren Report that the President's wounds were inflicted from the rear. As part of standard procedure, they had photographs and X-rays taken as they proceeded.

Confusion continued at Bethesda, as it had reigned at Parkland. FBI agents submitted a report, later disclosed in Edward J. Epstein's book, *Inquest,* which said they had heard one pathologist state that he had found a wound in the President's back, and could not find an exit.

The Warren Report version was explicit, that there was no wound in the back, but one in the neck. However, details of these published sketches tended to indicate that there was a wound below what could be described as the neck.

The photographs and X-rays which might clear up the issue were in possession of the Kennedy family, and only officially turned over to the Archives on October thirty-first, 1966—with the provision that they not be made public for five years. Now, there the matter has rested until now. But Captain Humes, the senior pathologist at the autopsy, has since gone to the Archives and reexamined the X-rays and photographs. His conclusions we will hear later in an exclusive interview, the only one he's granted since that fateful night.

But first, the observations of Dr. Wecht, whom we heard earlier.

WECHT: This sketch that was made by Dr. Boswell, Mr. Rather, is a very important sketch. It shows the bullet hole which he diagrammed in at a point approximately several inches below the collar level, although he does give other measurements to the side—which would place it at a higher level.

RATHER: Now, the Commission Report accepted that the bullet entered very near the neck, did it not?

WECHT: Yes. Take a look at this sketch, if you would, please. This was made by a medical illustrator at Bethesda Naval Hospital. This sketch shows the one that was accepted by the Warren Commission. It shows the point of entrance in the back at a much higher level, and it shows the point of exit again at approximately the level of the knot of the tie. You can then see why it was very important to accurately determine whether or not the bullet wound in the back was at this point, or whether it was five and a half inches below the collar level.

CRONKITE: Since the X-rays and films were turned over to the Archives, Captain Humes has reexamined them. And tonight, for the first time, he discusses with Dan Rather what is contained in them.

RATHER: Commander—now Captain Humes, have you had a look at the pictures and X-rays from the autopsy since the time that you submitted them to the Warren Commission?

HUMES: Yes, Mr. Rather, we have.

RATHER: And do you have any different conclusion, any different ideas, any different thoughts now, after seeing them again, than you had at that time?

HUMES: No, we think they bear up very well, and very closely, our testimony before the Warren Commission.

RATHER: How many wounds in the President's body?

HUMES: There were two wounds of entrance, and two of exit.

RATHER: And the two wounds of entry were where?

HUMES: Posteriorly, one low in the right posterior scalp, and one in the base of the neck, on the right.

RATHER: Let's talk about those two wounds, Captain. Both of these are blowups from the Warren Commission Report, these sets of drawings. Now, there are people who think they see discrepancies in these two drawings from the Warren Commission Report, in that this drawing shows the—what you called an entry wound at the base of the neck of the President—shows it to be, or seems to show it to be, in the upper back, near the shoulder blade—considerably below the base of the neck. Whereas, this drawing does show the entry wound to be at the base of the neck. Now could you talk about these, and reconcile that?

HUMES: Yes, sir. This first drawing is a sketch that—in which the outlines of the figure are already prepared. These are on sheets of paper present in the room in which the examination is conducted, and are routinely used to mark in general where certain marks or scars or wounds may be in conducting a post mortem examination. They are never meant to be accurate or precisely to scale.

RATHER: This is a routine in—in preparing autopsy reports, to use this kind of drawing, and at this stage for them not to be prepared precisely?

HUMES: No. No precise measurements are made. They are used as an *aide memoire*, if you will, to the pathologist as he later writes his report.

More importantly, we feel, that the measurements which are noted here at the margins of the drawing are the precise measurements which we took. One states that—we draw two lines, points of reference—from bony points of reference. We note that there were—the wound was fourteen centimeters from the tip of the right acrominion, and fourteen centimeters below the tip of the right mastoid. Now the acromion is the extreme outermost portion of the shoulder. The tip of the mastoid is the bony prominence just behind the ear. And where these two lines intersect was, in actuality, where this wound was situated. And if we would try and draw that to scale, which we weren't trying to do as this mark was made, this, I think, would appear a little bit higher.

RATHER: Now, you examined this whole area of the back?

HUMES: Yes, sir.

RATHER: Were there any other wounds except one at the base of the neck, and one up in the skull?

HUMES: No, sir, there were not. Now the second drawing, which you mentioned, was prepared as we were preparing to testify before the Warren Commission, to rather schematically and as accurately as we possibly could depict the story for the members of the Warren Commission.

RATHER: In this drawing you were trying to be precise?

HUMES: Yes, sir, we were. We were trying to be precise, and refer back to our measurements that we had made and noted in the margins of the other drawing.

Also, of course, since this time we have had opportunity to review the photographs which we made at that time. And these photographs show very clearly that the wound was exactly where we stated it to be in our testimony before the Warren Commission, and as it is shown in this drawing.

RATHER: Your reexamination of the photographs verify that the wounds were as shown here?

HUMES: Yes, sir, they do.

RATHER: About the—the head wound . . .

HUMES: Yes, sir.

RATHER: . . . there was only one?

HUMES: There was only one entrance wound in the head. Yes, sir.

RATHER: And that was where?

HUMES: That was posterior, about two and a half centimeters to the right of the midline, posteriorly.

RATHER: And the exit wound?

HUMES: And the exit wound was a large irregular wound to the front and side—right side of the President's head.

RATHER: Now, can you be absolutely certain that the wound you described as the entry wound was, in fact, that?

HUMES: Yes, indeed, we can—very precisely and incontrovertibly. The missile traversed the skin, and then traversed the bony skull. And as it passed through the skull it produced a characteristic coning, or beveling effect on the inner aspect of the skull—which is scientific evidence that the wound was made from behind and passed forward through the President's skull.

RATHER: This is very important. You say the scientific evidence— is it conclusive scientific evidence?

HUMES: Yes, sir, it is.

RATHER: How many autopsies have you performed?

HUMES: I—I would estimate approximately one thousand.

RATHER: Is there any doubt that the wound at the back of the President's head was the entry wound?

HUMES: There is absolutely no doubt, sir.

CRONKITE: So the chief pathologist at the Kennedy autopsy, after reexamining the X-rays and photographs, states without the slightest qualification that the shots which killed the President came from the rear.

In answer to our major question as to whether shots came from a direction other than the Book Depository Building, indicating other gunmen and a conspiracy, we have eye—or ear witnesses inside the building saying the shots came from there. Now, Mr. Holland who was on the railroad overpass, here, insists that he heard a shot from here. And in Mark Lane's book, *Rush to Judgment*, he writes that fifty-eight out of ninety people who were asked about the shots thought they came from the grassy knoll.

Now, expert opinions differ. All the experts agree that the shots could have come from the rear. But where some experts, such as Dr. Humes, say bluntly that they did, others—such as Dr. Wecht—find it highly unlikely.

CBS News concludes that the most reasonable answer is that the shots came from the Book Depository building, behind the President and Governor Connally. But if the shots came from the rear, and if there were only three of them, can all the wounds be accounted for? The President was struck at least twice. Governor Connally was wounded in the chest, the wrist, and the thigh. One bullet was recovered intact, as well as two large fragments. The Warren Commission concluded that of the three bullets fired, one missed entirely, one struck the President's skull and fragmented, and the third—this one—passed through the President's neck and went on to inflict all the governor's wounds. This is the single-bullet theory. And so we must ask: Could a single bullet have wounded both President Kennedy and Governor Connally?

Now, this is what the Report says: "Although it is not necessary to any essential findings of the Commission to determine just which shot hit Governor Connally, there is very persuasive evidence from the experts to indicate that the same bullet which pierced the President's throat, also caused Governor Connally's wounds. However, Governor Connally's testimony and certain other factors have given rise to some difference of opinion as to this probability but there is no question in the minds of any member of the Commission that all the shots which caused the President's and Governor Connally's wounds were fired from the sixth floor of the Texas School Book Depository."

Well, through the tortured English of that paragraph, a sentence that begins with *however,* and has *but* in the middle, we can make out the Commission's struggling to paper over internal dissension. It's unfruitful to try to puzzle out the meaning of the statement.

Instead, we asked Arlen Specter, assistant counsel to the Commission, and now district attorney of Philadelphia, and the author of the single-bullet theory.

SPECTER: The possibility of one bullet having inflicted the wounds on both the President's neck and the Governor's body came in a very gradual way. For example, the first insight was given when Dr. Humes testified, based on his autopsy findings. And at that time it was made clear for the first time that the bullet that went through the President's neck hit no bone, hit no solid muscle. And, according to Dr. Humes, came out with great velocity.

Now, it was at that juncture that we wondered for the first time what happened to the bullet. Where did the bullet go? The probability is that it went into Governor Connally, because it struck nothing else in the car. That is the single most convincing piece of evidence that the one bullet hit both men, because looking down the trajectory, as I did through Oswald's own rifle, and others did too, the trajectory was such that it was almost certain that the bullet which came out of the President's neck with great velocity would have had to have hit either the car or someone in the car.

RATHER: It stated in the Warren Commission Report that belief in the single-bullet theory is "not essential" to support in the conclusion of the Warren Commission Report.

Now, can you describe for us any other theory, besides the single-bullet theory, that would support the conclusions in the Report?

SPECTER: The Commission concluded that it was probable that one bullet inflicted the wound on the President's neck, and all of the wounds on Governor Connally. But you could have three separate bullets striking under the sequence as we know them. For example, the President could have been struck at frame 186 of the Zapruder film, which is a number given to the Zapruder film. Then Governor Connally could have been struck some forty-two frames later, which would be a little over two and a quarter seconds at about frame 228 or 229; and then the third shot could have hit President Kennedy's head at frame 313, which was pretty clearly established. So that it is not indispensable to have the single-bullet conclusion in order to come to the basic finding that Oswald was the sole assassin.

CRONKITE: The Commission's dilemma lay in the fact that it had to choose between two unpalatable alternatives in order to make its case stand up. Having decided that three shots were fired, and having three sets of wounds to explain, the Commission could only find either that all three shots hit their marks, or that one of the three bullets hit two men.

But, if all three shots hit, then one of them would have had to pass through the President's neck, emerge at 1800 feet per second, headed on a downward path toward the midst of the Presidential car and the six people in it, and vanish in mid air, hitting nothing and leaving no mark. Well, this was more than the Commission could stomach. Despite its own words, the single-bullet theory is essential to its finding.

The bullet was found after it rolled off a stretcher at Parkland Hospital during the tumult that followed the arrival of the two wounded men. The man who found it was Darrell C. Tomlinson, senior engineer at Parkland.

DARRELL C. TOMLINSON: There was a doctor that went into the Doctors' Lounge and he had to pull this stretcher out, the one I'd taken off the elevator, and whenever he came out he failed to push it back up against the wall, so I just stepped over and gave it a little kick to get it back in line, and then I turned to walk away and I heard a rattle, and I turned around and looked. I didn't see anything at that time, but I walked back over to the stretcher, and there was this bullet was layin' there. So, I picked it up, looked at it, put it in my pocket.

BARKER: Do you recall, was there any blood on the bullet, or was it—how did the bullet look?

TOMLINSON: Well, it was copper colored bullet and I couldn't tell whether it had blood on it or not. I—I really didn't look for it.

BARKER: It was a spent shell?

TOMLINSON: Yes.

BARKER: Well, now, as you think back, is there any doubt in your mind today that the stretcher on which you found that bullet was the stretcher that came off of the elevator?

TOMLINSON: Well, I know that. That I know. I just don't know who was on that stretcher.

BARKER: But, the stretcher was on the elevator?

TOMLINSON: Right.

BARKER: And this was the elevator that Governor Connally would have taken, or would have been placed on to go to the operating room, is that right?

TOMLINSON: Yes, sir, that's—that's the one he went up on.

CRONKITE: Critics have claimed that in fact the bullet came from the President's stretcher, which would rule out the single-bullet theory. But the President's stretcher was never in that elevator, and consequently Mr. Tomlinson's recollection disposes of that particular dispute. It does not dispose of another claim, however, the claim that the bullet was planted on the governor's stretcher as part of a plot to link Oswald to the assassination. And that claim can never be disproved.

The bullet is almost intact, only slightly flattened, with a little cone of lead missing from the rear end. Could such a bullet have penetrated successively, a human neck, a human torso, a wrist, and a thigh, and emerged in this condition? The Commission used animal carcasses and blocks of gelatin to test the bullet's penetrating power, firing repeated shots from Oswald's rifle. Now, this is standard technique. But, because of the difficulty of lining up such a shot, the Commission experts fired their bullets separately through the various simulators. Each time they measured how much speed the bullet had lost from its initial two thousand feet per second, and in the end, concluded that the bullet would have retained enough velocity to penetrate the Governor's thigh.

But, it seemed to us that the only completely valid test would be a single shot directly through a series of objects with the same thickness and density as the two bodies. We decided to make that shot.

RATHER: Dr. Alfred G. Olivier, chief of Wound Ballistics at Edgewood Arsenal, who conducted the tests for the Warren Commission, served as consultant to CBS News in these experiments at the H. P. White Ballistics Laboratory, Dr. Oliver suggested using gelatin blocks to simulate human tissue. The main object was to line up targets simulating the President's neck and the Governor's chest, wrist, and thigh, spaced as far apart as Mr. Zapruder's film indicated they were in the limousine, and then to see how far a 6.5 Mannlicher-Carcano bullet would penetrate.

Extensive research at Edgewood Arsenal has shown that gelatin, in a twenty per cent concentration, gives a good simulation of human tissue. The first gelatin block was made five and a half inches thick to simulate the President's neck, with cloth added to represent his coat and shirt. Set two feet or so away was a twelve-inch block representing the governor's chest, also with appropriate clothing. This high speed sequence, taken at 22,000 frames a second, shows the chest simulation block and how the bullet, slightly unstable after passing through neck simulation, begins to turn off course as it tears through the gelatin, exiting in an attitude pointing down.

The wrist block was two and a half inches thick, inset with masonite to represent bone. Beyond was a fourth gelatin target representing the Governor's thigh. Dr. Olivier told reporter Walter Lister about the tests.

OLIVIER: When the bullet struck the simulated neck, it was perfectly stable, passed through making a small track in the gelatin. This—this very closely simulates the wound received by the President. It was a small entrance and a small exit, as described on the autopsy report.

WALTER LISTER: This is about the way it would look through human muscle tissue?

OLIVIER: Yes. After the bullet left this simulated neck, and passed from this dense medium into air, which is less dense, then it had a chance to start to tip, and by the time it struck this block it was tipped, and you can see the difference: a much larger track in the gelatin block, which represents a more serious wound, as the governor received. In his case, the bullet passed along the rib, fractured the rib, throwing fragments into the lung. Of course, we have no rib here, but it still simulates passing through the flesh.

By the time it had passed through here, it had lost considerable velocity and entered the simulated wrist. In some cases it passed through the wrist; in other cases, it lodged in the wrist. Behind this wrist, we had another gelatin block, representing the Governor's thigh. In none of the cases did this thing actually penetrate that, but it would have taken very little more velocity to have caused a similar wound.

LISTER: What do you think that these tests have indicated here?

OLIVIER: Well, that they—I think they very strongly show that this one bullet could have caused all the wounds.

LISTER: Did someone outline these experiments for you?

OLIVIER: No, I'm afraid I'm guilty of the whole business.

CRONKITE: Our tests confirm that a single bullet could indeed have wounded both men. But conceding that it is possible, we must also ask if it is probable. We asked two distinguished pathologists, both experienced in the study of wounds, to give us their best judgment. They are Dr. William F. Enos of Northern Virginia Doctors Hospital, who has studied wounds both as a military and civilian pathologist; and Dr. Cyril Wecht, from whom we heard earlier. First, Dr. Enos with Dan Rather:

ENOS: I have had cases in which the missiles have gone through relatively heavy bone and very little deformity. The fact that it went through two men is perfectly acceptable because of its velocity.

RATHER: Now, most of us have an idea that the minute a bullet hits a bone that it shatters that bullet.

ENOS: No, not necessarily. Again, it depends on the construction of the missile, of the bullet. If it's a full-jacketed bullet it can remain intact with very little or no deformity.

RATHER: Is it impossible that the bullet would have gone through President Kennedy, gone through Governor Connally, and not suffered any more damage than is shown in this photograph?

ENOS: No, without hedging. In medicine we always fall back upon the trite expression; we never like to say that something is impossible. I—I would say that it is highly improbable. I—I—I would hesitate, really, to say that it's absolutely one hundred per cent impossible, but it is highly improbable. Another one, you see, another one of the very many highly improbables that we are asked to accept by the Warren Commission, if we are to accept the validity of their full Report.

CRONKITE: The most persuasive critic of the single-bullet theory is the man who might be expected to know best, the victim himself, Texas Governor John Connally. Although he accepts the Warren Report's conclusion, that Oswald did all the shooting, he has never believed that the first bullet could have hit both the President and himself.

CONNALLY: The only way that I could ever reconcile my memory of what happened and what occurred, with respect to the one bullet theory, is that it had to be the second bullet that might have hit us both.

BARKER: Do you believe, Governor Connally, that the first bullet could have missed, the second one hit both of you, and the third one hit President Kennedy?

CONNALLY: That's possible. That's possible. Now, the best witness I know doesn't believe that.

BARKER: Who is the best witness you know?

CONNALLY: Nellie was there, and she saw it. She believes the first bullet hit him, because she saw him after he was hit. She thinks the second bullet hit me, and the third bullet hit him.

MRS. CONNALLY: The first sound, the first shot, I heard, and turned and looked right into the President's face. He was clutching his throat, and just slumped down. He just had a—a look of nothingness on his face. He—he didn't say anything. But that was the first shot.

The second shot, that hit John—well, of course, I could see him covered with—with blood, and his—his reaction to a second shot. The third shot, even though I didn't see the President, I felt the matter all over me, and I could see it all over the car.

So I'll just have to say that I think there were three shots, and that I had a reaction to three shots. And—that's just what I believe.

CONNALLY: Beyond any question, and I'll never change my opinion, the first bullet did not hit me. The second bullet did hit me. The third bullet did not hit me.

Now, so far as I'm concerned, all I can say with any finality is that if there is—if the single-bullet theory is correct, then it had to be the second bullet that hit President Kennedy and me.

CRONKITE: The Governor insists that he heard a shot before he was struck, and that therefore he could not have been struck by the first bullet, as the Warren Commission supposes.

Those of you who were with us last night remember that we cited indications in the Zapruder film that it was Oswald's first shot, fired earlier than the Commission believed, which missed. Now if that is so, then the Governor could indeed have heard a shot and begun reacting to it before he himself was hit. We have, in fact, three theories to explain the same facts—the single-bullet theory, the second-assassin theory, the theory that all three bullets that were fired found their targets.

Our own view, on the evidence, is that it is difficult to believe the single-bullet theory. But, to believe the other theories is even more difficult. If the Governor's wounds were caused by a separate bullet, then we must believe that a bullet passed through the President's neck, emerged at high velocity on a course that was taking it directly into the middle of the automobile, and then vanished without a trace.

Or, we can complicate matters even further, as some do, by adding a second assassin, who fires almost simultaneously with Oswald, and whose bullet travels miraculously a trajectory identical with Oswald's, and that second assassin, too, vanishes without a trace. Difficult to believe as the single-bullet theory may be, it seems to be the least difficult of all those that are available. In the end, like the Commission, we are persuaded that a single bullet wounded both President Kennedy and Governor Connally.

The Warren Report's contention that there was only one assassin rests on the conviction that all the wounds suffered by both men were inflicted by no more than three shots, fired from behind and above them. We have heard Captain Humes, as well as other doctors and experts. We have looked hard at the single-bullet theory. The case is a strong one.

There is not a single item of hard evidence for a second assassin. No wound that can be attributed to him. No one who saw him, although he would have been firing in full view of a crowded plaza. No bullets. No cartridge cases. Nothing tangible.

If the demands for certainty that are made upon the Commission were applied to its critics, the theory of a second assassin would vanish before it was spoken.

As for the Governor, he now concedes he might have been struck by the bullet that pierced the President's throat. And our own investigation makes it likely that the bullet was the second, and not the first, that Oswald fired. The Governor's objections, which were the most troubling of all, now disappear. CBS News concludes, therefore, that Oswald was the sole assassin.

But was he truly alone? Or were there others in dark shadows behind him, coauthors of a plot in which Oswald was cast as a triggerman? Tomorrow we will look into those charges, and concern ourselves with Officer Tippit, with Jack Ruby, and the murky accounts and strange personages introduced into the case by District Attorney Jim Garrison in New Orleans.

GARRISON: He did not touch a gun on that day. He was a decoy at first, and then he was a patsy, and then he was a victim.

CRONKITE: We will hear Garrison, and some of those whom he has involved. And we will try to answer the third of our major questions: Was Lee Harvey Oswald part of a conspiracy?

CBS NEWS INQUIRY: "The Warren Report"

PART III *As broadcast over the* CBS TELEVISION NETWORK *Tuesday, June 27, 1967*

CRONKITE: For two nights we have been looking for answers to major questions concerning the assassination of President John F. Kennedy. Sunday night we asked: Did Lee Harvey Oswald take a rifle to the Book Depository building? Our answer was *yes.* Where was Oswald on the day President Kennedy was shot? In the building on the sixth floor. Was Oswald's rifle fired from the building? *Yes.* How many shots were fired? Most likely, three. How fast could Oswald's rifle be fired? Fast enough. What was the time span of the shots? At least as large as the Warren Commission reported? Most likely the assassin had more time, not less.

And so, we concluded Sunday night that Lee Harvey Oswald fired three shots at the motorcade. And then, last night, we began to look into the question of conspiracy. Were there others also firing at the President? We interviewed eyewitnesses. They told conflicting stories. We tested in our own investigation the critical single-bullet theory and found one bullet might well have wounded both men. Captain James Humes, who conducted the autopsy on the President, broke a three-and-a-half-year silence to report that he has reexamined the X-rays and photographs and stands firm that the shots came from behind. We heard Governor Connally and heard that his recollections conform with our own reconstruction of the assassination. And we concluded that there was no second gunman.

Tonight we look further into the question of conspiracy. Was

Oswald acting alone, or was he the agent of others? Was the assassination the sole work of a twisted, discontented man, seeking a place in history? Or were there dark forces behind Oswald?

Continuing to seek an answer to the question of whether Lee Harvey Oswald was involved in a conspiracy leads us to a second murder. Oswald was taken into custody in a movie theatre at 1:50 P.M., eighty minutes after President Kennedy was shot. But he was first charged, not with the murder of the President, but with the murder of Dallas Police Officer J. D. Tippit.

Our next question: Could Oswald have made his way to the scene of Officer Tippit's murder?

RATHER: To solve the Tippit killing, it is vital to reconstruct Lee Harvey Oswald's actions from the moment of the assassination to the moment of Tippit's death. Yet for three and a half years, all news media have been barred from the Texas School Book Depository where the first critical few moments of Oswald's flight occurred. Depository officials have agreed to lift the ban for these special broadcasts, and so, for the first time, we have been able to follow the path of Oswald's movements from his sniper's nest on the sixth floor.

Taking his rifle with him, Oswald went between the stacks of book cartons to the opposite corner of the sixth floor. He tucked the rifle down between stacks, and at this point probably discovered that the elevator could not be brought up, that Charles Givens, eager to see the parade, had forgotten to close the gate. So Oswald turned to the stairs and went down four flights to the second floor and to the lunchroom there, where he was next seen at about 12:31 P.M., barely a minute and a half after his third shot.

In front of a coke machine a policeman at gunpoint actually stopped Oswald. But Depository Superintendent Roy Truly told the officer Oswald was an employee, and Oswald was released. Free to go, Oswald apparently crossed the second floor through this office, went down the front stairs, perhaps three minutes after the assassination, and continued out through the glass front door, well before police sealed off the Depository building.

CRONKITE: Here is how the Warren Commission reconstructed Oswald's movements after he left the Depository. He walked seven blocks down Elm Street, then took a bus on Murphy, headed for Oak Cliff. But the bus quickly became tangled in the traffic jam caused by the assassination itself. And Oswald got off, walked two blocks to Lamar, then took a cab several blocks past his rooming house on Beckley.

The Commission believes he then walked back to his apartment, picked up a revolver and a lightweight jacket, and set off on foot down Beckley.

POLICE RADIO: Attention all squads. Attention all squads. The suspect in the shooting at Elm and Houston is reported to be an unknown white man, approximately thirty, slender build, is possibly armed with what is thought to be a thirty caliber rifle. No further description at this time, or information. 12:45. KTB

CRONKITE: During this period, the Dallas police radio broadcast a description of a suspect, and critics have made much of the speed with which it was sent out—just fifteen minutes after the shots were fired. It asked officers to be on the lookout for a white man, slender, weighing about 165, standing about five feet ten inches, in his early thirties.

Well, how did police get the description on the air in fifteen minutes? Critics have questioned both the source of the description and the speed with which it was sent out. The Warren Commission admitted the source could only be guessed at. Its own guess was that it came from Howard L. Brennan, an eyewitness. The critics doubt Brennan had a good enough view of Oswald in the window to arrive at a good description. They also doubt he passed the information on to a Secret Serviceman within ten minutes, as he later claimed.

At 1:15 P.M., forty-five minutes after the assassination, the Commission Report says, Officer Tippit stopped Oswald, whether because of the description or not will never be known, and was shot down. But did Oswald have time to get to Tenth and Patton in time for the fatal encounter with Tippit?

RATHER: A CBS newsman, following the Warren Commission blueprint, found that forty-five minutes was ample time.

CRONKITE: The answer is *yes*. He could have made his way there.

CRONKITE: Why was Officer Tippit in Oak Cliff off his normal beat? Those who believe there was a conspiracy involving the Dallas police force have maintained that the meeting between Oswald and Tippit was not an accident, that Tippit may have been looking for Oswald or vice versa. They say Tippit should not have been where he was and should not have been alone in the squad car. Eddie Barker talked to police radio dispatcher, Murray Jackson:

BARKER: Officer Jackson, a lot of critics of the Warren Report have made quite a thing out of the fact that Officer Tippit was not in his district when he was killed. Could you tell us how he happened to be out of his district?

MURRAY JACKSON: Yes, sir. I have heard this several times since the incident occurred. He was where he was because I had assigned him to be where he was in the central Oak Cliff area. There was the shooting involving the President, and we immediately dispatched every available unit to the triple underpass where the shot was reported to have come from.

I realized that we were draining the Oak Cliff area of available police officers, so if there was an emergency such as an armed robbery or a major accident to come up, we wouldn't have anybody there that would be in any close proximity to answer the call. And since J. D. was the outermost unit—actually I had two units: eighty-seven, which was Officer Nelson, and seventy-eight, which was Officer Tippit.

BARKER: Well, now, is—you got down to the time when Officer Tippit met his death. What transpired right prior to that? Did you—were you aware of where he was all the time?

JACKSON: No, I asked him once again what his location was sometime after and to determine that he was in the Oak Cliff area, he said he was at Lancaster and Eighth, which is on the east side of Oak Cliff, on the—in the main business district. And I did ask him once again, a few minutes later what his—I called him to ask him his location, so I could keep track of him, where he was, in my mind, but he didn't answer.

BARKER: When did you realize that he was dead?

JACKSON: We had received a call from a citizen. They called us on the telephone and the call sheet came—came to me, and there was a disturbance in the street in the 400 block of East Tenth. And I had called. I said, "seventy-eight," and he didn't answer. And almost immediately to this, a citizen came in on the police radio and said, "Send me some help. There's been an officer shot out here." And knowing that J. D. was the only one that should have been in Oak Cliff, my reaction was to call seventy-eight, and of course, J. D. didn't answer. So, we asked the citizen to look at the—the number on the side of the car. This was the equipment number that determined which car, which patrol car, was to be on each assigned district, and they said that it was Number Ten. And since I had worked with J. D. in this particular car, well, I determined to myself that with him not answering, and the equipment number, that this was Officer Tippit.

CRONKITE: The answer to this question is that he had been sent to Oak Cliff by the police dispatcher. Opponents of the Warren Report maintain that Officer Tippit was shot, not by Oswald, but by others. Who shot Officer Tippit? Eddie Barker talked to two witnesses who were on the scene of the Tippit murder. First, Domingo Benavides, who was at the wheel of a truck across the street from the scene.

DOMINGO BENAVIDES: As I was driving down the street, I seen this police car, was sitting here, and the officer was getting out of the car, and apparently he'd been talking to the man that was standing by the car. The policeman got out of the car, and as he walked past the windshield of the car, where it's kind of lined up over the hood of the car, where this other man shot him. And, of course, he was reaching for his gun.

And so, I was standing there, you know, I mean sitting there in the truck, and not in no big hurry to get out because I was sitting there watching everything. This man turned from the car then, and took a couple of steps, and as he turned to walk away I believe he was unloading his gun, and he took the shells up in his hand, and as he took off, he threw them in the bushes more or less like nothing really, trying to get rid of them. I guess he didn't figure he'd get caught anyway, so he just threw them in the bushes.

But he—as he started to turn to walk away, well, he stopped and looked back at me, and I don't know if he figured, well, I'll just let this poor guy go, or he had nothing to do with it, or, you know, I'm not out to kill everybody, just, you know, whoever gets in my way, I guess. I gave him enough time to get around the house. Thinking he might have went in the house, I set there for maybe a second or two and then jumped out of the truck and run over. As I walked by, I didn't even slow down, I seen the officer's dead. So I just walked on—got in the car and I figured that would be the fastest way—in fact, I don't know why I called him on the radio. I just figured now that it was the fastest way to —to get a police officer out.

POLICE RADIO: Hello, police operator [STATIC], go ahead. Hello, we've got a shooting out here. Where's it at? This is the police radio. What location is it at? Between Marsalis and Beckley. It's a police officer. Somebody shot him. What—what—it's in a police car, Number Ten. Hello, police operator, did you get that? Police officer, 510 East Jefferson. Thank you. Thirty-five, assist the police . . .

BARKER: Well, now, did several other people come up later?

BENAVIDES: Immediately afterwards. I mean, it was just—all I had to do was—people I asked a block away like Mr. Callaway, he come up and he says, let's go get him, or something. And then this cab pulled up right afterwards, and so Callaway went over and took the guns—the officer's gun out of his hand.

BARKER: Callaway did go after him, did he?

BENAVIDES: Yeah, Callaway took off to go try to catch him.

TED CALLAWAY: Well, Eddie, I was standing on the front porch of the used car lot that I worked on here, and all of a sudden I heard some shooting.

In fact, I heard five shots coming from the direction behind the lot, out on Tenth Street there. Well, I come running off the side of the porch and out to the sidewalk here, and I looked up the street, and I saw this man run through this hedge up here on the corner. And I saw right away that he had a gun in his hand. And he continued across the street coming in this direction. So when he got right across from me over here, just, oh, about thirty yards or less, why, I called to him and just asked him, "Hey, man, what the hell's goin' on, fella?" That's just exactly what I wondered. I didn't know who it was at the time, of course. And he looked in my direction and paused, almost stopped, and said something to me, but I couldn't make out what he said. But he had this pistol in his hand, carrying it in what we used to call in the Marine Corps a raised pistol position, and then he slowed down and started walking.

Then, I ran to the corner of Tenth and Patton, and when I got there, I saw this squad car parked near the curb. And then I walked around in front of the squad car, and this policeman was lying in front of the squad car.

BARKER: Dom, what about those expended shells?

BENAVIDES: Well, they were looking all over the place for evidence, I guess, and taking fingerprints and what have you. So, I guessed they was going to walk off and leave them, you know, not knowing they was there. And seeing that I knew where they was at, I walked over and—and picked up a stick and picked them up and put them in a waistcoat pocket. I think I picked up two and put them in a waistcoat pocket, and then, as I was walking up, I picked the other one up by hand, I believe. And I picked them up with a stick, you know, to keep from leaving fingerprints on them, because I figured they might need them.

CRONKITE: The cartridges that Benavides picked up were positively identified as being fired in Oswald's revolver. But, only one of the four lead bullets removed from Officer Tippit's body could be positively identified with that revolver by Illinois ballistics identification expert, Joseph Nicol.

NICOL: In the examination of the projectiles, the tests and the—and the evidence projectiles were not easily matched because of a certain mechanical problem with the weapon. The—the barrel was over-sized for the size of the ammunition used, since this was a weapon originally intended for British use, and it was reimported into America.

This means that the bullet, instead of touching on all surfaces going down the barrel, actually wobbles a little bit as it goes through the barrel. As a consequence, it is difficult to have it strike the same places every time that it goes through the barrel.

So that the—the match on the—on the projectiles was extremely difficult.

I did find, however, that on the driving edge of the lense there were certain groups of lines which I could match on one bullet. I wasn't able to identify the others, although there was nothing to exclude them insofar as the class characteristics. All of them could have been fired in that particular weapon.

CRONKITE: One of the bullets that killed Officer Tippit was fired in Oswald's revolver. The other three could have been, according to the ballistics identification expert. Ted Callaway went to the police station that night and made a positive identification of Oswald in a line-up. But Mr. Benavides did not do so. Eddie Barker asked him if he were sure Oswald did the shooting.

BARKER: Is there any doubt in your mind that Oswald was the man you had seen shoot Tippit?

BENAVIDES: No, sir, there was no doubt at all. I could even tell you how he combed his hair and the clothes he wore and what have you, all the details. And if he had a scar on his face, I could probably have told you about it, but—you don't forget things like that.

CRONKITE: The answer to this question, despite the problem of the ballistic evidence, is that Lee Harvey Oswald shot J. D. Tippit.

What of the theory that Tippit actually knew Oswald? It's not easy to prove that someone did not know someone else. But every attempt to pin down the rumor that the two men knew each other has ended in failure. There is nothing in the circumstances surrounding Tippit's death to suggest any kind of conspiracy.

Mrs. Tippit says flatly that neither she nor her husband knew Oswald. Officer Jackson was among Tippit's closest friends and had been for years. Eddie Barker put the question to him.

BARKER: Do you have any reason to believe that Officer Tippit knew Lee Harvey Oswald?

JACKSON: I don't believe there is a possible connection at all. No. I don't think that he knew Oswald.

BARKER: Did you know Oswald?

JACKSON: No, I didn't either.

RATHER: Thirty-five minutes after Officer Tippit's murder Oswald was captured in the Texas Theatre. Johnny Brewer, a shoe clerk, had spotted him in the doorway, and watched while he slipped into the theatre. Brewer spoke to the cashier. She called police.

The next forty-eight hours were filled with confusion. An army of newsmen jammed into the Dallas Police Building. Oswald was paraded through the halls, to and from questioning sessions.

Police Chief Jesse Curry and District Attorney Henry Wade said repeatedly they expected to prove Oswald guilty, although he maintained to the last he was not.

No record was made of his interrogation.

Sunday, November twenty-fourth, the mob scene continues, as Oswald is brought into the basement of the Police Building for transfer to the jail. And then, in full sight of millions of television viewers, a man named Jack Ruby surges through the crowd and shoots Lee Oswald dead.

CRONKITE: Why? A fateful meeting of deranged minds? Or some twisted conspiracy? Why did Ruby kill Oswald?

RATHER: This is the world of Jack Ruby. A world of neon and female flesh, of bumps and grinds, and watered drinks.

Ruby operated a pair of sleazy nightclubs, The Carousel and The Vegas. In the free and easy atmosphere that seemed to characterize the boom city, Ruby was also a hanger-on of the police, entertaining off-duty officers in his strip joints, often carrying sandwiches over to the Police Building for his on-duty friends.

These are some of the people of Jack Ruby's world—his roommate, a competing nightclub owner, and two of Jack Ruby's girls.

Mr. Weinstein, why do you think Jack Ruby shot Lee Harvey Oswald?

BARNEY WEINSTEIN: I think it was on the spur of the moment, that he really wanted to make himself look like a big man. And he thought that would make him above everybody else, that the people would come up and thank him for it, that people would come around and want to meet him and want to know him, "This is the man that shot the man that shot the President."

RATHER: Why do you think Jack shot Oswald?

ALICE: Oh, I think that it was mostly an impulsive act. And Jack also, I believe, felt that so many people at the time were saying, "They ought to kill him," and this and that, that he—in my personal opinion, Jack thought this would just bring him a—a sensational amount of business, and he would just really be a hero.

RATHER: Diana, why do you think Jack shot Oswald?

DIANA: I think that he came down there just to see what was going on, and when he saw that sneer on Oswald's face—that's all it would take to snap Jack, the way Oswald's mouth was curled up, you could even see it in the picture. I think when he saw that look was when he decided to shoot him. Not when he was coming down. And I think he did it because he thought that it was a service to his country, in his way of thinking. That was the way he thought.

GEORGE SENATOR: I don't believe that Jack Ruby ever took any secrets to his grave. I've been—I've been around him too long, and I've lived with him too long. And I'm certain he told the truth right up until his death. And I'll never can be—and I'll never be convinced otherwise. There is nothing he ever hid. The public knew everything he ever said, or heard.

CRONKITE: Jack Ruby was convicted of the murder of Oswald, but the conviction was reversed by an Appeals Court which held that an alleged confession should not have been admitted.

Ruby died six months ago of cancer, maintaining to the last that he was no conspirator, that he had killed Oswald out of anger and a desire to shield Jacqueline Kennedy from the ordeal of a trial at which she would have had to appear as a witness.

Dallas police had alerted the press that Oswald would be moved to the County Jail shortly after 10:00 A.M. on November twenty-fourth. That departure was delayed. Yet a receipt shows that Ruby was sending a money order to one of his strippers from a Western Union office across from the courthouse at 11:17 A.M., when anyone premeditating murder in the courthouse basement would already have stationed himself there. In fact, it was probably the activity around the courthouse entrance which caught Jack Ruby's eye as he left the Western Union office. Ruby was carrying a pistol because he was carrying money. He was accustomed to wander in and out of the Police Building at will.

The Oswald murder today still appears to have been not a conspiracy, but an impulse—meaningless violence born of meaningless violence.

But the most recent, most spectacular development in the Oswald case involves the CIA. It involves, too, the spectacular district attorney of New Orleans, a man they call the *Jolly Green Giant*. It involves an arrest, hypnotism, truth serum, bribery charges, and for the first time, an outline of a conspiracy. It certainly accounts for the recent national upsurge of suspicion concerning the conclusions of the Warren Report. And it raises a new question: Was the assassination plotted in New Orleans?

Mike Wallace reports.

WALLACE: New Orleans District Attorney Jim Garrison quietly began his own investigation of the assassination last fall. In a sense he picked up where the Warren Commission had left off. Warren investigators questioned a number of people in New Orleans after the assassination, and they failed to implicate any of them. But the more Garrison went back over old ground, apparently, the more fascinated he became with the possibility that a plot to kill President Kennedy actually began in New Orleans. By the time the story of his investigation broke four months ago, he seemed supremely confident that he could make a case, that he had solved the assassination.

GARRISON: Because I certainly wouldn't say with confidence that we would make arrests and have convictions afterwards if I did not know that we had solved the assassination of President Kennedy beyond any shadow of a doubt. I can't imagine that people would think that—that I would guess and say something like that rashly. There's no question about it. We know what cities were involved, we know how it was done in—in the essential respects. We know the key individuals involved. And we're in the process of developing evidence now. I thought I made that clear days ago.

WALLACE: He shocked New Orleans four months ago by arresting the socially prominent Clay Shaw, former director of the New Orleans International Trade Mart.

Garrison's charge was that Shaw had conspired with two other men to plot the assassination of President Kennedy. Garrison said Shaw had known David Ferrie, an eccentric former airline pilot who was found dead a week before Garrison had planned to arrest him. Incidentally, the coroner said Ferrie died of natural causes. But Garrison called it suicide.

He said Shaw also knew Lee Harvey Oswald; that Ferrie, Oswald, and Shaw met one night in the summer of 1963 and plotted the President's death. Clay Shaw said it was all fantastic.

SHAW: I am completely innocent of any such charges. I have not conspired with anyone, at any time, or any place, to murder our late and esteemed President John F. Kennedy, or any other individual. I have always had only the highest and utmost respect and admiration for Mr. Kennedy.

The charges filed against me have no foundation in fact or in law. I have not been apprised of the basis of these fantastic charges, and assume that in due course I will be furnished with this information, and will be afforded an opportunity to prove my innocence.

I did not know Harvey Lee Oswald, nor did I ever see or talk with him, or anyone who knew him at any time in my life.

WALLACE: A preliminary hearing for Shaw was held two weeks after his arrest. The hearing was complete with a surprise mystery witness, Perry Raymond Russo, twenty-five-year-old insurance salesman, and friend of the late David Ferrie. Through three days of intense cross-examination Russo held doggedly to his story, that he himself had been present when Shaw, Ferrie, and Oswald plotted the Kennedy assassination. Russo admitted at the hearing that he had been hypnotized three times by Garrison men.

A writer for the *Saturday Evening Post* said he read transcripts of what went on at those sessions. The writer suggested that Russo's entire performance at the hearing was the product of post-hypnotic suggestion. Clay Shaw was ordered held for trial. It could be months before the trial actually takes place.

Meanwhile, various news organizations have reported serious charges against Jim Garrison and his staff, alleging bribery, intimidation, and efforts to plant and/or manufacture evidence against Shaw. Last month *Newsweek* magazine said Garrison's office had tried to bribe Alvin Beauboeuf, the twenty-one-year-old former friend of David Ferrie. Beauboeuf, the magazine said, was offered three thousand dollars to supply testimony that would shore up the conspiracy charge against Shaw.

Garrison promptly released an affidavit Beauboeuf had signed. The affidavit said no one working for Garrison had ever asked Beauboeuf to tell anything but the truth.

Subsequently, New Orleans police investigated the Beauboeuf charge and said Garrison's men had been falsely accused. But that was just the beginning. Three more bribery accusations have since come to light, two involving Louisiana prison inmates, one involving a nightclub and Turkish Bath operator. In each of those cases the charges are that rewards were offered in return for allegedly false testimony or other help that would implicate Clay Shaw. We will hear Garrison's comment on those charges later in the broadcast.

Meanwhile, Garrison has gone on to include Jack Ruby in the alleged conspiracy involving Shaw and Lee Harvey Oswald. Garrison says Jack Ruby's unlisted telephone number in 1963 appears in code in address books belonging to Shaw and Oswald. He says both books note the Dallas Post Office box number 19106. Ruby's unlisted phone number was WHitehall 1-5601. And Garrison furnished a complicated formula for converting PO 19106 to WH 1-5601.

Louisiana Senator Russell Long, appearing on *Face the Nation* a few days later, explained how the code works.

LONG: . . . so if you take the P and the O, and you use a telephone dial, P gives you seven, O gives you six. You add seven and six together and you get thirteen. Then you take the 19106, and you work on a A B C D E F—the A B C D E basis, so you put A—A falls—comes ahead of E. Then you put D behind C. And you reconstruct the numbers, and that—and then you subtract thirteen hundred, which you got for the P O, and that gives you Ruby's unlisted telephone number.

WALLACE: A Dallas businessman named Lee Odom had that Dallas Post Office box for a while in 1966. He said he didn't know how the number got in Oswald's address book, but he could explain how it got in Shaw's. Odom said he met Shaw when he went to New Orleans looking for a place to hold a bloodless bullfight.

ODOM: When I got to New Orleans, and I got there—it was late, and so I wanted to see what New Orleans—my first trip to New Orleans. And I went to Pat O'Brien's, and that's where I met Mr. Shaw. I was sitting, drinking at the bar, and he was sitting next to me, and I got to talking to him about the—if he thought a bullfight might go over good in—in New Orleans. And he said that he thought it would, and we introduced each other. He was in the real estate business, and said he might be able to help me. So the next day, why, we had lunch together, and tried to find out about a place to have a bullfight. Made two or three phone calls, and— we didn't find any place. So when I got ready to leave there, I give him my name and my box number, which I saw him write in his little book. And I never heard from him after that. But that's how the number got in the book.

WALLACE: The number 19106 does appear in Oswald's address book, although some say the letters in front of it are not P O, but Russian letters. No one knows when Oswald made the entry.

Garrison has expanded the scope of his charges to include not only a Shaw-Oswald-Ruby link, but the CIA as well. Further, Garrison says he knows that five anti-Castro Cuban guerrillas, not Lee Harvey Oswald, killed President Kennedy. He says the CIA is concealing both the names and the whereabouts of the Cubans.

In an interview with Bob Jones of WWL-TV, New Orleans, he discussed proof that the guerrillas were there at Dealey Plaza in Dallas.

GARRISON: We have even located photographs in which we can— we have found the—the men behind the grassy knoll, and the—and the stone wall, before they dropped completely out of sight. There were five of them. Three behind the stone wall, and two behind the grassy knoll. And they're not quite out of sight. And they've been located in other photographs, by process of bringing them out. Although they're not distinct enough you can make an identification from their faces.

WALLACE: This is one of the photographs Garrison is talking about, shown first with an overlay. Those roughly-drawn figures at the bottom of the page could be the men Garrison believes he sees through the little holes at the top. Now we remove the overlay to see the photograph itself—a hazy blowup of an area from a larger picture. If there are men up there behind the wall, they definitely cannot be seen with the naked eye.

I asked Garrison if he would sort it all out, if he could summarize his investigation, and put it in perspective.

GARRISON: About the New Orleans part, I don't like to sound coy, but it is impossible to talk about the New Orleans details without touching somehow on the case. And I'm not going to take any chances about reflecting on Mr. Shaw, or this case. We've worked too hard for me to ruin it by casual comment.

WALLACE: Four months ago you said that you had solved the assassination. At that time you didn't even know Perry Russo. And yet Perry Russo, it turns out, is your main witness in the preliminary hearing.

GARRISON: Right.

WALLACE: Is he still your main witness?

GARRISON: No.

WALLACE: Are there others?

GARRISON: No. There are others, and I would not describe Perry Russo as the main witness. But let me say this, that the major part of our case, up to that time, was circumstantial. Again, I don't want to touch in any way on the case against the defendant, but we knew months before that the key people involved but there was no basis for moving at that time.

WALLACE: You say that Lee Harvey Oswald did not kill President Kennedy. Who, then, did kill him?

GARRISON: Well, first of all, if I knew the names of the individuals behind the grassy knoll, where we know they were, and the stone wall, I certainly would not tell you, and couldn't here. There is no question about the fact they were there. There's no question in our minds what the dominant race of these individuals was. And there's no question about the motive. In the course of time we will have the names of every one of them. The reason for Officer Tippit's murder is simply this: It was necessary for them to get rid of the decoy in the case—Lee Oswald . . . Lee Oswald. Now, in order to get rid of him—so that he would not later describe the people involved in this, they had what I think is a rather clever plan. It's well known that police officers react violently to the murder of a police officer. All they did was arrange for an officer to be sent out to Tenth Street, and when Officer Tippit arrived there he was murdered, with no other reason than that. Now, after he was murdered, Oswald was pointed to, sitting in the back of the Texas Theater where he'd been told to wait, obviously.

Now, the idea was, quite apparently, that Oswald would be killed in the Texas Theater when he arrived, because he'd killed a "bluecoat." That's the way the officers in New Orleans use the phrase. "He killed a bluecoat." But the Dallas police, at least the arresting Dallas police, fooled them, becaues they had, apparently, too much humanity in them, and they did not kill him.

WALLACE: All right, there is Lee Harvey Oswald at the back of the Texas Theater—then what?

GARRISON: Well, then notification is gotten to the police of this suspicious man in the back of the theater, and you know the rest. But the—the Dallas police, apparently, at least the arresting police officers, had more humanity in them than the planners had in mind. And this is the first point at which the plan did not work completely. So Oswald was not killed there. He was arrested. This left a problem, because if Lee Oswald stayed alive long enough, obviously he would name names and talk about this thing that he'd been drawn into. It was necessary to kill him.

WALLACE: That's where Jack Ruby comes into the picture.

GARRISON: That's right. It was necessary for one of the people involved to kill him.

WALLACE: Mr. Garrison, obviously we're not going to try the case of Clay Shaw here on television, but some people, some journalists and others, have charged that you have tried to bribe, to hypnotize, to drug witnesses in order to prove your case against Shaw.

GARRISON: That's right. I understand that the latest—latest news by a *New York Times* writer is that we offered an ounce of heroin and three months' vacation to one—as a matter of fact, this is part of our incentive program for convicts. We also have six weeks in the Bahamas, and give them some LSD to get there.

This—this—this attitude of skepticism on the part of the press is an astonishing thing to me, and a new thing to me. They have a problem with my office. And one of the problems is that we have no political appointments. Most of our men are selected by recommendations of deans of law schools. They work 9:00 to 5:00, and we have a highly professional office. I think one of the best in the country. So they're reduced to making up these fictions. We have not intimidated a witness since the day I came in office.

WALLACE: One question is asked again and again: Why doesn't Jim Garrison give his information, if it is valid information, why doesn't he give it to the federal government? Now that everything is out in the open, the CIA could hardly stand in your way again, could they? Why don't you take this information that you have and cooperate with the federal government?

GARRISON: Well, that would be one approach, Mike. Or I could take my files and take them up on the Mississippi River Bridge and throw them in the river. It'd be about the same result.

WALLACE: You mean, they just don't want any other solution from that in the Warren Report?

GARRISON: Well, isn't that kind of obvious? Where do you think that pressure's coming from, that prevents witnesses and defendants from being brought back to our state?

WALLACE: Where is that pressure coming from?

GARRISON: It's coming from Washington, obviously.

WALLACE: For what reason?

GARRISON: Because there are individuals in Washington who do not want the truth about the Kennedy murder to come out.

WALLACE: Where are those individuals? Are they in the White House? Are they in the CIA? Are they in the FBI? Where are they?

GARRISON: I think the probability is that you'll find them in the Justice Department and the Central Intelligence Agency.

WALLACE: You're asking a good many questions, but you haven't got the answers to those questions. You have a theory as to why indeed the President might have been assassinated by a group of dissidents. . . .

GARRISON: No. Your statement is incorrect. We have more than a theory. We have conversations about the assassination of the President of the United States, and it does not include only the conversation brought out at the preliminary hearing.

We have money passed, with regard to the assassination of the President of the United States. We have individuals involved in the planning. And we can make the case completely. I can't make any more comments about the case, except to say anybody that thinks it's just a theory is going to be awfully surprised when it comes to trial.

WALLACE: Garrison says Clay Shaw used the alias Clay Bertrand, or Clem Bertrand. At Shaw's preliminary hearing Perry Russo testified that Shaw used the name Clem Bertrand the night of the alleged meeting to plot the assassination. It was obviously a crucial point in Garrison's presentation at that hearing.

But a week ago NBC said it has discovered that Clay Bertrand is not Clay Shaw. NBC said the man who uses that alias is a New Orleans homosexual, whose real name—not disclosed in the broadcast—has been turned over to the Justice Department.

CRONKITE: Garrison's problems multiplied yesterday. His chief aide, William Gurvich, who conferred recently with Senator Robert Kennedy, abruptly resigned.

Gurvich was questioned by Bill Reed, News Director of WWL-TV, New Orleans, and CBS News reporter Edward Rabel.

RABEL: Mr. Gurvich, why did you resign as Mr. Garrison's chief aide in this investigation?

GURVICH: I was very dissatisfied with the way the investigation was being conducted, and I saw no reason for the investigation— and decided that if the job of an investigator is to find the truth, then I was to find it. I found it. And this led to my resignation.

RABEL: Well, what then is the truth?

GURVICH: The truth, as I see it, is that Mr. Shaw should never have been arrested.

RABEL: Why did you decide to see Senator Robert Kennedy?

GURVICH: Ed, I went to Senator Kennedy because he was a brother of the late President Kennedy, to tell him we could shed no light on the death of his brother, and not to be hoping for such. After I told him that, he appeared to be rather disgusted to think that someone was exploiting his brother's death, and—by bringing it up, over and over again, and doing what has been done in this investigation.

REED: There's been talk of allegations, of wrong-doing, of coercion, of possible bribery on the part of investigators—of certain investigators for the district attorney. To your knowledge, are these allegations true?

GURVICH: Unquestionably, things have happened in the district attorney's office that definitely warrants an investigation by the Parish Grand Jury, as well as the Federal Grand Jury.

REED: Would you say these methods were illegal?

GURVICH: I would say very illegal, and unethical.

REED: Can you give us any specifics?

GURVICH: I would rather save that for the grand juries, Bill, if I may.

REED: Is this on the part of just one or two investigators, or does it involve the whole staff, or perhaps Mr. Garrison . . .

GURVICH: It involves more than two people.

REED: More than two people. Do you believe Mr. Garrison had knowledge of these activities?

GURVICH: Yeah—of course, he did. He ordered it.

REED: He ordered it?

GURVICH: He ordered it. Yes, sir.

RABEL: Why did he feel it was necessary to order such activities?

GURVICH: That I cannot explain. I am not a psychiatrist.

REED: Mr. Garrison said the CIA has attempted to block his investigation . . .

GURVICH: His purpose for bringing the CIA in, Bill, is this: As he put it, they can't afford to answer. He can say what he damn well pleases about that agency, and they'll never reply.

CRONKITE: Mr. Garrison is the only critic who has been in a position to act on his beliefs. He has brought Clay Shaw before the courts of Louisiana, and until that case is tried we cannot, with propriety, go deep into the details of the evidence, or reach any final conclusions concerning the case or the allegations concerning Clay Shaw.

Mr. Garrison's public statements, however—and there's been no shortage of them—are fair targets. They have consistently promised startling proof, but until the trial Mr. Garrison's promises remain just that, and cannot be tested.

But the whole atmosphere of his investigations, and the charges that have been made by news organizations concerning it, are not such as to inspire confidence. It may be that Garrison will finally show that there was a lunatic fringe in dark and devious conspiracy. But, so far, he has shown us nothing to link the events he alleges to have taken place in New Orleans, and the events we know to have taken place in Dallas.

Those events, events surrounding the assassination itself, we have now examined to the best of our ability. On Sunday night we considered whether Lee Harvey Oswald had shot the President. We concluded that he had. Last night we asked if there was more than one assassin. We concluded there was not, and that Oswald was a sole assassin.

Tonight we've asked if there was a conspiracy involving perhaps Officer Tippit, Jack Ruby, or others. The answer here cannot be as firm as our other answers, partly because of the difficulty, cited in the Warren Report, of proving something did not happen. But partly, too, because there remains a question as to just what Jim Garrison will produce in that New Orleans courtroom.

But on the basis of the evidence now in hand at least, we still can find no convincing indication of such a conspiracy. If we put those three conclusion together, they seem to CBS News to tell just one story—Lee Harvey Oswald, alone, and for reasons all his own, shot and killed President Kennedy. It is too much to expect that the critics of the Warren Report will be satisfied with the conclusions CBS News has reached, any more than they were satisfied with the conclusions the Commission reached.

Mark Lane, for example, the most vocal of all the critics, has a theory of his own.

BILL STOUT: If you would give us, briefly, Mr. Lane, your version of what happened there that day.

LANE: Well, I think—if I can use this model, I think the evidence indicates—of course, the car came down Main, up here, and down to Elm Street, and was approximately here when the first shot was fired. The first shot struck the President in the back of the right shoulder, according to the FBI report, and indicates therefore that it came from some place in the rear—which includes the possibility of it coming from the Book Depository building.

The second bullet struck the President in the throat from the front, came from behind this wooden fence, high up on a grassy knoll. Two more bullets were fired. One struck the Elm—the Main Street curb, and caused some concrete, or lead, to scatter up and strike a spectator named James Tague in the face. Another bullet, fired from the rear, struck Governor Connally in the back. As the limousine moved up to approximately this point, another bullet was fired from the right front, struck the President in the head, drove him—his body, to the left and to the rear, and drove a portion of his skull backward, to the left and to the rear. Five bullets, fired from at least two different directions, the result of a conspiracy.

CRONKITE: An even more elaborate account is given by William Turner, a former FBI agent, who has become a warm supporter of District Attorney Garrison.

TURNER: Now, what happened there was that the Kennedy motorcade coming down there, the Kennedy limousine—there were shots from the rear, from either the Dallas School Book Depository building, or the Dell Mart, or the courthouse; and there were shots from the grassy knoll. This is triangulation. There is no escape from it, if it's properly executed.

I think that the massive head wound, where the President's head was literally blown apart, came from a quartering angle on the grassy knoll. The bullet was a low velocity dum-dum mercury fulminate hollow-nose, which were outlawed by The Hague Convention, but which are used by paramilitary groups. And that the whole reaction is very consistent to this kind of weapon. That he was struck, and his head—doesn't go directly back this way, but it goes back and over this way, which would be consistent with the shot from that direction, and Newton's Law of Motion.

Now, I feel also that the escape was very simple. Number one, using a revolver or a pistol, the shells do not eject, they don't even have to bother to pick up their discharged shells. Number two, they can slip—put the gun under their coat, and when everybody comes surging up there they can just say, "He went that-a-way." Very simple. In fact, it's so simple that it probably happened that way.

CRONKITE: In the light of what we have exposed over the past three evenings, it's difficult to take such versions seriously. But unquestionably there are those who will do so, and it is their privilege.

Our own task is not yet over. We must still ask whether the Warren Commission did all that was asked of it, whether other arms of the government acted as they should have acted, whether another commission might cast new light upon the assassination. We must ask also whether there are fundamental and profound human reasons for the aura of disbelief that surrounds the Warren Report. We will deal with all those matters tomorrow night, in the last portion of this inquiry.

But this is a natural moment to pause, and to sum up what we think we have learned.

Dan, you were in Dealey Plaza on the day of the assassination. You've been back there several times since, when we did the first Warren Report, and now in recent days to prepare this report. You've been up in that window. We've looked out that window with you. But, subjectively, what is the Oswald-eye view of the assassination site?

RATHER: It was an easy shot. A much easier shot than even it looks in our pictures. The range was such, the angle was such, that it did not take an expert shot, one man, to do what the Warren Commission says was done from there.

CRONKITE: Eddie, as news director of our esteemed affiliate, KRLD-TV in Dallas, you've been right in the vortex of this thing since the moment of the assassination. What about the people of Dallas themselves? Do they agree with the Warren Commission Report?

BARKER: Walter, I think that on a cross-section basis, the percentage that had some doubt about it would be about what it would be across the country. Certainly there are people who have some doubts about it. But most of the doubters, I think, are those who come to Dallas, and who come into our newsroom, as a matter of fact. They bring a lot of questions. But so far none of them have brought any answers.

CRONKITE: That's the problem we all have, isn't it? And let me ask each of you in turn this question: Are you contented with the basic finding of the Warren Commission?

RATHER: I'm contented with the basic finding of the Warren Commission, that the evidence is overwhelming that Oswald fired at the President, and that Oswald probably killed President Kennedy alone. I am not content with the findings on Oswald's possible connections with government agencies, particularly with the CIA. I'm not totally convinced that at some earlier time, unconnected with the assassination, that Oswald may have had more connections than we've been told about, or that have been shown. I'm not totally convinced about the single-bullet theory. But I don't think it's absolutely necessary to the final conclusion of the Warren Commission Report. I would have liked more questioning, a more thorough going into Marina Oswald's background. But as to the basic conclusion, I agree.

CRONKITE: Eddie?

BARKER: I agree with it, Walter. It's too bad, of course, that Oswald didn't have his day in court. But I felt the night of

November twenty-second that he was the one who had shot the President, and nothing has come to light since then to change my opinion a bit.

CRONKITE: It is difficult to be totally content. Yet experience teaches all of us that any complex human event that is examined scrupulously and in detail will reveal improbabilities, inconsistencies, awkward gaps in our knowledge. Only in fiction do we find all the loose ends neatly tied. That is one of the ways we identify something as fiction.

Real life is not all that tidy. In 1943 Lieutenant John F. Kennedy came under enemy fire behind Japanese lines in the Pacific. His PT boat was destroyed. His back, already weak, was reinjured. Yet he swam three miles, towing a wounded shipmate, found shelter on an island, escaped Japanese search, encountered natives who carried messages back to American forces, crossed undetected through enemy waters as enemy planes hovered overhead, and survived to become President.

The account of his survival is full of improbabilities, coincidences, unknowns. So is the account of his death. So would be the account of your life, or mine, or the life of any one of us.

Concerning the events of November twenty-second, 1963, in Dealey Plaza, the report of the Warren Commission is probably as close as we can ever come now to the truth. And yet if the Warren Commission had acted otherwise three years ago, if other government agencies had done differently then, would we today be even closer to the truth?

Tomorrow we will consider not the assassination, but the work of the Commission that was appointed to study it. For the first time a member of that Commission, John J. McCloy, will publicly discuss its work and its findings. Members of the Commission staff, and one of the Commission's most persuasive critics, Edward J. Epstein, will be heard. And we will ask, although we may not be able to answer, two last questions:

Should America believe the Warren Report?

Could America believe the Warren Report?

CBS NEWS INQUIRY: "The Warren Report"

PART IV   *As broadcast over the* CBS TELEVISION NETWORK
Wednesday, June 28, 1967

WALTER CRONKITE: Good evening. For the past three nights we have been examining the circumstances of the assassination of President John F. Kennedy. On Sunday, we returned to Dealey Plaza to re-create that fatal motorcade ride beneath the windows of the Texas School Book Depository.

Believing that rifle tests conducted by the Warren Commission were less than adequate, we conducted new tests, more closely simulating the conditions of the actual murder. We found hitherto undiscovered evidence in film of the murder itself, that the killer had more time than the minimal 5.6 seconds indicated in the Warren Report to get the shots off. And we concluded that beyond reasonable doubt, Oswald was indeed at least one of the killers.

But was there more than one? On Monday night we interviewed eyewitnesses who said all the shots came from the School Book Depository; and others equally insistent that there were shots from the grassy knoll overlooking the motorcade itself.

We tested more exhaustively than did the Warren Commission the extremely controversial single-bullet theory, found that one bullet could, indeed, have wounded both the President and Governor Connally. We heard autopsy surgeon, James Humes, break three and a half years of silence to report that he has re-examined the X-rays and photographs of the President's body, and still has no doubt that all the shots struck from behind.

We concluded that in the absence of solid evidence that there were other assassins, and with the indications that one killer could account for all the shots, there was no second gunman. But, even as the only gunman, was Oswald, as the Warren Report suggests, a lone madman? Or was he the trigger-man for a conspiracy to kill the President?

On Tuesday we considered such frequently mentioned indications of conspiracy as the murder of Officer J. D. Tippit, found that he was legitimately ordered from his normal patrol area as part of a redeployment of police forces to cope with the assassination; found, too, that a partial description of the assassin, broadcast on police radio, could account for Tippit's stopping Oswald.

We found the nightclub owner, Jack Ruby, the man who killed Oswald, was a strange, mercurial creature given to hitting first and asking questions afterward. And none of his closest associates would credit Ruby with the ability to keep a secret very long.

We presented the conspiracy theories of New Orleans District Attorney Jim Garrison, theories which Garrison says he will present in a court of law, but which today remain a series of largely unsupported statements. And we concluded that, for now at least, no conspiracy theory of the assassination has been proved.

Tonight we turn from the assassination to the Warren Commission itself. Having found that the Commission's conclusions, in the main, still stand up almost three years after published, we now ask our fourth and last fundamental question: Why doesn't America believe the Warren Report?

Tonight, as in our preceding reports, my colleague Dan Rather and I are going to break this fundamental question into subsidiary questions. For the first part of the broadcast, we will ask: *Should* America believe the Warren Report? We will explore just how well and honestly the Warren Commission operated, to what extent it deserves belief.

The second question will be: *Could* America believe the Warren Report? And we'll try to determine whether there are elements in the way people, and particularly Americans, think about great events, which would prevent their accepting the Warren Report, however trustworthy it might be.

But this final broadcast will be different. The questions we will ask tonight, we can only ask. Tonight's answers will be not ours, but yours.

RATHER: As we take up whether or not America should believe the Warren Report, we'll hear first from the man who perhaps more than any other is responsible for the question being asked. Mark Lane, lawyer and former New York state assemblyman, was the gadfly of the Warren Commission. He demanded the right to appear before it as a defense counsel for the dead Lee Harvey Oswald. Refused, he began his own investigation of the President's death, a study that produced first the best-selling attack on the Warren Commission, *Rush To Judgment*, and now a movie of the same name.

Mark Lane has lectured all over the world on his own theories of the assassination, theories which he spelled out for Bill Stout.

MARK LANE: There was one conclusion, one basic conclusion that the Commission reached, I think, which can be supported by the facts, and that was the Commission's conclusion that Ruby killed Oswald. But, of course, that took place on television. It would have been very difficult to deny that. But, outside of that there's not an important conclusion which can be supported by the facts and—and this is the problem.

And what the Commission was thinking and what they were doing is still hidden from us, of course. The minutes of the Commission meetings are locked up in the National Archives, and no one can see them. A vast amount of the evidence, FBI reports, CIA reports, which may be directly related to the information we should have, are also locked up in the Archives. No one can see that.

The photographs and X-rays of the President's body, taken at the autopsy in Bethesda, Maryland, taken just before the autopsy was begun, taken by Naval technicians, which in and of themselves might resolve the whole question as to whether or not there was a conspiracy, cannot be seen by anyone today, and in fact, not one member of the Warren Commission ever saw the most important documents in the case, the photographs and the X-rays. And not one lawyer for the Commission ever saw—was curious enough to examine the most important evidence.

I think the villain was the desire of government officials to be nice, to see to it that nothing would upset the American people, that the apathy which has seized us for all of these years be permitted to remain uninterrupted by a factual presentation of what happened. The American people would have been upset surely if they were told there was a conspiracy which took the life of your President.

CRONKITE: But Mr. Lane, who accuses the Commission of playing fast and loose with the evidence, does not always allow facts to get in the way of his own theories. In *Rush To Judgment,* for example, he writes: "The statements of eyewitnesses close to the President tended to confirm the likelihood that the shot came from the right and not from the rear." Lane then quotes Associated Press photographer James Altgens, and another eyewitness, Charles Brehm, as giving testimony that would support the idea of a killer on the grassy knoll. Yet Mr. Altgens, as we saw Monday night, is entirely certain that all of the shots came from behind, a fact that Mr. Lane does not mention.

As for Mr. Brehm, Eddie Barker discovered that he holds no brief either for the grassy knoll theory or for the use of his words by Mark Lane.

EDDIE BARKER: Well now, some critics of the Warren Report have taken your testimony, or interviews with you, to indicate that you thought the shots came from behind the fence over there. What about that?

CHARLES BREHM: Well, as I say, it was not a number of critics. It was one critic, Mark Lane, who takes very great liberties with adding to my quotation. I never said that the—any shot came from here like I was quoted by Mr. Lane. Mr. Lane would like me to have positively identified the—what I saw fly over here—his skull —although I told him I could not—I did not—I thought it was but I could not. So, he has added his interpretations to what I said, and consequently that's where the story comes from that—that I said that the shots come from up there. No shot came from up there at any time during the whole fiasco that afternoon.

CRONKITE: Nor are these the only examples of Mr. Lane lifting remarks out of context to support his theories. Perhaps the most charitable explanation is that Mark Lane still considers himself a defense attorney for Lee Harvey Oswald—and a defense attorney's primary duty is not to abstract truth, but to his client.

There exists, however, a less partisan, and therefore perhaps more disturbing critique of the Warren Commission Report.

RATHER: One of the most influential attacks on the work of the Commission is the book, *Inquest*, by a young scholar named Edward J. Epstein. It began as a thesis in Political Science, Mr. Epstein deciding to find out just how the Warren Commission had gone about solving this crime of the century.

He studied the twenty-six volumes of hearings, then interviewed five of the seven Commission members, General Counsel J. Lee Rankin and some of the Commission's top investigators. And the pattern that began to emerge disturbed him.

EPSTEIN: Well, there were three, I think, levels of complaint. The first one was the institutional, you might say: the general problem that a government has when it searches for truth. The problem of trying to have an autonomous investigation, free from political interference, and at the same time, it's dealing by its very nature with a political problem.

The second level might be called the organizational level of— was the Warren Commission organized in a way that prevented it from finding facts? And here my findings were that by using a part time staff and by the Commission's detaching themselves from the investigation—in other words, not actively partaking in the investigation—it raised some problems as to whether the Warren Commission's investigation went deep enough, so that if there was evidence of a conspiracy, they would have in fact found it.

The third level of my criticism concerned the evidence itself, and this concerned the problem of when the Warren Commission was come—confronted with a very complex problem. For example, the contradiction between the FBI summary report on the autopsy and the autopsy report they had in hand—how they solved this problem, whether they simply glossed over it or whether they called witnesses, and—and this—this, of course, brought up the questions of—of a second assassin.

RATHER: One of the men Mr. Epstein interviewed for his *Inquest* is Arlen Specter, now district attorney of Philadelphia, but in

1964, one of the principal investigators for the Warren Commission, charged with establishing the basic facts of the assassination. Mr. Specter thinks the Commission did its job well and came up with the right answers.

SPECTER: I would say after having prosecuted a great many cases that seldom would you ever find a case which was as persuasive that Oswald was the assassin, and in fact, the lone assassin, and and we convict people in the criminal courts every day right here in City Hall, Philadelphia. And the times the death penalties are imposed or life imprisonment—so that—so that the case does fit together.

RATHER: In separate interviews we asked critic Epstein and investigator Specter to discuss some of the central issues that must determine how well or how badly the Warren Commission did its work.

EPSTEIN: Part of the job of the Warren Commission was restoring confidence in the American Government. And for this he had to pick seven very respectable men, men who would lend their name and lend probity to the report. And so that the problem was, in any seven men he picked of this sort, they would have very little time for the investigation.

They would also have two purposes. One purpose would be to find the truth, all the facts. The other purpose would be to allay rumors, to dispel conspiracy theories and material of that sort.

SPECTER: My view is that there is absolutely no foundation for that type of a charge. When the President selected the commissioners, he chose men of unblemished reputation and very high standing. The Chief Justice of the Supreme Court of the United States would have no reason whatsoever to be expedient or to search for political truths. Nor would Allen W. Dulles, the former head of the CIA, nor would John McCloy, with his distinguished service in government, nor would the Congressional or Senatorial representatives.

Now, the same thing was true of the staff members. When it came time to select the individuals to serve as assistant counsel and general counsel, men were chosen from various parts of the United States who had no connection with government.

EPSTEIN: For example, there were rumors concerning the FBI or various intelligence agencies. I noticed that there were a number of memorandums where the—where—from Warren to the Secretary of the Treasury, who was in charge of the Secret Service, assuring that their findings wouldn't impair the efficiency or the morale of the Secret Service. And the same thing again with the FBI, a question of whether there was ever any possible connection between Oswald—and by connection I don't mean anything sinister, I simply meant that he was furnishing information and there were some rumors to this effect—and they, rather than investigating these rumors, they preferred to give it to the FBI to investigate the rumors themselves. As J. Lee Rankin, their general counsel, said, they would rather that agency clear its own skirts. Well, what this meant, of course, is that if the FBI would have discretion if it did find a connection between Oswald and itself, the discretion of either reporting it or not reporting it.

SPECTER: In the main, the FBI conducted the basic line of investigation. But the Commission used its independent judgment wherever, say, the FBI or the Secret Service was involved itself so that they would not investigate themselves on the subjects where they were directly involved, and I think the Commission showed its independence in that regard by criticizing the Federal Bureau of Investigation and by criticizing the Secret Service where the facts warranted such criticism.

On every subject where the Federal Bureau of Investigation had contact with the area of investigation with which I was intimately connected, I was fully satisfied with their thoroughness and with their competency and with their integrity.

CRONKITE: Despite Mr. Specter's defense, it is the opinion of CBS News that the role of the FBI as well as the Secret Service, both in the assassination and its aftermath, has been less than glorious. And, to some extent, the performance of these agencies weakens the credibility of the Warren Report. As to what the FBI and the Secret Service did wrong before the assassination, we need look no further than the Report itself.

It notes the Secret Service agents assigned to protect the President had been drinking beer and liquor into the early hours of the morning, that no search was made of buildings along the route, and that: "The procedures of the Secret Service, designed to identify and protect against persons considered serious threats to the President, were not adequate prior to the assassination." That is, the Secret Service should have known about Lee Harvey Oswald.

But the Report goes on to point out that if the Secret Service did not know about him, the FBI did, and did not see fit to mention his existence to the Secret Service. The report issues a mildly phrased yet devastating rebuke to the FBI, charging that it took an unduly restrictive view of its responsibilities. Knowing what the FBI knew about Oswald, the Report says, an alert agency should have listed him as a potential menace to the President. Yet, after the assassination, the Commission itself relied heavily on these two agencies as its investigative arms.

Did their performance improve? We know that some of the tests conducted by them for the Warren Commission were unsatisfactory. In the first of these broadcasts we pointed out that to simulate Oswald's problem of hitting a moving target from a sixty-foot-high perch, the FBI conducted its firing tests on a fixed target, from a thirty-foot height. Certainly, if CBS News could duplicate the conditions of the actual assassination for a firing test, the feat's not beyond the capability of the FBI.

RATHER: There is also the case of the famous exhibit 399, the bullet which the Commission thought wounded both the President and Governor Connally, winding up on the Governor's stretcher in Parkland Hospital. Critics of the Report, you will remember, insist it couldn't have hit both men, but must have been found on the President's stretcher. Yet, part of the now permanent confusion surrounding the bullet and where it was found, must be charged to the cavalier attitude of agents of both the FBI and the Secret Service at Parkland Hospital.

On Monday night, hospital attendant Darrell Tomlinson described how, in shoving a stretcher into place, he dislodged a spent rifle bullet. Mr. Tomlinson quite properly sent at once for the hospital's chief of security, O. P. Wright. Mr. Wright describes what happened then:

WRIGHT: I told him to withhold and not let anyone remove the bullet, and I would get a hold of either the Secret Service or the

FBI, and turn it over to them. Thereby, it wouldn't have come through my hands at all. I contacted the FBI and they said they were not interested because it wasn't their responsibility to make investigations. So, I got a hold of a Secret Serviceman and they didn't seem to be interested in coming and looking at the bullet in the position it was then in.

So I went back to the area where Mr. Tomlinson was and picked up the bullet and put it in my pocket, and I carried it some thirty or forty minutes. And I gave it to a Secret Serviceman that was guarding the main door into the emergency area.

BARKER: Mr. Wright, when you gave this bullet to the Secret Service agent, did he mark it in any way?

WRIGHT: No, sir.

BARKER: What did he do with it?

WRIGHT: Put it in his lefthand coat pocket.

BARKER: Well now, did he ask your name or who you were or any question at all about the bullet?

WRIGHT: No, sir.

BARKER: How did the conversation go? Do you remember?

WRIGHT: I just told him this was a bullet that was picked up on a stretcher that had come off the emergency elevator that might be involved in the moving of Governor Connally. And I handed him the bullet, and he took it and looked at it and said, "OK," and put it in his pocket.

CRONKITE: There is little to praise in such treatment by the FBI and the Secret Service of perhaps the most important single piece of evidence in the assassination case. Moreover, the Warren Commission seriously compromised itself by allowing the Secret Service, the FBI, and the CIA to investigate questions involving their own actions.

RATHER: The Commission had before it the hard fact that Oswald's notebook contained the name, phone number, and license plate number of Dallas FBI agent, James Hosty. The FBI's explanation was that Hosty had asked Ruth Paine, with whom Marina Oswald was living, to let him know where Oswald was staying, that he jotted down his phone number, and that Marina, under prior instructions from her husband, also copied down Hosty's license plate.

CRONKITE: The question of a link between the killer and the FBI was indeed a legitimate part of the investigation. The Commission's handling of that question is scarcely justifiable. What it did was to accept as conclusive, sworn affidavits from J. Edgar Hoover, and other FBI officials, that Oswald was never employed in any capacity by the FBI.

The Commission says it also checked the FBI's own files, but mentions no other investigation. It followed the same curious procedure with the CIA, taking the word of top CIA officials that Oswald had no connection with that agency either. The Commission then came to the sweeping conclusion that there was absolutely no type of informant or undercover relationship between an agency of the U.S. Government and Lee Harvey Oswald at any time.

Now, elsewhere the Warren Report argues persuasively the difficulty of proving a negative, of proving in that case that Oswald was not a member of a conspiracy. You will remember that it hedged its conclusion, saying only that there was no evidence of a conspiracy.

Yet the Commission had no hesitation in asserting another far-reaching negative: that Oswald was not involved with any agency of the U.S. Government ever. Oswald's mother, Marguerite, has always maintained that her son was a government agent—she favors the CIA—and that he was innocent of the assassination.

BARKER: Mrs. Oswald, what sort of proof do you have that your son was an agent of this government?

MARGUERITE C. OSWALD: Now, proof, Eddie—that's a very strong question. I think the Warren Commission members themselves gave Marguerite Oswald the proof. They want us to believe that Lee Harvey Oswald went to Russia as a defector. And yet he got out of the Marine Corps three years before his hitch was up on a Dire Need discharge. Now, this is documented. This is what they tell the American people. They go into great details, that Lee Harvey Oswald got out of the Marine Corps three months ahead of time because his mother had an accident—which was the truth, and it all went through the Red Cross legitimately.

And when he came home, he stayed with his mother three days. We sort of know that story. And then he left for Russia. And so, this is supposed to be all cut and dried. But when you read the Warren Report, and when you know the case—and this is my case, and my son's—so I know it, then you see a little part where the Warren Commission says, the documentation says, that Lee Harvey Oswald was given a passport by the State Department to travel to Russia, the Dominican Republic, Cuba, and et cetera; and at that time these countries were not restricted.

Now, how can Lee Harvey Oswald get out of the Marine Corps three months ahead of time on a Dire Need discharge, and at the same time be issued a passport to travel?

CRONKITE: The evidence is overwhelming that Mrs. Oswald is wrong as to whether her son did assassinate the President. Yet, there remain disturbing indications that she may not be quite so wrong about some kind of link between Oswald and various intelligence agencies of the United States. The question of whether Oswald had any relationship with the FBI or the CIA is not frivolous. The agencies, of course, are silent.

Although the Warren Commission had full power to conduct its own independent investigation, it permitted the FBI and the CIA to investigate themselves—and so cast a permanent shadow on the answers.

RATHER: More than one critic of the Warren Report has attacked it over the question of witnesses: which ones it heard, and which of those it decided to believe.

Once again Edward Jay Epstein:

EPSTEIN: I'm not sure that the Commission went below the surface, but then no one could be sure of whether they did or not, because from what's visible, what we can see, the Commission did seem to bring forth most of the testimony, most of the relevant witnesses. Whether these witnesses were saying all they knew, or whether there were other witnesses they should have called is another. I think there are. You can show examples of other witnesses the Commission didn't call.

There was a witness, Mrs. Eric Walther.

MRS. CAROLYN WALTHER: When I saw this man in the window with a gun, and there was another man beside him, and he was holding the gun down. His arms were resting on the window.

EPSTEIN: Well, they never called her, nor did a Commission lawyer ever investigate her, or go down and ask her any questions.

RATHER: The Warren Commission and its staff interviewed 552 witnesses. Their testimony takes up these twenty-six thick volumes. Yet the question of whether it interviewed the right witnesses, and how it evaluated the testimony it did hear, are basic to any decision on how well it did its job.

For instance, what about Mrs. Carolyn Walther, who saw two men and a gun in a different window of the School Book Depository, and who never got to tell her story to the Commission?

CRONKITE: David Belin, an attorney for the Commission staff, who had a hand in the decision not to call Mrs. Walther after her interviews with the FBI, has said that the Commission simply could not hear every single person who had been in the Plaza that day. He pointed out that Mrs. Walther's woman companion, standing next to her, told investigators Mrs. Walther had never mentioned seeing any men. Nevertheless, among those 552 witnesses who were called by the Commission were many whose testimony was considerably less relevant than Mrs. Walther's.

Perhaps the Commission should have had the chance to decide whether or not she saw what she says she did.

RATHER: Right now, long after the fact of the Commission Report being out, right now, what bothers you most about the Report? Are there any—is there a central question, or central questions that bother you most?

EPSTEIN: There is one central question that does bother me, and that is—involves the autopsy that was performed on President Kennedy. And there was a conflict—really, a contradiction, between the FBI report on the autopsy, which the FBI says they received from the autopsy doctors—at least they said in these reports, and the autopsy report published by the Warren Commission. And I don't think we have to get into the exact details, but it wasn't absolute—if one was true, the other couldn't be true. It concerned the path of the bullet through President Kennedy's body. The FBI said it didn't go through, it only went in a short distance. The Warren Report said it went—or the autopsy in the Warren Report said it went clean through and exited.

There was evidence, evidence that I think any lawyer or law court would have demanded, and that is the actual photographs of the autopsy and the X-rays.

CRONKITE: Almost from the day the Warren Commission published its report, its decision to omit those vital X-rays and photographs has been under attack. Only that physical evidence, say the critics, can finally resolve the debate over how many bullets struck the President, where they came from, and where they went —the central questions in the argument over how many assassins opened fire in Dealey Plaza.

More than one critic has charged that the autopsy record in the Warren Report is not the original autopsy, but has been changed to conform with the Commission's theories. You will remember that after a silence of three and a half years the doctor who headed the autopsy team at Bethesda Naval Hospital agreed to reexamine those disputed photographs and X-rays, and review his findings for these broadcasts. And here is what Captain James Humes told Dan Rather.

HUMES: The Report, as I stated, is exactly the way it was delivered, and the way it was written.

CRONKITE: Yet it seems to CBS News that one of the most serious errors made by the Warren Commission was its decision not to look at those photographs and X-rays, an error now compounded. For the Kennedy family, which had possession of the autopsy pictures, agreed last year to donate them to the National Archives, but only with the stipulation that the pictures be locked away for five years—with only certain authorized government personnel allowed to see them.

Now, no one would propose that those grim and tragic relics be made generally available, to be flashed across television screens and newspaper pages. But in view of their crucial bearing on the entire assassination we believe that those films should now be made available for independent examination by expert pathologists, with the high qualifications of Captain Humes—but without his status as a principal in the case.

There is one further piece of evidence which we feel must now be made available to the entire public: Abraham's Zapruder's film of the actual assassination. The original is now the private property of *Life* magazine. A *Life* executive refused CBS News permission to show you that film at any price, on the grounds that it is "an invaluable asset of Time, Inc." although these broadcasts have demonstrated that the film may contain vital undiscovered clues to the assassination.

Life's decision means you cannot see the Zapruder film in its proper form, as motion picture film. We believe that the Zapruder film is an invaluable asset, not of Time, Inc.—but of the people of the United States.

Until now we have heard a great deal about the Warren Commission from its friends and its foes. But what of the Warren Commission itself? Where do its seven members stand amidst this torrent of controversy over their performance?

Chief Justice Warren, who headed the Commission, has refused to discuss the Warren Report publicly, with CBS News, or indeed with anyone. But one Commissioner has agreed to participate in this broadcast. He is John McCloy, internationally known lawyer, Presidential adviser, and former high commissioner for Germany.

Mr. McCloy, however objectively the Commission may have set about its work, the Report itself—it seems to us—may have just as well have been entitled *The Case Against Lee Harvey Oswald*.

Now, are you satisfied that as much effort was put into challenging that case, as into establishing it? In other words, did the accused man get a fair trial?

MCCLOY: I'll answer that in just a moment. If I may just say one thing, I—which I'd like to say. In the first place, I had some question as to the propriety of my appearing here as a former member of the Commission, to comment on the evidence of the Commission—seems to be some question, and I think there is some question about the advisability of doing that. But I'm quite prepared to talk about the procedures and the attitudes of the Commission. And I'm—the scope of its conclusions, and so forth. But I will now try to answer your question by pointing out that this was an investigation, and not a trial.

We didn't have any plaintiff and defendant. This wasn't what is known as an adversary proceeding. We were all called upon to come down there to—I believe the wording was—the directive from the President, "to satisfy yourself," that is the Commission, "what were the relevant facts in relation to this assassination." And that's the base from which we started.

There've been a number of suggestions that the Commission, for example, was only motivated by a desire to put—to make things quiet, so as to give comfort to the Administration, or give comfort to the people of the country, that there was nothing vicious about this. Well, that wasn't the attitude that we had at all.

I know what my attitude, when I first went down, I was convinced that there was something phony between the Ruby and the Oswald affair, that forty-eight hours after the assassination, here's this man shot in the police station. I was pretty skeptical about that. But as time went on and we heard witnesses and weighed the witnesses—but just think how silly this charge is.

Here we were seven men, I think five of us were Republicans. We weren't beholden to any Administration. Besides that, we—we had our own integrity to think of. A lot of people have said that you can rely upon the distinguished character of the Commission. You don't need to rely on the distinguished character of the Commission. Maybe it was distinguished, and maybe it wasn't. But you can rely on common sense. And you know that seven men aren't going to get together, of that character, and concoct a conspiracy, with all of the members of the staff we had, with all of the investigative agencies—it would have been a conspiracy of a character so mammoth and so vast that it transcends any—even some of the distorted charges of conspiracy on the part of Oswald.

CRONKITE: What did you do on those visits to Dallas?

MCCLOY: Well, we went there and walked over the Dealey Plaza, almost—it seems to me—foot by foot. We went into the School Book Depository. We talked to all of the police officers there— that were there, a number of the witnesses; visited the boarding house—the boarding houses that Oswald had lived in; retraced,

step by step, his—his movements from the School Book Depository
to the point at which he was apprehended in the theater. We
chased ourselves up and down the stairs, and timed ourselves. I
sat in the window and held the very rifle, with a four power scope
on it, and sighted down across it—seeing—must have been at the
exact spot that whoever the assassin was sat, with the carton of
boxes as a headrest; snapped the trigger many times; saw the—
we had a car moving at the alleged rate—well, I can go on.

But I'm just trying to give you the—the impression of what
was the fact that we did, assiduously, follow this evidence, and
work out as best we could our own judgments in relation to it.

CRONKITE: Mr. McCloy, the Commission came into being late in
1963, went through to September '64—when you were dissolved.
Could you have used more time? There is the charge that it was—
your conclusions were rushed, that there was some stringent time
scale imposed.

MCCLOY: The conclusions weren't rushed at all. If there's any
charge that can be made—and maybe this is an unjust charge,
because I wasn't in charge of it—I'm inclined to think that we
perhaps rushed to print a little too soon. But the conclusions we
arrived at in our own good time.

I think that if there's one thing I would do over again, I would
insist on those photographs and the X-rays having been produced
before us. In the one respect, and only one respect there, I think
we were perhaps a little oversensitive to what we understand was
the sensitivities of the Kennedy family against the production of
colored photographs of the body, and so forth.

But those exist. They're there. We had the best evidence in
regard to that—the pathology in respect to the President's wounds.
It was our own choice that we didn't subpoena these photographs,
which were then in the hands of the Kennedy family. I say, I
wish—I don't think we'd have subpoenaed them. We could have
gotten—Mr. Justice Warren was talking to the Kennedy family
about that at that time. I thought that he was really going to
see them, but it turned out that he hadn't.

CRONKITE: It's not surprising that there should be some skeptics,
quite obviously, to any such report. But how do you account for

the fact that the disbelievers outnumber the believers by such a wide margin?

MCCLOY: I think that—if you want me to speculate on it, first place, there's the credulity of people generally. This is pretty spicy, pretty scandalous. Bear in mind that there have been an enormous amount of books written now, a large number of books written, pamphlets written—with the most shocking and distorted statements in regard to the evidence; with all of the blurbs and all of the propaganda. You know the business that goes with selling books.

Many more thousands of those have been distributed and read than the rather limited distribution of the Report, with the rather prosaic accounts. So, that I suppose this tends to build the thing up. There are other—there are other things that I suppose you can talk about—strange attitudes—the people associate their politics with their belief, or their disbelief, in the Report.

I've gone to a number of campuses, for example. I'm astounded to find that they—the professors, as well as students—in many of the cases, I don't say the majority, think that it's illiberal to come to the conclusion that a communist inclined defector could have been the assassin of the President. It's liberal to feel that it was the result of a right-wing conspiracy in the hostile atmosphere of Texas. And nothing that you can say or do seems to be able to dispel their viewpoint.

Maybe there's a general distrust of government and government agencies. I don't know. You can speculate, Mr. Cronkite, as much as I can about it. I—I—what I do resist, in a way it irritates me, is any suggestion that the Commission were motivated other than by—and I'll leave myself out, there were competent people in that Commission, people who—who were experienced in investigation, like the senators and the congressmen, have been through many types of investigation; Dulles, who was—people who were used to dealing with FBI reports, appraising them, weighing them, taking many of them for something less than their face value.

They went at this thing, and they came to this conclusion—and there was nothing fraudulent about it, there was nothing sinister about it—either conscious or subconscious, in my judgment. And

I think that, as I say, that common sense would tell you that this must be the case. We may have erred somewhere along the line, but so far I haven't seen any credible evidence which dispels the soundness of the fundamental conclusions that we came to.

CRONKITE: In a way, we have come to the end of this report on the Warren Report. For some three and a half hours now we have presented what seemed to us the most significant new evidence concerning the assassination itself, and the President's Commission to investigate the assassination.

Yet over these months, as we prepared this report, we began to realize that there is one more question to be answered. That question does not really involve the assassination, or the Warren Commission—except indirectly. It involves the people of the United States. We began to wonder how it is possible that so many more Americans disbelieve the Warren Report than have ever read it.

Why, for instance, when fewer than two million copies of the Report have been sold, a Gallup Poll indicates that six Americans out of every ten think they know enough about it to mistrust it? Or why, by a considerable margin, more people have bought copies of books attacking the Report than have bought the Report itself?

Such indications begin to suggest that, completely apart from the merits of the Warren Report itself, there may be something abroad in the land that wants not to believe the Report's conclusion, that President Kennedy was the victim of a lone madman, and not of a conspiracy.

Our final question then: Could America believe the Warren Report? Dr. Seymour Lipset of Harvard is a distinguished sociologist whose special field of interest is American behavior. And Dan Rather asked him about this national reaction of disbelief to the Warren Report.

LIPSET: Sort of thing, you know, we're terribly bothered by murders. You know, when you get the kind of Jack the Ripper thing, or this fellow in Texas who shot down—if someone's killed because —for his money, if someone's kidnapped for money, if—this is OK. I mean, not that you—we don't want it. But at least you can understand what happened. If it—and therefore, an assassination which is a consequence of a plot is like a murder in the context of a crime for more money by a gang. But if somebody's just shot down in the street by some fellow who just picked up a gun and shot him, well, if it happened to him, it can happen to you.

If the President is assassinated, not because of a rational plot, but because of just a nut who has a gun, then any—not only any President can be assassinated this way—which he can be—but anybody else can. It becomes a much less controlled world.

CRONKITE: A man who looks into the American spirit from another viewpoint, but with equally keen interest, is historian Henry Steele Commager, whose book *Search for a Usable Past* is considered a major insight into what we are, and how we got that way.

COMMAGER: But I do think that there has come up in recent years, particularly since the coming of the Cold War, something that might be called a conspiracy psychology. A feeling that great events can't be explained by ordinary processes, that if anything goes wrong—whether it's a great thing, like the so-called loss of China, or a minor—a particular thing, like a discovery of espionage somewhere, or the terrible fact of the assassination—is not to be explained as other historical events, but by some special standard of explanation, to be applied to the United States. And the point is that the ordinary rules for the rest of the world don't hold for us.

And so with a great number of the things that are ordinarily explained by the normal processes of history are not to be explained by this, because they don't apply to the United States. We are expected always to be victorious, and always to triumph, and so forth and so forth.

And to this came the—added to this came the McCarthy era, with the miasma of suspicion, with the ceaseless insistence on conspiracy, and dirty work at the crossroads, everywhere. And we were—I think we have been persuaded very largely since the beginnings of the Cold War to be more receptive to conspiracy theories. I don't think we'd become paranoid. But we were on the road to a paranoid explanation of things.

MORLEY SAFER: Do you think that a second investigation, an independent investigation, into the assassination of the President is any more likely to be believed than the Warren Commission?

COMMAGER: No. I see no reason to suppose that anyone who doesn't believe the first will believe a second, or a third, or a fourth. The conspiracy theory, the conspiracy mentality, will not accept ordinary evidence, any more than the conspiracy mentality accepts the ordinary explanation of the assassination of Lincoln, and the death of Booth. It has—there's some psychological requirement that forces them to reject the ordinary, and find refuge in the extraordinary. And if another investigation were to be held, and came up—came to the same conclusion, as I'm inclined to think it would, who knows—I think it would be found just as unsatisfactory, and the critics would say, "Well, of course, this too is part of the Establishment. The Establishment appointed this; they want this kind of an explanation, and we don't believe any of it, because we know there's dirty work at the crossroads somewhere. They're covering things up." So I see no value, really, in another investigation.

CRONKITE: In Washington, Eric Sevareid has been watching these four programs with you, and we turn to him now for his thoughts on the Warren Commission and its work.

SEVAREID: When this reporter returned home after the first year of World War II in Europe, I made a few speeches to American groups: intelligent, middle-class, Town Hall kind of audience. But almost invariably some man, or group of men, would get me aside after the speech and say, in effect, "Now tell us the real low-down."

This was my first adult encounter with that strain of permanent skepticism about what they read or hear that runs through so much of the American people. This distrust governs peoples' feelings toward government and public events more than their feelings toward one another in their daily life. Part of the impulse is simply that traditional Yankee horse trader desire not to be taken in. Part is the wish to be personally "in the know," one up on the other fellow.

But this automatic reaction that there must be conspiracy

somewhere, the prevalence of this devil theory of politics, this probably has increased among us, as Professor Commager suggests, as a result of World War II and the Cold War that followed.

Roosevelt must have sold out East Europe at Yalta, so many people thought: Obscure Reds in the State Department, teachers and writers here and there must have delivered vast China to Communist hands. Indeed, one or two otherwise reputable personages argued that Roosevelt conspired with the Japanese to bring about the Pearl Harbor attack.

What fed the conspiracy notion about the Kennedy assassination among many Americans was the sheer incongruity of the affair. All that power and majesty wiped out in an instant by one skinny, weak-chinned, little character. It was like believing that the Queen Mary had sunk without a trace, because of a log floating somewhere in the Atlantic, or that AT&T's stock had fallen to zero because a drunk somewhere tore out his telephone wires.

But this almost unbelievable incongruity has characterized nearly every one of the asassinations and attempted assassinations of American Presidents. Deranged little men killed Lincoln, Garfield, McKinley, tried to kill Presidents Theodore and Franklin Roosevelt. Only the Puerto Rican attempt on President Truman represented a real conspiracy.

There are still people who think Adolph Hitler is alive, people who think the so-called learned Elders of Zion are engaged in a Jewish plot to control the world. The passage of years, the failure of anybody anywhere to come up with respectable evidence does not shake the people who cling to these illusions.

And so, three and a half years later, there are people who still think some group of men are living somewhere, carrying in their breasts the most explosive secret conceivable, knowledge of a plot to kill Mr. Kennedy. These imagined men supposedly go about their lives under iron self-discipline, never falling out with each other, never giving out a hint of suspicion to anyone else.

And nearly three years after the Warren inquiry finished its painful and onerous work, there are not only the serious critics who point to the various mistakes of commission or omission, mistakes of a consequence one can only guess at, and of a kind that has probably plagued every lengthy, voluminous official investigation ever staged; there are also people who think the

Commission itself was a conspiracy to cover up something.

In the first place it would be utterly impossible in the American arena of a fierce and free press and politics to conceal a conspiracy among so many individuals who live in the public eye. In the second place the deepest allegiance of men like Chief Justice Warren, or of John McCloy, does not lie with any President, political party, or current cause—it lies with history, their name and place in history. That is all they live for in their later years. If they knowingly suppressed or distorted decisive evidence about such an event as a Presidential murder, their descendants would bear accursed names forever. The notion that they would do such a thing is idiotic.

CRONKITE: Three years ago, after we had studied for the first time the Report of the Warren Commission, we summed up our feelings about it. In the end, we find confronting each other, we said, the liar, the misfit, the defector, on the one hand, and seven distinguished Americans on the other. And yet, exactly here we must be careful that we do not say too much. Oswald was never tried for any crime and perhaps, therefore, there will forever be questions of substance and detail, raised by amateur detectives, professional skeptics, and serious students as well.

For the Warren Commission could not give Lee Harvey Oswald his day in court and the protection of our laws. Suspects are not tried by seven distinguished Americans. Their cases are heard under law by twelve ordinary citizens. If it had not been for Jack Ruby's revolver in the basement of the Dallas police station, twelve such citizens would have heard the evidence, would have heard Oswald, if he had chosen to speak.

That jury would have represented our judgment, our conscience, and in the end would have spoken for us. Now, we do not have that reliance. We must depend on our own judgments and look into our own consciences. The Warren Commission cannot do that for us. We are the jury, all of us, in America and throughout the world.

We found no reason to withdraw what we said then. But, now we have studied the report again, this time with the benefit of three years of controversy, of all of these books, of our own investigations. We have found that wherever you look at the Report closely and without preconceptions, you come away convinced that the story it tells is the best account we are ever likely to have of what happened that day in Dallas.

We have found that most objections to the Report—and certainly all objections that go to the heart of the Report—vanish when they are exposed to the light of honest inquiry. It is a strange kind of tribute to the Warren Report that every objection that can be raised against it is to be found in the Report itself. It is true that the answers to some questions leave us restless. The theory that a single bullet struck down both the President and the Governor, for example, has too much of the long arm of coincidence about it for us to be entirely comfortable. But would we be more comfortable believing that a shot was fired by a second assassin who materialized out of thin air for the purpose, fired a shot, and then vanished again into thin air, leaving behind no trace of himself, his rifle, his bullet, or any other sign of existence.

Measured against the alternatives, the Warren Commission Report is the easiest to believe, and that is all the Report claims. But, we have found also that there has been a loss of morale, a loss of confidence among the American people toward their own government and the men who serve it. And that is perhaps more wounding than the assassination itself. The damage that Lee Harvey Oswald did the United States of America, the country he first denounced and then appeared to reembrace, did not end when the shots were fired from the Texas School Book Depository. The most grievous wounds persist, and there is little reason to believe that they will soon be healed.

PRODUCER	Leslie Midgley
DIRECTOR	Vern Diamond
PRODUCER IN DALLAS	Bernard Birnbaum
DALLAS SEQUENCES DIRECTED BY	Don Hewitt
WRITTEN BY	Ron Bonn, Clinton McCarty, Leslie Midgley, Stephen White
ASSOCIATE PRODUCERS	Jane Bartels, Ron Bonn, Walter Lister, Clinton McCarty, Robert Richter, Sam Roberts, Joseph Wershba, Stephen White
FILM EDITORS	David McCruden, Jack Drescher, Jerome McCarthy, Mitchell Rudick, Herbert J. Schwartz
FILM CAMERAMEN	Walter Dombrow, Herbert J. Schwartz
UNIT MANAGER	Grace Diekhaus
PRODUCTION SUPERVISOR	Arthur Schotz
ASSOCIATE DIRECTOR	Joe Gorsuch
VIDEO TAPE EDITORS	Harold Bailey, W. Matwichuk, Ed Smith
TECHNICAL DIRECTORS	Hal Classon, Bill Guyon, George Keck

INDEX